To Jayce 30/11/99.
With Love
Mum

Daughters of God

Messages Especially for Women

Ellen G. White

REVIEW AND HERALD® PUBLISHING ASSOCIATION
HAGERSTOWN, MD 21740

Prepared by the Ellen G. White Estate
12501 Old Columbia Pike
Silver Spring, Maryland 20904, U.S.A.

At the time Ellen White wrote, mostly in the nineteenth century, "men" and the masculine pronoun "he" were commonly used to include both men and women. This was Mrs. White's custom. No doubt if she were writing today, she would use more gender-inclusive language. This is evident by the fact that some file copies of her letters and manuscripts contain the handwritten words "and women" inserted after the word "men."

Texts credited to NKJV are from the New King James Version. Copyright © 1979, 1980, 1982, Thomas Nelson, Inc., Publishers. Used by permission. All rights reserved.

Bible texts credited to RV are from the Revised Version, Oxford University Press, 1911.

This book was
Copyedited by Jocelyn Fay, William Cleveland, James Cavil
Designed by Patricia S. Wegh
Cover photo by PhotoDisc
Typeset: Palatino 10/13

R&H Cataloging Service
White, Ellen Gould Harmon, 1827-1915
    Daughters of God: messages especially for women

    1. Women—Religious life.   I. Title.
                    248.843

ISBN 0-8280-1358-6

Other books by Ellen G. White

Thoughts From the Mount of Blessing (Pacific Press)
The Truth About Angels (Pacific Press)
The Upward Look
The Voice in Speech and Song (Pacific Press)
Welfare Ministry
William Miller: Herald of the Blessed Hope
Ye Shall Receive Power
Your Mind and Your Health (Pacific Press)

To order, call 1-800-765-6955.

Visit us at www.rhpa.org for more information on
Review and Herald products.

List of Abbreviations

Contents

A Word to the Reader

During the last half of the nineteenth century women were given greater leadership roles in some Protestant churches. This was true of the Seventh-day Adventist Church.

Three of the first 10 treasurers of the General Conference (1863-1883) were women. Of the 12 editors of *The Youth's Instructor* who served between 1852 and 1899, nine were women. L. Flora Plummer headed the Sabbath School Department of the General Conference for 23 years. The Adventist Church during 1878-1910 licensed 31 women to preach.

Ellen White often pointed out that "the Lord has a work for women, as well as for men. . . . They can come close to the hearts of those whom men cannot reach" (RH, Aug. 26, 1902).

Significant portions of Ellen White's counsel to women in the work of God have been brought together in this volume. Included also are chapters on self-respect and on balance in all aspects of life. Most of the counsel in these chapters, though originally directed to men, is equally applicable to women. In today's high-pressure society many women are wage earners, often single mothers trying to provide for their families. The content of these chapters will go far toward restoring and sustaining a sense of self-respect, helping women to know that they are important and valued in God's sight.

A few of the statements in this book must be understood in the light of their cultural, social, and time context. "Regarding the testimonies, nothing is ignored; nothing is cast aside; but time and place must be considered" (1SM 57). To assist the reader, we have endeavored to provide enough context for a complete understanding. We also have given the date and source of publication, or the original date of writing when publication was after Ellen White's death. In a few cases, when the original publication is not readily available, we have given a more recent source, along with the date of writing. Subheadings throughout the book have been supplied by the compilers.

Daughters of God is designed to be an encouragement, inspiration, and affirmation to women around the world. It includes counsels that lead women to strive for the highest ideals in whatever walk of life they find themselves, be it personal or professional. Every woman is of inestimable value in the sight of our heavenly Father. He created woman to stand by the side of man, equal in value before God, and associated with him in the work he was given to do. The Father gave His only begotten Son to die for the entire human race, individually and collectively, male and female.

It is our hope that church members around the world will gain new insights and blessings from reading this volume. God needs the talents of all His people to help finish His work on earth.

The Trustees of the Ellen G. White Estate

*A*ll who work for God should have the Martha and the Mary attributes blended—a willingness to minister and a sincere love of the truth. Self and selfishness must be put out of sight. God calls for earnest women workers, workers who are prudent, warmhearted, tender, and true to principle. He calls for persevering women who will take their minds from self and their personal convenience, and will center them on Christ, speaking words of truth, praying with the persons to whom they can obtain access, laboring for the conversion of souls.

—Testimonies, *vol. 6, p. 118*

The Lord Calls Women to His Service

1

In the various branches of the work of God's cause, there is a wide field in which our sisters may do good service for the Master. . . . Among the noble women who have had the moral courage to decide in favor of the truth for this time are many who have tact, perception, and good ability, and who may make successful workers. The labors of such Christian women are needed."

—Evangelism, *p. 466*

WOMEN AS CHRISTIAN LABORERS

He who died to redeem man from death loves with a divine love; and He says to His followers: "This is my commandment, That ye love one another, as I have loved you." Christ showed His love for the fallen race by His actions.

The true child of God will be Christlike; and as he grows in the knowledge of the truth, and is sanctified through the truth, he will be more and more like Christ, and more desirous to save souls, the purchase of His blood.

Some can do more than others; but all can do something. Women should not feel that they are excused because of their domestic cares. They should become intelligent as to how they can work most successfully and methodically in bringing souls to Christ. If all would realize the importance of doing to the utmost of their ability in the work of God, having a deep love for souls, feeling the burden of the work upon them, hundreds would be engaged as active workers who have hitherto been dull and uninterested, accomplishing nothing, or at most but very little.

In many cases the rubbish of the world has clogged the channels of the soul. Selfishness controls the mind and warps the character. Were the life hid with Christ in God, His service would be no drudgery. If the whole heart were consecrated to God, all would find something to do, and would covet a part in the work. They would sow beside all waters, praying and believing that the fruit would appear. The practical, God-fearing workers will be growing upward, praying in faith for grace and heavenly wisdom that they may do the work devolving upon them with cheerfulness and a willing mind. They will seek the divine rays of light that they may brighten the paths of others.

Those who are colaborers with God will have no disposition to engage in the various expedients for amusement; they will not be seeking after happiness and enjoyment. In taking up their work in the fear of God, and doing service to the Master, they will secure the most substantial happiness. Connected with Jesus Christ, they will be wise unto salvation. They will be fruit-bearing trees. They will develop a blameless life, a beauteous character. The great work of redemption will be their first consideration. Eating and drinking and dressing, houses and lands, will be secondary matters. The peace of God within will force off the withered or gnarled branches of selfishness, vanity, pride, and indolence. It is faith and practice that make up the Christian's life. We do not meet the standard of Christianity in merely professing Christ and having our names upon the church book. We should be individual workers for Christ. By personal effort we can show that we are connected with Him.

Christian women are called for. There is a wide field in which they may do good service for the Master. There are noble women who have had moral courage to decide in favor of the truth from the weight of evidence. They have tact, perception, and good ability, and could make successful Christian workers. There is work neglected or done imperfectly that could be thoroughly accomplished through

The Lord Calls Women to His Service

the help that they are able to give. They could reach a class that ministers cannot reach. There are offices in the church that they could fill acceptably, and many branches of the church work that they could attend to if properly instructed.

Women can do good work in the missionary field, by writing to friends, and learning their true feelings in relation to the cause of God. Very valuable items are brought to light through this means. The workers should not seek for self-exaltation, but to present the truth in its simplicity wherever they shall have an opportunity. The money that has been spent for needless trimmings and useless ornaments should be devoted to the cause of God, and used to bring the light of truth to those who are in the darkness of error. The souls saved through their efforts will be more precious to them than costly and fashionable dress. The white robes and jeweled crown given them by Christ as the reward for their unselfish efforts in the salvation of souls, will be more valuable than needless adornments. The stars in their crowns will shine forever and ever, and will a thousand times repay them for the self-denial and self-sacrifice they have exercised in the cause of God.

Women of firm principle and decided character are needed, women who believe that we are indeed living in the last days, and that we have the last solemn message of warning to be given to the world. They should feel that they are engaged in an important work in spreading the rays of light which Heaven has shed upon them. When the love of God and His truth is an abiding principle, they will let nothing deter them from duty, or discourage them in their work. They will fear God, and will not be diverted from their labors in His cause by the temptation of lucrative situations and attractive prospects. They will preserve their integrity at any cost to themselves. These are the ones who will correctly represent the religion of Christ, whose words will be fitly spoken, like apples of gold in pictures of silver. Such persons can in many ways do a precious work for God. He calls upon them to go out into the harvest field, and help gather in the sheaves.

Intelligent Christian woman may use their talents to the very highest account. They can show by their life of self-denial, and by their willingness to work to the best of their ability, that they believe the truth, and are being sanctified through it. Many need a work of this kind to develop the powers they possess. Wives and mothers should in no case neglect their husbands and their children; but they can do much without neglecting home duties, and all have not these responsibilities.

Who can have so deep a love for the souls of men and women for whom Christ died as those who are partakers of His grace? Who can better represent the religion of Christ than Christian women, women who are earnestly laboring to bring souls to the light of truth? Who else is so well adapted to the work of the Sabbath school? The true mother is the true teacher of children. If with a heart imbued with the love of Christ, she teaches the children of her class, praying with them and for them, she may see souls converted, and gathered into the fold of Christ. I do not recommend that woman should seek to become a voter* or officeholder; but as a missionary, teaching the truth by epistolary correspondence, distributing reading matter, conversing with families and praying with the mother and children, she may do much, and be a blessing.

The Lord of the vineyard is saying to many women who are now doing nothing, "Why stand ye here all the day idle?" They may be instruments of righteousness, rendering holy service. It was Mary who first preached a risen Jesus; and the refining, softening influence of Christian women is needed in the great work of preaching the truth now. If there were twenty women where now there is one who would make the saving of souls their cherished work, we should see many more converted to the truth. Zealous and continued diligence in the cause of God would be wholly successful, and would astonish them with its results. The work must be accomplished through patience and perseverance, and in this is manifested the real devotion to God. He calls for deeds, and not words only.

The work of God is worthy of our best efforts. In fulfillment of the divine plan, the Son of man came to seek and to save that which was lost. He taught the erring and sinful ones whom He came to save, and wrestled in earnest prayer to His Father in their behalf; and we should engage in the same work. If it was not beneath the dignity of the Son of God, the Creator of worlds, should it be considered too humiliating or too self-sacrificing for His followers? No, indeed. However aspiring we may be, there is no calling that is higher, holier, and more ennobling than to be a colaborer with the Son of God.

Often we are so wrapped up in our selfish interests that our hearts are not allowed to take in the needs and wants of humanity; we are lacking in deeds of sympathy and benevolence, in sacred and social ministering to the needy, the oppressed, and the suffering. Women are needed who are not self-important, but gentle in manners and lowly of heart, who will work with the meekness of Christ wherever they can find anything to do for the salvation of souls. All who have been made partakers of the heavenly benefits should be earnest and anxious that others, who do not have the privileges which they have enjoyed, should have the evidences of the truth presented before them. And they will not merely desire that others should have this benefit, but will see that they do have it, and will do their part toward the accomplishment of this object.

Those who become colaborers with God will increase in moral and spiritual power, while those who devote their time and energies to serving themselves will dwarf, and wither, and die. Christian women, the youth, the middle-aged, and those of advanced years, may have a part in the work of God for this time; and in engaging in this work as they have opportunity, they will obtain an experience of the highest value to themselves. In forgetfulness of self, they will grow in grace. By training the mind in this direction, they will learn how to bear burdens for Jesus, and will realize the blessedness of the service. And soon the time will come when "they that sow in tears shall reap in joy."—ST, Sept. 16, 1886.

The Lord has a work for women, as well as for men. They may take their places in His work at this crisis, and He will work through them. If they are imbued with a sense of their duty, and labor under the influence of the Holy Spirit, they will have just the self-possession required for this time. The Saviour will reflect upon these self-sacrificing women the light of His countenance, and will give them a power that exceeds that of men. They can do in families a work that men cannot do, a work that reaches the inner life. They can come close to the hearts of those whom men cannot reach. Their labor is needed.—RH, Aug. 26, 1902.

We hear much of the education of women, and it is a subject that is deserving of careful attention. The highest education for woman is to be found in the thorough and equal cultivation of all her talents and powers. The heart, the mind, the spirit, as well as the physical being, should be properly developed. There are many who are uncultured in mind and manners. Many are full of affectation, and the aim of their life seems to be to make a display. When we see this state of affairs, we cannot help breathing a prayer that God will bless the world with women who are developed as they should be in mind and character, women who have a true realization of their God-given responsibility.—ST, Mar. 23, 1891.

If those who have had great light will not respond to the invitation to become laborers with God, then God will take and use those who have had far less light and much fewer opportunities. Those who will work out their own salvation with fear and trembling will realize that it is God that worketh in them, to will and to do of His own pleasure. There should be thousands fully awake and in earnest in the work of God, who should be bright and shining lights. There should be thousands who know the time in which we are living, and who wait not to be urged, but who are constrained by the power of God to diffuse light, to open to others the truth that is so distinctly revealed in the Word of God. There is no time to lose.

Men and women should be ministering in unenlightened communities in regions beyond. After they have awakened an interest, they should find the living preacher who is skillful in the presentation of the truth, and qualified to instruct families in the Word of God. Women who have the cause of God at heart can do a good work in the districts in which they reside. Christ speaks of women who helped Him in presenting the truth before others, and Paul also speaks of women who labored with him in the gospel. But how very limited is the work done by those who could do a large work if they would! There are families that have means which they could use for God's glory in going to distant lands to let their light shine forth in good works to those who need help. Why do not men and women engage in the missionary work, following the example of Christ?—RH, July 21, 1896.

Women were not granted the right to vote in the United States until 1920. When this was written some already were attempting by various means to change the law.

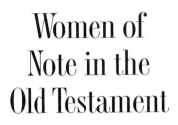

Women of Note in the Old Testament

2

A study of women's work in connection with the cause of God in Old Testament times will teach us lessons that will enable us to meet emergencies in the work today. We may not be brought into such a critical and prominent place as were the people of God in the time of Esther; but often converted women can act an important part in more humble positions. This many have been doing, and are still ready to do.

—Special Testimonies, *Series B, No. 15, p. 2.*

EVE, MOTHER OF ALL
Genesis 1 and 2

"By the word of the Lord were the heavens made; and all the host of them by the breath of his mouth." "For he spake, and it was done; he commanded, and it stood fast." Psalm 33:6, 9. He "laid the foundations of the earth, that it should not be removed for ever." Psalm 104:5.

As the earth came forth from the hand of its Maker, it was exceedingly beautiful. . . . The angelic host viewed the scene with delight, and rejoiced at the wonderful works of God.

After the earth with its teeming animal and vegetable life had been called into existence, man, the crowning work of the Creator, and the one for whom the beautiful earth had been fitted up, was brought upon the stage of action. To him was given dominion over all that his eye could behold; for "God said, Let us make man in our image, after our likeness: and let them have dominion over . . . all the earth. . . . So God created man in his own image, . . . male and female created he them." Here is clearly set forth the origin of the human race; and the divine record is so plainly stated that there is no occasion for erroneous conclusions. God created man in His own image. Here is no mystery. There is no ground for the supposition that man was evolved by slow degrees of development from the lower forms of animal or vegetable life. Such teaching lowers the great work of the Creator to the level of man's narrow, earthly conceptions. Men are so intent upon excluding God from the sovereignty of the universe that they degrade man and defraud him of the dignity of his origin. He who set the starry worlds on high and tinted with delicate skill the flowers of the field, who filled the earth and the heavens with the wonders of His power, when He came to crown His glorious work, to place one in the midst to stand as ruler of the fair earth, did not fail to create a being worthy of the hand that gave him life. The genealogy of our race, as given by inspiration, traces back its origin, not to a line of developing germs, mollusks, and quadrupeds, but to the great Creator. Though formed from the dust, Adam was "the son of God." . . .

Man was to bear God's image, both in outward resemblance and in character. . . . He was holy and happy in bearing the image of God and in perfect obedience to His will.

As man came forth from the hand of his Creator, he was of lofty stature and perfect symmetry. His countenance bore the ruddy tint of health and glowed with the light of life and joy. Adam's height was much greater than that of men who now inhabit the earth. Eve was somewhat less in stature; yet her form was noble, and full of beauty. The sinless pair wore no artificial garments; they were clothed with a covering of light and glory, such as the angels wear. So long as they lived in obedience to God, this robe of light continued to enshroud them. . . .

God Himself gave Adam a companion. He provided "an help meet for him"—a helper corresponding to him—one who was fitted to be his companion, and who could be one with him in love and sympathy. Eve was created from a rib taken from the side of Adam, signifying that she was not to control him as the head, nor to be trampled under his feet as an inferior, but to stand by his side as an equal, to be loved and protected by him. A part of man, bone of his bone, and flesh of his flesh, she was his second self, showing the close union and the affectionate attachment that should exist in this relation. "For no man ever yet hated his own flesh; but nourisheth and cherisheth it." Ephesians 5:29. "Therefore shall a man leave his father and his mother, and shall cleave unto his wife; and they shall be one." . . .

The creation was now complete. "The heavens and the earth were finished, and all the host of them." "And God saw everything that he had made, and, behold, it was very good." Eden bloomed on earth. Adam and Eve had free access to the tree of life. No taint of sin or shadow of death marred the fair creation. "The morning stars sang together, and all the sons of God shouted for joy." Job 38:7.

Our first parents, though created innocent and holy, were not placed beyond the possibility of wrongdoing. God made them free moral agents, capable of appreciating the wisdom and benevolence of His character and the justice of His requirements, and with full liberty to yield or to withhold obedience. They were to enjoy communion with God and with holy angels; but before they could be rendered eternally secure, their loyalty must be tested. . . .

While they remained true to God, Adam and his companion were to bear rule over the earth. Unlimited control was given them over every living thing. The lion and the lamb sported peacefully around them or lay down together at their feet. The happy birds flitted about them without fear; and as their glad songs ascended to the praise of their Creator, Adam and Eve united with them in thanksgiving to the Father and the Son. . . .

The angels had cautioned Eve to beware of separating herself from her husband while occupied in their daily labor in the garden; with him she would be in less danger from temptation than if she were alone. But absorbed in her pleasing task, she unconsciously wandered from his side. . . . She soon found herself gazing with mingled curiosity and admiration upon the forbidden tree. The fruit was very beautiful, and she questioned with herself why God had withheld it from them. Now was the tempter's opportunity. As if he were able to discern the workings of her mind, he addressed her: "Yea, hath God said, Ye shall not eat of every tree of the garden?" . . .

The tempter intimated that the divine warning was not to be actually fulfilled; it was designed merely to intimidate them. . . .

Eve really believed the words of Satan, but her belief did not save her from the penalty of sin. She disbelieved the words of God, and this was what led to her fall. In the judgment men will not be condemned because they conscientiously believed a lie, but because they did not believe the truth, because they neglected the opportunity of learning what is truth. . . .

When she [Eve] "saw that the tree was good for food, and that it was pleasant to the eyes, and a tree to be desired to make one wise, she took of the fruit thereof, and did eat." It was grateful to the taste, and as she ate, she seemed to feel a vivifying power, and imagined herself entering upon a higher state of existence. Without a fear she plucked and ate. And now, having herself transgressed, she became the agent of Satan in working the ruin of her husband. In a state of strange, unnatural excitement, with her hands filled with the forbidden fruit, she sought his presence, and related all that had occurred.

An expression of sadness came over the face of Adam. He appeared astonished and alarmed. To the words of Eve he replied that this must be the foe against whom they had been warned; and by the divine sentence she must die. In answer she urged him to eat, repeating the words of the serpent, that they should not surely die. She reasoned that this must be true, for she felt no evidence of God's displeasure, but on the contrary realized a delicious, exhilarating influence, thrilling every faculty with new life, such, she imagined, as inspired the heavenly messengers.

Adam understood that his companion had transgressed the command of God, disregarded the only prohibition laid upon them as a test of their fidelity and love. There was a terrible struggle in his mind. He mourned that he had permitted Eve to wander from his side. But now the deed was done; he must be separated from her whose society had been his joy. How could he have it thus? . . .

He resolved to share her fate; if she must die, he would die with her. After all, he reasoned, might not the words of the wise serpent be true? Eve was before him, as beautiful and apparently as innocent as before this act of disobedience. She expressed greater love for him than before. No sign of death appeared in her, and he decided to brave the consequences. He seized the fruit and quickly ate.—PP 44-57 (1890).

Had Adam and Eve never disobeyed their Creator, had they remained in the path of perfect rectitude, they could have known and understood God. But when they listened to the voice of the tempter, and sinned against God, the light of the garments of heavenly innocence departed from them; and in parting with the garments of innocence, they drew about them the dark robes of ignorance of God. The clear and perfect light that had hitherto surrounded them had lightened everything they approached; but deprived of that heavenly light, the posterity of Adam could no longer trace the character of God in His created works.—RH, Nov. 8, 1898.

SARAH, WIFE OF ABRAHAM, MOTHER OF NATIONS
Genesis 11-23

There was given to Abraham the promise, especially dear to the people of that age, of a numerous posterity and of national greatness: "I will make of thee a great nation, and I will bless thee, and make thy name great; and thou shalt be a blessing." And to this was added the assurance, precious above every other to the inheritor of faith, that of his line the Redeemer of the world should come: "In thee shall all families of the earth be blessed." Yet, as the first condition of fulfillment, there was to be a test of faith; a sacrifice was demanded.

The message of God came to Abraham, "Get thee out of thy country, and from thy kindred, and from thy father's house, unto a land that I will shew thee." In order that God might qualify him for his great work as the keeper of the sacred oracles, Abraham must be separated from the associations of his early life. The influence of kindred and friends would interfere with the training which the Lord purposed to give His servant. Now that Abraham was, in a special sense, connected with heaven, he must dwell among strangers. His character must be peculiar, differing from all the world. He could not even explain his course of action so as to be understood by his friends. Spiritual things are spiritually discerned, and his motives and actions were not comprehended by his idolatrous kindred.

"By faith Abraham, when he was called to go out into a place which he should after receive for an inheritance, obeyed; and he went out, not knowing whither he went." Hebrews 11:8. . . .

Besides Sarah, the wife of Abraham, only Lot, the son of Haran long since dead, chose to share the patriarch's pilgrim life. . . .

During his stay in Egypt, Abraham gave evidence that he was not free from human weakness and imperfection. In concealing the fact that Sarah was his wife, he betrayed a distrust of the divine care, a lack of that lofty faith and courage so often and nobly exemplified in his life. Sarah was fair to look upon, and he doubted not that the dusky Egyptians would covet the beautiful stranger, and that in order to secure her, they would not scruple to slay her husband. He reasoned that he was not guilty of falsehood in representing Sarah as his sister, for she was the daughter of his father, though not of his mother.

But this concealment of the real relation between them was deception. No deviation from strict integrity can meet God's approval. Through Abraham's lack of faith, Sarah was placed in great peril. The king of Egypt, being informed of her beauty, caused her to be taken to his palace, intending to make her his wife. But the Lord, in His great mercy, protected Sarah by sending judgments upon the royal household. By this means the monarch learned the truth in the matter, and, indignant at the deception practiced upon him, he reproved Abraham and restored to him his wife, saying, "What is this that thou hast done unto me? . . . Why saidst thou, She is my sister? So I might have taken her to me to wife: now therefore behold thy wife, take her, and go thy way." . . .

Abraham returned to Canaan "very rich in cattle, in silver, and in gold." Lot was still with him, and again they came to Bethel, and pitched their tents by the altar which they had before erected. . . .

In a vision of the night the divine Voice was again heard. "Fear not, Abram" were the words of the Prince of princes; "I am thy shield, and thy exceeding great reward." But his mind was so oppressed by forebodings that he could not now grasp the promise with unquestioning confidence as heretofore. He prayed for some tangible evidence that it would be fulfilled. And how was the covenant promise to be realized, while the gift of a son was withheld? "What wilt thou give me," he said, "seeing I go childless?" "And, lo, one born in my house is mine heir." He proposed to make his trusty servant Eliezer his son by adoption, and the inheritor of his possessions. But he was assured that a child of his own was to be his heir. Then he was led outside his tent, and told to look up to the unnumbered stars glittering in the heavens; and as he did so, the words were spoken, "So shall thy seed be." "Abraham believed God, and it was counted unto him for righteousness." Romans 4:3. . . .

Abraham had accepted without question the promise of a son, but he did not wait for God to fulfill His word in His own time and way. A delay was permitted, to test his faith in the power of God; but he failed to endure the trial. Thinking it impossible that a child should be given her in her old age, Sarah suggested, as a plan by which the divine purpose might be fulfilled, that one of her handmaidens should be taken by Abraham as a secondary wife. Polygamy had become so widespread that it had ceased to be regarded as a sin, but it was no less a violation of the law of God, and was fatal to the sacredness and peace of the family relation. Abraham's marriage with Hagar resulted in evil, not only to his own household, but to future generations. . . .

When Abraham was nearly one hundred years old, the promise of a son was repeated to him, with the assurance that the future heir should be the child of Sarah. But Abraham did not yet understand the promise. His mind at once turned to Ishmael, clinging to the belief that through him God's gracious purposes were to be accomplished. In his affection for his son he exclaimed, "O that Ishmael might live before thee!" Again the promise was given, in words that could not be mistaken: "Sarah thy wife shall bear thee a son indeed; and thou shalt call his name Isaac: and I will establish my covenant with him." . . .

The birth of Isaac, bringing, after a lifelong waiting, the fulfillment of their dearest hopes, filled the tents of Abraham and Sarah with gladness. . . .

The instruction given to Abraham touching the sacredness of the marriage relation was to be a lesson for all ages. It declares that the rights and happiness of this relation are to be carefully guarded, even at a great sacrifice. Sarah was the only true wife of Abraham. Her rights as a wife and mother no other person was entitled to share. She reverenced her husband, and in this she is presented in the New Testament as a worthy example. But she was unwilling that Abraham's affections should be given to another, and the Lord did not reprove her for requiring the banishment of her rival. Both Abraham and Sarah distrusted the power of God, and it was this error that led to the marriage with Hagar.

God had called Abraham to be the father of the faithful, and his life was to stand as an example of faith to succeeding generations. But his faith had not been perfect. He had shown distrust of God in concealing the fact that Sarah was his wife, and again in his marriage with Hagar.—PP 125-147 (1890).

The heritage that God has promised to His people is not in this world. Abraham had no possession in the earth, "no, not so much as to set his foot on." Acts 7:5. He possessed great substance, and he used it to the glory of God and the good of his fellow men; but he did not look upon this world as his home. The Lord had called him to leave his idolatrous countrymen, with the promise of the land of Canaan as an everlasting possession; yet neither he nor his son nor his son's son received it. When Abraham desired a burial place for his dead, he had to buy it of the Canaanites. His sole possession in the Land of Promise was that rock-hewn tomb in the cave of Machpelah.—PP 169 (1890).

["Sarah lived one hundred and twenty-seven years; these were the years of the life of Sarah. So Sarah died in Kirjath Arba (that is, Hebron) in the land of Canaan, and Abraham came to mourn for Sarah and to weep for her.

["Then Abraham stood up from before his dead, and spoke to the sons of Heth, saying: 'I am a foreigner and a visitor among you. Give me property for a burial place among you, that I may bury my dead out of my sight.' . . .

["Hear us, my lord: You are a mighty prince among us; bury

your dead in the choicest of our burial places. None of us will with-hold from you his burial place, that you may bury your dead."—Genesis 23:1-6, NKJV.]

REBEKAH

Abraham sent his servant Eliezar to choose a wife for his son Isaac. In answer to Eliezar's prayer, God led him to the one He had chosen to be Isaac's wife, Rebekah. Genesis 24.

The Canaanites were idolaters, and the Lord had commanded that His people should not intermarry with them, lest they should be led into idolatry. Abraham was old, and he expected soon to die. Isaac was yet unmarried. Abraham was afraid of the corrupting influence surrounding his son, and was anxious to have a wife selected for him who would not lead him from God. He committed this matter to his faithful, experienced servant who ruled over all that he had. Abraham required his servant to make a solemn oath to him before the Lord, that he would not take a wife for Isaac of the Canaanites, but that he would go to Abraham's kindred, who believed in the true God, and select a wife for the young man. He charged him not to take Isaac to the country from which he came; for they were nearly all affected with idolatry. If he could not find a wife for Isaac who would leave her kindred and come where he was, then he should be clear of the oath which he had made.—ST, Apr. 10, 1879.

This important matter was not left with Isaac, for him to select [a wife] for himself, independent of his father. Abraham tells his servant that God will send His angel before him to direct him in his choice. The servant to whom this mission was entrusted started on his long journey. As he entered the city where Abraham's kindred dwelt, he prayed earnestly to God to direct him in his choice of a wife for Isaac. He asked that certain evidence might be given him, that he should not err in the matter.

He rested by a well which was a place of the greatest gathering. Here he particularly noticed the engaging manners and courteous conduct of Rebekah, and all the evidence he has asked of God he receives that Rebekah is the one whom God has been pleased to select to become Isaac's wife. She invites the servant to her father's house.

He then relates to Rebekah's father, and her brother, the evidences he has received from the Lord, that Rebekah should become the wife of his master's son, Isaac.

Abraham's servant then said to them, "And now if ye will deal kindly and truly with my master, tell me: and if not, tell me; that I may turn to the right hand, or to the left." The father and son answered, "The thing proceedeth from the Lord: we cannot speak unto thee bad or good. Behold, Rebekah is before thee, take her, and go, and let her be thy master's son's wife, as the Lord hath spoken. And it came to pass, that, when Abraham's servant heard their words, he worshipped the Lord, bowing himself to the earth."—3SG 109, 110 (1864).

After the consent of the family had been obtained, Rebekah herself was consulted as to whether she would go to so great a distance from her father's house, to marry the son of Abraham. She believed, from what had taken place, that God had selected her to be Isaac's wife, and she said, "I will go."

The servant, anticipating his master's joy at the success of his mission, was impatient to be gone; and with the morning they set out on the homeward journey. Abraham dwelt at Beersheba, and Isaac, who had been attending to the flocks in the adjoining country, had returned to his father's tent to await the arrival of the messenger from Haran. "And Isaac went out to meditate in the field at the eventide: and he lifted up his eyes, and saw, and, behold, the camels were coming. And Rebekah lifted up her eyes, and when she saw Isaac, she lighted off the camel. For she had said unto the servant, What man is that that walketh in the field to meet us? And the servant had said, It is my master: therefore she took a veil, and covered herself. And the servant told Isaac all things that he had done."—PP 173 (1890).

Isaac was highly honored by God in being made inheritor of the promises through which the world was to be blessed; yet when he was forty years of age he submitted to his father's judgment in appointing his experienced, God-fearing servant to choose a wife for him. And the result of that marriage, as presented in the Scriptures, is a tender and beautiful picture of domestic happiness: "Isaac brought her into his mother Sarah's tent, and took Rebekah, and she became his wife; and he loved her: and Isaac was comforted after his mother's death."—PP 175 (1890).

JOCHEBED, MOTHER OF MOSES
Exodus 2

The [Egyptian] king and his counselors had hoped to subdue the Israelites with hard labor, and thus decrease their numbers and crush out their independent spirit. Failing to accomplish their purpose, they proceeded to more cruel measures. Orders were issued to the women whose employment gave them opportunity for executing the command, to destroy the Hebrew male children at their birth. Satan was the mover in this matter. He knew that a deliverer was to be raised up among the Israelites; and by leading the king to destroy their children he hoped to defeat the divine purpose. But the women feared God, and dared not execute the cruel mandate. The Lord approved their course, and prospered them. The king, angry at the failure of his design, made the command more urgent and extensive. The whole nation was called upon to hunt out and slaughter his helpless victims. "And Pharaoh charged all his people, saying, Every son that is born ye shall cast into the river, and every daughter ye shall save alive."

While this decree was in full force a son was born to Amram and Jochebed, devout Israelites of the tribe of Levi. The babe was "a goodly child"; and the parents, believing that the time of Israel's release was drawing near, and that God would raise up a deliverer for His people, determined that their little one should not be sacrificed. Faith in God strengthened their hearts, "and they were not afraid of the king's commandment." Hebrews 11:23.—PP 242 (1890).

When this cruel decree was in full force, Moses was born. His mother hid him as long as she could with any safety, and then prepared a little vessel of bulrushes, making it secure with pitch, that no water might enter the little ark, and placed it at the edge of the water, while his sister should be lingering around the water with apparent indifference. She was anxiously watching to see what would become of her little brother.

Angels were also watching that no harm should come to the

helpless infant, which had been placed there by an affectionate mother, and committed to the care of God by her earnest prayers mingled with tears. And these angels directed the footsteps of Pharaoh's daughter to the river, near the very spot where lay the innocent little stranger. Her attention was attracted to the little strange vessel, and she sent one of her waiting-maids to fetch it to her. And when she had removed the cover of this singularly constructed little vessel, she saw a lovely babe, "and, behold, the babe wept. And she had compassion on him." She knew that a tender Hebrew mother had taken this singular means to preserve the life of her much-loved babe, and she decided at once that it should be her son. The sister of Moses immediately came forward and inquired, "Shall I go and call to thee a nurse of the Hebrew women, that she may nurse the child for thee? And Pharaoh's daughter said to her, Go."—1SP 162, 163 (1870).

Jochebed was a woman and a slave. Her lot in life was humble, her burden heavy. But through no other woman, save Mary of Nazareth, has the world received greater blessing. Knowing that her child must soon pass beyond her care, to the guardianship of those who knew not God, she the more earnestly endeavored to link his soul with heaven. She sought to implant in his heart love and loyalty to God. And faithfully was the work accomplished. Those principles of truth that were the burden of his mother's teaching and the lesson of her life, no after influence could induce Moses to renounce.—Ed 61 (1903).

MIRIAM, SISTER OF MOSES
Book of Exodus; Numbers 12

Miriam watched over Moses as their mother hid him in the bulrushes. Later she was associated with Moses and Aaron in the deliverance of God's people from Egypt. She was talented and gifted in many ways, but jealousy of her position with Moses led her to make serious mistakes.

At Hazeroth, the next encampment after leaving Taberah, a still more bitter trial awaited Moses. Aaron and Miriam had occupied a position of high honor and leadership in Israel. Both were endowed with the prophetic gift, and both had been divinely associated with Moses in the deliverance of the Hebrews. "I sent before thee Moses,

Aaron, and Miriam" (Micah 6:4) are the words of the Lord by the prophet Micah.

Miriam's force of character had been early displayed when as a child she watched beside the Nile the little basket in which was hidden the infant Moses. Her self-control and tact God had made instrumental in preserving the deliverer of His people. Richly endowed with the gifts of poetry and music, Miriam had led the women of Israel in song and dance on the shore of the Red Sea. In the affections of the people and the honor of Heaven she stood second only to Moses and Aaron. But the same evil that first brought discord in heaven sprang up in the heart of this woman of Israel, and she did not fail to find a sympathizer in her dissatisfaction.—PP 382 (1890).

God had chosen Moses, and had put His Spirit upon him; and Miriam and Aaron, by their murmurings, were guilty of disloyalty, not only to their appointed leader, but to God Himself. The seditious whisperers were summoned to the tabernacle, and brought face to face with Moses. "And Jehovah came down in the pillar of the cloud, and stood in the door of the tabernacle, and called Aaron and Miriam." Their claim to the prophetic gift was not denied; God might have spoken to them in visions and dreams. But to Moses, whom the Lord Himself declared "faithful in all mine house," a nearer communion had been granted. With *him* God spake mouth to mouth. "Wherefore then were ye not afraid to speak against my servant Moses? And the anger of the Lord was kindled against them; and he departed."

The cloud disappeared from the tabernacle in token of God's displeasure, and Miriam was smitten. She "became leprous, white as snow." Aaron was spared, but he was severely rebuked in Miriam's punishment. Now, their pride humbled in the dust, Aaron confessed their sin, and entreated that his sister might not be left to perish by that loathsome and deadly scourge. In answer to the prayers of Moses the leprosy was cleansed. Miriam was, however, shut out of the camp for seven days. Not until she was banished from the encampment did the symbol of God's favor again rest upon the tabernacle. In respect for her high position, and in grief at the blow that had fallen upon her, the whole company abode in Hazeroth, awaiting her return.

This manifestation of the Lord's displeasure was designed to be a warning to all Israel, to check the growing spirit of discontent and insubordination. If Miriam's envy and dissatisfaction had not been signally rebuked, it would have resulted in great evil. Envy is one of the most satanic traits that can exist in the human heart, and it is one of the most baleful in its effects. . . . It was envy that first caused discord in heaven, and its indulgence has wrought untold evil among men. "Where envying and strife is, there is confusion and every evil work." James 3:16.—PP 384, 385 (1890).

From Kadesh the children of Israel had turned back into the wilderness; and the period of their desert sojourn being ended, they came, "even the whole congregation, into the desert of Zin in the first month: and the people abode in Kadesh." Numbers 20:1.

Here Miriam died and was buried. From that scene of rejoicing on the shores of the Red Sea, when Israel went forth with song and dance to celebrate Jehovah's triumph, to the wilderness grave which ended a lifelong wandering—such had been the fate of millions who with high hopes had come forth from Egypt. Sin had dashed from their lips the cup of blessing.—PP 410 (1890).

ZIPPORAH, WIFE OF MOSES
Exodus 2
When Moses fled from Egypt to the land of Midian, he met and married Jethro's daughter, Zipporah.

Yielding to the spirit of dissatisfaction, Miriam found cause of complaint in events that God had especially overruled. The marriage of Moses had been displeasing to her. That he should choose a woman of another nation, instead of taking a wife from among the Hebrews, was an offense to her family and national pride. Zipporah was treated with ill-disguised contempt.

Though called a "Cushite woman" (Numbers 12:1, RV), the wife of Moses was a Midianite, and thus a descendant of Abraham. In personal appearance she differed from the Hebrews in being of a somewhat darker complexion. Though not an Israelite, Zipporah was a worshiper of the true God. She was of a timid, retiring disposition, gentle and affectionate, and greatly distressed at the sight of suffering.—PP 383 (1890).

On the way [to Egypt] from Midian, Moses received a startling and terrible warning of the Lord's displeasure. An angel appeared to him in a threatening manner, as if he would immediately destroy him. No explanation was given; but Moses remembered that he had disregarded one of God's requirements; yielding to the persuasion of his wife, he had neglected to perform the rite of circumcision upon their youngest son. He had failed to comply with the condition by which his child could be entitled to the blessings of God's covenant with Israel; and such a neglect on the part of their chosen leader could not but lessen the force of the divine precepts upon the people. Zipporah, fearing that her husband would be slain, performed the rite herself, and the angel then permitted Moses to pursue his journey. In his mission to Pharaoh, Moses was to be placed in a position of great peril; his life could be preserved only through the protection of holy angels. But while living in neglect of a known duty, he would not be secure; for he could not be shielded by the angels of God.

In the time of trouble just before the coming of Christ, the righteous will be preserved through the ministration of heavenly angels; but there will be no security for the transgressor of God's law. Angels cannot then protect those who are disregarding one of the divine precepts.—PP 255, 256 (1890).

RAHAB

Joshua 2 and 6; Hebrews 11:30, 31

Rahab was a harlot who lived on the wall of Jericho. She hid the two Israelite spies sent to check out the defenses of that city. Because of her kindness to them, and her declaration of belief in God, the spies promised that the lives of Rahab and her family would be spared when the attack came on Jericho.

A few miles beyond the [Jordan] river, just opposite the place where the Israelites were encamped, was the large and strongly fortified city of Jericho. This city was virtually the key to the whole country, and it would present a formidable obstacle to the success of Israel. Joshua therefore sent two young men as spies to visit this city and ascertain something as to its population, its resources, and the strength of its fortifications. The inhabitants of the city, terrified and suspicious, were constantly on the alert, and the messengers were in great danger.

Daughters of God

They were, however, preserved by Rahab, a woman of Jericho, at the peril of her own life. In return for her kindness they gave her a promise of protection when the city should be taken.—PP 482 (1890).

Jericho was a city devoted to the most extravagant idolatry. The inhabitants were very wealthy. All the riches that God had given them they accredited to the gifts of their gods. Gold and silver were in abundance. Like the people before the Flood, they were corrupt and blasphemous. They insulted and provoked the God of heaven by their wicked works. God's judgments awakened against Jericho. It was a stronghold. But the Captain of the Lord's host came Himself from heaven to lead the armies of heaven in the attack upon the city. Angels of God laid hold of the massive walls and brought them to the ground. God had said that the city of Jericho should be accursed, and that all should perish except Rahab and her household. They should be saved because of the favor that Rahab showed the messengers of the Lord.—RH, Sept. 16, 1873.

In the deliverance of Israel from Egypt a knowledge of the power of God spread far and wide. The warlike people of the stronghold of Jericho trembled. "As soon as we had heard these things," said Rahab, "our hearts did melt, neither did there remain any more courage in any man, because of you: for Jehovah your God, he is God in heaven above, and in earth beneath." Joshua 2:11.—PP 369 (1890).

All the inhabitants of the city [Jericho], with every living thing that it contained, "both man and woman, young and old, and ox, and sheep, and ass," were put to the sword. Only faithful Rahab, with her household, was spared, in fulfillment of the promise of the spies. The city itself was burned.—PP 491 (1890).

See Matthew 1:1-16 for genealogy of Jesus, whose ancestor was Rahab.

DEBORAH

Judges 4 and 5

Deborah the prophet governed Israel during the reign of Jabin, a Canaanite king who was very cruel to the children of Israel. Life in the villages was harsh. The people were plundered and fled to the fortified cities for protection. Then the Lord raised up Deborah, who was like a loving mother to Israel. God sent a message through her to Barak that he should prepare to meet Sisera,

Jabin's general, in battle. Barak refused to go unless Deborah went with him. She agreed, but warned him that because of his lack of faith in the words of the Lord, the honor of killing Sisera would go to a woman, not to Barak.

The Israelites, having again separated themselves from God by idolatry, were grievously oppressed by [their] enemies. The property and even the lives of the people were in constant danger. Hence the villages and lonely dwellings were deserted, and the people congregated in the walled cities. The highroads were unoccupied, and the people went from place to place by unfrequented byways. At the places for drawing water, many were robbed and even murdered, and to add to their distress, the Israelites were unarmed. Among forty thousand men, not a sword or a spear could be found.

For twenty years, the Israelites groaned under the yoke of the oppressor; then they turned from their idolatry, and with humiliation and repentance cried unto the Lord for deliverance. They did not cry in vain. There was dwelling in Israel a woman illustrious for her piety, and through her the Lord chose to deliver His people. Her name was Deborah. She was known as a prophetess, and in the absence of the usual magistrates, the people had sought to her for counsel and justice.

The Lord communicated to Deborah His purpose to destroy the enemies of Israel, and bade her send for a man named Barak, of the tribe of Naphtali, and make known to him the instructions which she had received. She accordingly sent for Barak, and directed him to assemble ten thousand men of the tribes of Naphtali and Zebulun, and make war upon the armies of King Jabin.

Barak knew the scattered, disheartened, and unarmed condition of the Hebrews, and the strength and skill of their enemies. Although he had been designated by the Lord Himself as the one chosen to deliver Israel, and had received the assurance that God would go with him and subdue their enemies, yet he was timid and distrustful. He accepted the message from Deborah as the word of God, but he had little confidence in Israel, and feared that they would not obey his call. He refused to engage in such a doubtful undertaking unless Deborah would accompany him, and thus support his efforts by her influence and counsel. Deborah consented, but assured him that because of his lack of faith, the victory gained should not bring honor to him; for Sisera would be betrayed into the hands of a woman. . . .

The Israelites had established themselves in a strong position in the mountains, to await a favorable opportunity for an attack. Encouraged by Deborah's assurance that the very day had come for signal victory, Barak led his army down into the open plain, and boldly made a charge upon the enemy. The God of battle fought for Israel, and neither skill in warfare, nor superiority of numbers and equipment, could withstand them. The hosts of Sisera were panic-stricken; in their terror they sought only how they might escape. Vast numbers were slain, and the strength of the invading army was utterly destroyed. The Israelites acted with courage and promptness; but God alone could have discomfited the enemy, and the victory could be ascribed to Him alone.

When Sisera saw that his army was defeated, he left his chariot, and endeavored to make his escape on foot, as a common soldier. Approaching the tent of Heber, one of the descendants of Jethro, the fugitive was invited to find shelter there. In the absence of Heber, Jael, his wife, courteously offered Sisera a refreshing draught, and opportunity for repose, and the weary general soon fell asleep.

Jael was at first ignorant of the character of her guest, and she re-solved to conceal him; but when she afterward learned that he was Sisera, the enemy of God and of His people, her purpose changed. As he lay before her asleep, she overcame her natural reluctance to such an act, and slew him by driving a nail through his temples, pin-ning him to the earth. As Barak, in pursuit of his enemy, passed that way, he was called in by Jael to behold the vainglorious captain dead at his feet—slain by the hand of a woman.

Deborah celebrated the triumph of Israel in a most sublime and impassioned song. She ascribed to God all the glory of their deliver-ance, and bade the people praise Him for His wonderful works. She called upon the kings and princes of surrounding nations to hear what God had wrought for Israel, and to take warning not to do them harm. She showed that honor and power belong to God, and not to men, or to their idols. She portrayed the awful exhibitions of divine power and majesty displayed at Sinai. She set before Israel their helpless and distressed condition, under the oppression of their enemies, and related in glowing language the history of their deliverance.—ST, June 16, 1881.

HANNAH, MOTHER OF SAMUEL
1 Samuel 1; 2

Hannah, first and best-loved wife of Elkanah, a Levite, was barren and greatly desired a child. At the yearly feast at Shiloh she silently cried and prayed to the Lord to grant her a child. Eli, the priest, heard her and told her to "go in peace, and may the Lord, the God of Israel, answer your prayer."

The father of Samuel was Elkanah, a Levite, who dwelt at Ramah, in Mount Ephraim. He was a person of wealth and influence, a kind husband, and a man who feared and reverenced God. Hannah, the wife of Elkanah, was a woman of piety and devotion. Humility, conscientiousness, and a firm reliance upon God, were ruling traits in her character. Of Hannah it might truly be said, in the words of the wise man: "The heart of her husband doth safely trust in her."—ST, Oct. 27, 1881.

The blessing so earnestly sought by every Hebrew was denied this godly pair; their home was not gladdened by the voice of childhood; and the desire to perpetuate his name led the husband—as it had led many others—to contract a second marriage. But this step, prompted by a lack of faith in God, did not bring happiness. Sons and daughters were added to the household; but the joy and beauty of God's sacred institution had been marred and the peace of the family was broken. Peninnah, the new wife, was jealous and narrow-minded, and she bore herself with pride and insolence. To Hannah, hope seemed crushed and life a weary burden; yet she met the trial with uncomplaining meekness.

Elkanah faithfully observed the ordinances of God. The worship at Shiloh was still maintained, but on account of irregularities in the ministration his services were not required at the sanctuary, to which, being a Levite, he was to give attendance. Yet he went up with his family to worship and sacrifice at the appointed gatherings.

Even amid the sacred festivities connected with the service of God the evil spirit that had cursed his home intruded. After pre-

senting the thank offerings, all the family, according to the established custom, united in a solemn yet joyous feast. Upon these occasions Elkanah gave the mother of his children a portion for herself
and for each of her sons and daughters; and in token of regard for
Hannah, he gave her a double portion, signifying that his affection
for her was the same as if she had had a son. Then the second wife,
fired with jealousy, claimed the precedence as one highly favored of
God, and taunted Hannah with her childless state as evidence of the
Lord's displeasure.

This was repeated from year to year, until Hannah could endure
it no longer. Unable to hide her grief, she wept without restraint, and
withdrew from the feast. Her husband vainly sought to comfort her.
"Why weepest thou? and why eatest thou not? and why is thy heart
grieved?" he said; "am I not better to thee than ten sons?"

Hannah uttered no reproach. The burden which she could share
with no earthly friend she cast upon God. Earnestly she pleaded that
He would take away her reproach and grant her the precious gift of
a son to nurture and train for Him. And she made a solemn vow that
if her request were granted, she would dedicate her child to God,
even from its birth. Hannah had drawn near to the entrance of the
tabernacle, and in the anguish of her spirit she "prayed, . . . and wept
sore." Yet she communed with God in silence, uttering no sound. In
those evil times such scenes of worship were rarely witnessed.
Irreverent feasting and even drunkenness were not uncommon,
even at the religious festivals; and Eli the high priest, observing
Hannah, supposed that she was overcome with wine. Thinking to
administer a deserved rebuke, he said sternly, "How long wilt thou
be drunken? put away thy wine from thee."

Pained and startled, Hannah answered gently, "No, my lord, I
am a woman of a sorrowful spirit: I have drunk neither wine nor
strong drink, but have poured out my soul before the Lord. Count
not thine handmaid for a daughter of Belial: for out of the abundance
of my complaint and grief have I spoken hitherto."

The high priest was deeply moved, for he was a man of God; and
in place of rebuke he uttered a blessing: "Go in peace: and the God
of Israel grant thee thy petition that thou hast asked of Him."

Women of Note in the Old Testament

Hannah's prayer was granted; she received the gift for which she had so earnestly entreated. As she looked upon the child, she called him Samuel—"asked of God."—PP 569, 570 (1890).

During the first three years of the life of Samuel the prophet, his mother carefully taught him to distinguish between good and evil. By every familiar object surrounding him, she sought to lead his thoughts up to the Creator. In fulfillment of her vow to give her son to the Lord, with great self-denial she placed him under the care of Eli the high priest, to be trained for service in the house of God. Though Samuel's youth was passed at the tabernacle devoted to the worship of God, he was not free from evil influences or sinful example. The sons of Eli feared not God, nor honored their father; but Samuel did not seek their company nor follow their evil ways. His early training led him to choose to maintain his Christian integrity. What a reward was Hannah's! And what an encouragement to faithfulness is her example!—RH, Sept. 8, 1904.

From Shiloh, Hannah quietly returned to her home at Ramah, leaving the child Samuel to be trained for service in the house of God, under the instruction of the high priest. From the earliest dawn of intellect, she had taught her son to love and reverence God, and to regard himself as the Lord's. By every familiar object surrounding him, she had sought to lead his thoughts up to the Creator. When separated from her child, the faithful mother's solicitude did not cease. Every day he was the subject of her prayers. Every year she made, with her own hands, a robe of service for him; and as she went up with her husband to worship at Shiloh, she gave the child this reminder of her love. Every fiber of the little garment had been woven with a prayer that he might be pure, noble, and true. She did not ask for her son worldly greatness, but she earnestly pleaded that he might attain that greatness which Heaven values—that he might honor God and bless his fellowmen.—PP 572 (1890).

ABIGAIL

1 Samuel 25

Abigail was the beautiful, kind, and intelligent wife of Nabal, a mean and violent-tempered man. By her wise course she was able to avoid much bloodshed when her husband treated David and his men with contempt.

When David was a fugitive from the face of Saul, he had camped near the possessions of Nabal and had protected the flocks and the shepherds of this man. . . . In a time of need, David sent messengers to Nabal with a courteous message, asking for food for himself and his men, and Nabal answered with insolence, returning evil for good, and refusing to share his abundance with his neighbors. No message could have been more respectful than that which David sent to this man, but Nabal accused David and his men falsely in order to justify himself in his selfishness, and represented David and his followers as runaway slaves. When the messenger returned with this insolent taunt, David's indignation was aroused, and he determined to have speedy revenge.—21MR 213 (1891).

One of Nabal's servants hastened to Abigail, the wife of Nabal, after he had dismissed David's young men, and told her what had happened. "Behold," he said, "David sent messengers out of the wilderness to salute our master; and he railed on them. But the men were very good unto us, and we were not hurt, neither missed we any thing, as long as we were conversant with them, when we were in the fields. They were a wall unto us both by night and day, all the while we were with them keeping the sheep. Now therefore know and consider what thou wilt do; for evil is determined against our master, and against all his household."

Without consulting her husband or telling him of her intention, Abigail made up an ample supply of provisions, which, laded upon asses, she sent forward in the charge of servants, and herself started out to meet the band of David. She met them in a covert of a hill. "And when Abigail saw David, she hasted, and lighted off the ass, and fell before David on her face, and bowed herself to the ground, and fell at his feet, and said, Upon me, my lord, upon me let this iniquity be: and let thine handmaid, I pray thee, speak in thine audience." Abigail addressed David with as much reverence as though speaking to a crowned monarch. Nabal had scornfully exclaimed, "Who is David?" but Abigail called him, "my lord." With kind words she sought to soothe his irritated feelings, and she pleaded with him in behalf of her husband. With nothing of ostentation or pride, but full of the wisdom and love of God, Abigail revealed the strength of her devotion to her household; and she made it plain to David that the unkind course of her husband was in no wise premeditated against him as a personal affront, but was simply the outburst of an unhappy and selfish nature.

"Now therefore, my lord, as the Lord liveth, and as thy soul liveth, seeing the Lord hath withholden thee from coming to shed blood, and from avenging thyself with thine own hand, now let thine enemies, and they that seek evil to my lord, be as Nabal." Abigail did not take to herself the credit of this reasoning to turn David from his hasty purpose, but gave to God the honor and the praise. She then offered her rich provision as a peace offering to the men of David, and still pleaded as if she herself were the one who had so excited the resentment of the chief.—PP 665, 666 (1890).

Although Nabal had refused the needy company of David and his men, yet that very night he made an extravagant feast for himself and his riotous friends, and indulged in eating and drinking till he sunk in drunken stupor. The next day after the effects of his drunken debauch had somewhat passed away, his wife told him of how near he had been to death, and of how the calamity had been averted. As he listened, he realized what a course of evil would have resulted but for Abigail's discretion, and terror filled his heart. Palsied with horror, he sat down and never recovered from the shock.

From this history, we can see that there are circumstances under which it is proper for a woman to act promptly and independently, moving with decision in the way she knows to be the way of the Lord. The wife is to stand by the side of the husband as his equal, sharing all the responsibilities of life, rendering due respect to him who has selected her for his lifelong companion.—21MR 214, 215 (1891).

The Lord would have the wife render respect unto her husband, but always as it is fit in the Lord. In the character of Abigail, the wife of Nabal, we have an illustration of womanhood after the order of Christ, while her husband illustrates what a man may become who yields himself to the control of Satan.—21MR 213 (1891).

HULDAH, THE PROPHET
2 Kings 22

Josiah, from his earliest manhood, had endeavored to take advantage of his position as king to exalt the principles of God's holy law. And now, while Shaphan the scribe was reading to him out of the book of the law, the king discerned in this volume a treasure of knowledge, a powerful ally, in the work of reform he so much desired to see wrought in the land. He resolved to walk in the light of its counsels, and also to do all in his power to acquaint his people with its teachings and to lead them, if possible, to cultivate reverence and love for the law of heaven.

But was it possible to bring about the needed reform? Israel had almost reached the limit of divine forbearance; soon God would arise to punish those who had brought dishonor upon His name. Already the anger of the Lord was kindled against the people. Overwhelmed with sorrow and dismay, Josiah rent his garments and bowed before God in agony of spirit, seeking pardon for the sins of an impenitent nation.

At that time the prophetess Huldah was living in Jerusalem, near the temple. The mind of the king, filled with anxious foreboding, reverted to her, and he determined to inquire of the Lord through this chosen messenger to learn, if possible, whether by any means within his power he might save erring Judah, now on the verge of ruin.

The gravity of the situation and the respect in which he held the prophetess led him to choose as his messengers to her the first men of the kingdom. "Go ye," he bade them, "inquire of the Lord for me, and for the people, and for all Judah, concerning the words of this book that is found: for great is the wrath of the Lord that is kindled against us, because our fathers have not hearkened unto the words of this book, to do according unto all that which is written concerning us." 2 Kings 22:13.

Through Huldah the Lord sent Josiah word that Jerusalem's ruin could not be averted. Even should the people now humble themselves before God, they could not escape their punishment. So long had their senses been deadened by wrongdoing that, if judgment should not come upon them, they would soon return to the same sinful course. "Tell the man that sent you to me," the prophetess declared, "Thus saith the Lord, Behold, I will bring evil upon this place, and upon the inhabitants thereof, even all the words of the book which the king of Judah hath read: because they have forsaken me, and have burned incense unto other gods, that they might provoke me to anger with all the works of their hands; therefore my wrath shall be kindled against this place, and shall not be quenched." Verses 15-17.

But because the king had humbled his heart before God, the Lord would acknowledge his promptness in seeking forgiveness and mercy. To him was sent the message: "Because thine heart was tender, and thou hast humbled thyself before the Lord, when thou heardest what I spake against this place, and against the inhabitants thereof, that they should become a desolation and a curse, and hast rent thy clothes, and wept before me; I also have heard thee, saith the Lord. Behold therefore, I will gather thee unto thy fathers, and thou shalt be gathered into thy grave in peace; and thine eyes shall not see all the evil which I will bring upon this place." Verses 19, 20.—RH, July 29, 1915.

ESTHER

Book of Esther

Esther was a beautiful Jewish girl, cousin of Mordecai, who took her into his home after her parents died, and loved her as his own daughter. God used her to save the Jewish people in the land of Persia.

In ancient times the Lord worked in a wonderful way through consecrated women who united in His work with men whom He had chosen to stand as His representatives. He used women to gain great and decisive victories. More than once, in times of emergency, He brought them to the front and worked through them for the salvation of many lives. Through Esther the queen, the Lord accomplished a mighty deliverance for His people. At a time when it seemed that no power could save them, Esther and the women associated with her, by fasting and prayer and prompt action, met the issue, and brought salvation to their people.—SpT-B15 1, 2 (1911).

A study of women's work in connection with the cause of God in the Old Testament times will teach us lessons that will enable us to meet emergencies in the work today. We may not be brought into such a critical and prominent place as were the people of God in the time of Esther; but often converted women can act an important part in more humble positions. This many have been doing and are still ready to do.—LLM 570 (1911).

The great majority of the Israelites had chosen to remain in the land of their exile [Medo-Persia] rather than undergo the hardships of the return journey and the reestablishment of their desolated cities and homes. . . .

Through Haman the Agagite, an unscrupulous man high in authority in Medo-Persia, Satan worked at this time to counterwork the purposes of God. Haman cherished bitter malice against Mordecai, a Jew. Mordecai had done Haman no harm, but had simply refused to show him worshipful reverence. . . .

Misled by the false statements of Haman, Xerxes was induced to issue a decree providing for the massacre of all the Jews "scattered abroad and dispersed among the people in all the provinces" of the Medo-Persian kingdom. . . .

The plots of the enemy were defeated by a Power that reigns among the children of men. In the providence of God, Esther, a Jewess who feared the Most High, had been made queen of the Medo-Persian kingdom. Mordecai was a near relative of hers. In their extremity they decided to appeal to Xerxes in behalf of their people. Esther was to venture into his presence as an intercessor. "Who knoweth," said Mordecai, "whether thou art come to the kingdom for such a time as this?" Esther 4:14.

The crisis that Esther faced demanded quick, earnest action; but both she and Mordecai realized that unless God should work mightily in their behalf, their own efforts would be unavailing. So Esther took time for communion with God, the source of her strength. "Go," she directed Mordecai, "gather together all the Jews that are present in Shushan, and fast ye for me, and neither eat nor drink three days, night or day: I also and my maidens will fast likewise; and so will I go in unto the king, which is not according to the law: and if I perish, I perish" (verse 16).—PK 598-601 (1917).

The events that followed in rapid succession—the appearance of Esther before the king, the marked favor shown her, the banquets of the king and the queen with Haman as the only guest, the troubled sleep of the king, the public honor shown Mordecai, and the humiliation and fall of Haman upon discovery of his wicked plot against the Jewish people—all these are parts of a familiar story. In a marvelous manner God wrought in behalf of His penitent people; and a counter-decree issued by the king, allowing them to fight for their lives, was rapidly communicated to every part of the realm by mounted couriers who were "hastened and pressed on by the king's commandment." "And in every province, and in every city, whithersoever the king's commandment and his decree came, the Jews had joy and gladness, a feast and a good day. And many of the people of the land became Jews; for the fear of the Jews fell upon them." Esther 8:14, 17.—RH, Jan. 23, 1908.

Women of Note in the New Testament

3

During the years of Christ's ministry on earth, godly women assisted in the work that the Saviour and His disciples were carrying forward. If those who were opposing this work could have found anything out of the regular order in the conduct of these women, it would have closed the work at once. But while women were laboring with Christ and the apostles, the entire work was conducted on so high a plane as to be above the shadow of a suspicion. No occasion for any accusation could be found. The minds of all were directed to the Scriptures, rather than to individuals. The truth was proclaimed intelligently, and so plainly that all could understand.

—Evangelism, pp. 67, 68

ELISABETH, MOTHER OF JOHN THE BAPTIST
Luke 1

"There was in the days of Herod, the king of Judaea, a certain priest named Zacharias, of the course of Abia: and his wife was of the daughters of Aaron, and her name was Elisabeth. And they were both righteous before God, walking in all the commandments and ordinances of the Lord blameless. And they had no child, because that Elisabeth was barren, and they both were now well stricken in years. And it came to pass, that while he executed the priest's office before God in the order of his course, according to the custom of the priest's office, his lot was to burn incense when he went into the temple of the Lord. And the whole multitude of the people were praying without at the time of incense. And there appeared unto him an angel of the Lord standing on the right side of the altar of incense. And when Zacharias saw him, he was troubled, and fear fell upon him. But the angel said unto him, Fear not, Zacharias: for thy prayer is heard; and thy wife Elisabeth shall bear thee a son, and thou shalt call his name John. And thou shalt have joy and gladness; and many shall rejoice at his birth. For he shall be great in the sight of the Lord, and shall drink neither wine nor strong drink; and he shall be filled with the Holy Ghost, even from his mother's womb. And many of the children of Israel shall he turn to the Lord their God. And he shall go before him in the spirit and power of Elias, to turn the hearts of the fathers to the children, and the disobedient to the wisdom of the just; to make ready a people prepared for the Lord. . . . And the child grew, and waxed strong in spirit, and was in the deserts till the day of his showing unto Israel."

An angel from heaven came to instruct Zacharias and Elisabeth as to how they should train and educate their child, so as to work in harmony with God in preparing a messenger to announce the coming of Christ. As parents they were to faithfully cooperate with God in forming such a character in John as would fit him to perform the part God had assigned him as a competent worker. John was the son of their old age, he was a child of miracle, and the parents might have reasoned that he had a special work to do for the Lord, and the Lord would take care of him. But the parents did not thus reason; they moved to a retired place in the country, where their son would not be exposed to the temptations of city life, or induced to depart from the counsel and instruction which they as parents would give him. They acted their part in developing a character in the child that would in every way meet the purpose for which God had designed his life. By no careless neglect on their part shall their son fail to become good and wise, "to give light to them that sit in darkness and in the shadow of death, and to guide our feet into the way of peace." They sacredly fulfilled their obligation.—ST, Apr. 16, 1896.

MARY, THE MOTHER OF JESUS
Matthew, Mark, Luke, and John

When the Majesty of heaven became a babe and was entrusted to Mary, she did not have much to offer for the precious gift. She brought to the altar only two turtledoves, the offering appointed for the poor; but they were an acceptable sacrifice to the Lord. She could not present rare treasures such as the wise men of the East came to Bethlehem to lay before the Son of God; yet the mother of Jesus was not rejected because of the smallness of her gift. It was the willingness of her heart that the Lord looked upon, and her love made the offering sweet. So God will accept our gift, however small, if it is the best we have, and is offered from love to Him.—RH, Dec. 9, 1890.

The priest went through the ceremony of his official work. He took the child in his arms, and held it up before the altar. After handing it back to its mother, he inscribed the name "Jesus" on the roll of the firstborn. Little did he think, as the babe lay in his arms, that it was the Majesty of heaven, the King of glory. The priest did not think that this babe was the One of whom Moses had written, "A prophet shall the Lord your God raise up unto you of your brethren, like unto me; him shall ye hear in all things whatsoever he shall say unto you." Acts 3:22. He did not think that this babe was He whose glory Moses had asked to see. But One greater than Moses lay in the priest's arms; and when he enrolled the child's name, he was enrolling the name of One who was the foundation of the whole Jewish economy.—DA 52 (1898).

[From the first] Mary looked forward to the Messiah's reign on David's throne, but she saw not the baptism of suffering by which it must be won. Through Simeon [at Christ's dedication as a baby in the temple] it is revealed that the Messiah is to have no unobstructed passage through the world. In the words to Mary, "A sword shall pierce through thy own soul also," God in His tender mercy gives to the mother of Jesus an intimation of the anguish that already for His sake she had begun to bear.—DA 56 (1898).

The child Jesus did not receive instruction in the synagogue schools. His mother was His first human teacher. From her lips and from the scrolls of the prophets, He learned of heavenly things. The very words which He Himself had spoken to Moses for Israel He was now taught at His mother's knee. As He advanced from childhood to youth, He did not seek the schools of the rabbis. He needed not the education to be obtained from such sources; for God was His instructor.—DA 70 (1898).

Among the Jews the twelfth year was the dividing line between childhood and youth. On completing this year a Hebrew boy was called a son of the law, and also a son of God. He was given special opportunities for religious instruction, and was expected to participate in the sacred feasts and observances. It was in accordance with this custom that Jesus in His boyhood made the Passover visit to Jerusalem. Like all devout Israelites, Joseph and Mary went up every year to attend the Passover; and when Jesus had reached the required age, they took Him with them.—DA 75 (1898).

For the first time the child Jesus looked upon the temple. He saw the white-robed priests performing their solemn ministry. He beheld the bleeding victim upon the altar of sacrifice. With the worshipers He bowed in prayer, while the cloud of incense ascended before God. He witnessed the impressive rites of the paschal service. Day by day He saw their meaning more clearly. Every act seemed to be bound up with His own life. New impulses were awakening within Him. Silent and absorbed, He seemed to be studying out a great problem. The mystery of His mission was opening to the Saviour.

Rapt in the contemplation of these scenes, He did not remain beside His parents. He sought to be alone. When the paschal services were ended, He still lingered in the temple courts; and when the worshipers departed from Jerusalem, He was left behind.

In this visit to Jerusalem, the parents of Jesus wished to bring Him in connection with the great teachers in Israel. . . . An apartment connected with the temple was devoted to a sacred school, after the manner of the schools of the prophets. Here leading rabbis with their pupils assembled, and hither the child Jesus came. Seating Himself at the feet of these grave, learned men, He listened to their instruction.—DA 78 (1898).

The wise men were surprised at the questions that the child Jesus asked. They wanted to encourage Him in studying the Bible, and they wanted to see how much He knew about the prophecies. This is why they asked Him so many questions. Joseph and Mary were as much surprised at the wise answers of their son as were the wise men themselves. When there was a pause, Mary, the mother of Jesus, came up to her son, and asked, "Son, why hast thou thus dealt with us? Behold, thy father and I have sought thee sorrowing." Then a divine light shone from Jesus' face, as He lifted His hand and said, "How is it that ye sought me? Wist ye not that I must be about my Father's business? And they understood not the saying which he spake unto them." They did not know what He really meant by these words, but they knew He was a true son, who would be submissive to their commands. Though He was the Son of God, He went down to Nazareth and was subject to His parents. Though His mother did not understand the meaning of His words, she did not forget them, but "kept all these saying in her heart."—YI, Nov. 28, 1895.

As Joseph and Mary should return from Jerusalem alone with Jesus, He hoped to direct their minds to the prophecies of the suffering Saviour. Upon Calvary He sought to lighten His mother's grief. He was thinking of her now. Mary was to witness His last agony, and Jesus desired her to understand His mission, that she might be strengthened to endure, when the sword should pierce through her soul. As Jesus had been separated from her, and she had sought Him sorrowing three days, so when He should be offered up for the sins of the world, He would again be lost to her for three days. And as He should come forth from the tomb, her sorrow would again be turned to joy. But how much better she could have borne the anguish of His death if she had understood the Scriptures to which He was now trying to turn her thoughts!—DA 82 (1898).

For twelve years of His life He had walked the streets of Nazareth, and worked with Joseph at his trade, carefully performing the duties that devolved upon a son. Hitherto He had not given indications of His peculiar character, or made manifest the nature of His mission to earth as the Son of God. But upon this occasion He made known to His parents the fact that He had a higher, holier mission to perform than they thought, for He had a work to do which had been committed to Him by His heavenly Father. Mary knew that

Jesus had disclaimed relationship to Joseph, and claimed His sonship to the Eternal. She was perplexed; she did not fully comprehend the meaning of the words herself when He referred to His mission. She questioned in her mind as to whether anyone had told Jesus that Joseph was not His true father, but that God was His Father. Mary pondered these things in her heart.—YI, July 13, 1893.

Mary believed in her heart that the holy child born of her was the long-promised Messiah, yet she dared not express her faith. Throughout His life on earth she was a partaker in His sufferings. She witnessed with sorrow the trials brought upon Him in His childhood and youth. By her vindication of what she knew to be right in His conduct, she herself was brought into trying positions. She looked upon the associations of the home, and the mother's tender watchcare over her children, as of vital importance in the formation of character. The sons and daughters of Joseph knew this, and by appealing to her anxiety, they tried to correct the practices of Jesus according to their standard.—DA 90 (1898).

The life of Christ was marked with respect, devotion, and love for His mother. She often remonstrated with Him, and sought to have Him concede to the wishes of His brethren. His brethren could not persuade Him to change His habits of life in contemplating the works of God, in manifesting sympathy and tenderness toward the poor, the suffering, and the unfortunate, and in seeking to alleviate the sufferings of both men and dumb animals. When the priests and rulers came to Mary to persuade her to force Jesus to give allegiance to their ceremonies and traditions, she felt much troubled. But peace and confidence came to her troubled heart as her Son presented the clear statements of the Scriptures in upholding His practices.—ST, Aug. 6, 1896.

From the day when she heard the angel's announcement in the home at Nazareth, Mary had treasured every evidence that Jesus was the Messiah. His sweet, unselfish life assured her that He could be no other than the Sent of God. Yet there came to her also doubts and disappointments, and she had longed for the time when His glory should be revealed. Death had separated her from Joseph, who had shared her knowledge of the mystery of the birth of Jesus. Now there was no one to whom she could confide her hopes and fears.

The past two months had been very sorrowful. She had been parted from Jesus, in whose sympathy she found comfort; she pondered upon the words of Simeon, "A sword shall pierce through thy own soul also" (Luke 2:35); she recalled the three days of agony when she thought Jesus lost to her forever; and with an anxious heart she awaited His return.—DA 145 (1898).

The widowed mother had mourned over the sufferings that Jesus had endured in His loneliness. His Messiahship had caused her deep sorrow as well as joy. Yet strangely, as it appears to her, she meets Him at the marriage feast, the same tender, dutiful son, yet not the same, for His countenance is changed; she sees the marks of His fierce conflict in the wilderness of temptation, and the evidence of His high mission in His holy expression and the gentle dignity of His presence. She sees that He is accompanied by a number of young men who address Him with reverence, calling Him Master. These companions tell Mary of the wonderful things they have witnessed, not only at the baptism, but upon numerous other occasions, and they conclude by saying, "We have found Him of whom Moses in the law, and the prophets, did write, Jesus of Nazareth, who is the long-looked-for Messiah."—2SP 100 (1877).

Mary had heard of the manifestation at the Jordan, at His baptism. The tidings had been carried to Nazareth, and had brought to her mind afresh the scenes that for so many years had been hidden in her heart. In common with all Israel, Mary was deeply stirred by the mission of John the Baptist. Well she remembered the prophecy given at his birth. Now his connection with Jesus kindled her hopes anew. But tidings had reached her also of the mysterious departure of Jesus to the wilderness, and she was oppressed with troubled forebodings. . . .

As the guests assemble, many seem to be preoccupied with some topic of absorbing interest. A suppressed excitement pervades the company. Little groups converse together in eager but quiet tones, and wondering glances are turned upon the Son of Mary. As Mary had heard the disciples' testimony in regard to Jesus, she had been gladdened with the assurance that her long-cherished hopes were not in vain. Yet she would have been more than human if there had not mingled with this holy joy a trace of the fond mother's natural pride. As she saw the many glances bent upon Jesus, she longed to have Him prove to the company that He was really the Honored of God. She hoped there might be opportunity for Him to work a miracle before them.—DA 144, 145 (1898).

But though Mary had not a right conception of Christ's mission, she trusted Him implicitly. To this faith Jesus responded. It was to honor Mary's trust, and to strengthen the faith of His disciples, that the first miracle was performed. The disciples were to encounter many and great temptations to unbelief. To them the prophecies had made it clear beyond all controversy that Jesus was the Messiah. They looked for the religious leaders to receive Him with confidence even greater than their own. They declared among the people the wonderful works of Christ and their own confidence in His mission, but they were amazed and bitterly disappointed by the unbelief, the deepseated prejudice, and the enmity to Jesus, displayed by the priests and rabbis. The Saviour's early miracles strengthened the disciples to stand against this opposition.—DA 147 (1898).

It was the custom of the times for marriage festivities to continue several days. On this occasion, before the feast ended it was found that the supply of wine had failed. This discovery caused much perplexity and regret. It was unusual to dispense with wine on festive occasions, and its absence would seem to indicate a want of hospitality. As a relative of the parties, Mary had assisted in the arrangements for the feast, and she now spoke to Jesus, saying, "They have no wine." These words were a suggestion that He might supply their need. But Jesus answered, "Woman, what have I to do with thee? mine hour is not yet come."—DA 145 (1898).

In nowise disconcerted by the words of Jesus, Mary said to those serving at table, "Whatsoever he saith unto you, do it." Thus she did what she could to prepare the way for the work of Christ.—DA 148 (1898).

["After this he went down to Capernaum, he, and his mother, and his brethren, and his disciples: and they continued there not many days. And the Jews' passover was at hand, and Jesus went up to Jerusalem."—John 2:12, 13.

["There came then his brethren and his mother, and, standing without, sent unto him, calling him. And the multitude sat about him, and they said unto him, Behold, thy mother and thy brethren without seek for thee."—Mark 3:31, 32.]

❧

It is not clear from the Scriptures or from the Spirit of Prophecy writings how often, or whether, Mary saw Jesus again before His crucifixion.

"And when they were come to the place, which is called Calvary, there they crucified Him.". . . A vast multitude followed Jesus from the judgment hall to Calvary. The news of His condemnation had spread throughout Jerusalem. . . .

Arriving at the place of execution, the prisoners were bound to the instruments of torture. . . . The mother of Jesus, supported by John the beloved disciple, had followed the steps of her Son to Calvary. She had seen Him fainting under the burden of the cross, and had longed to place a supporting hand beneath His wounded head, and to bathe that brow which had once been pillowed upon her bosom. But she was not permitted this mournful privilege. . . . Her heart would sink as she recalled the words in which He had foretold the very scenes that were then taking place. . . . Must she give up her faith that Jesus was the Messiah? Must she witness His shame and sorrow, without even the privilege of ministering to Him in His distress? She saw His hands stretched upon the cross; the hammer and the nails were brought, and as the spikes were driven through the tender flesh, the heart-stricken disciples bore away from the cruel scene the fainting form of the mother of Jesus.—DA 741-744 (1898).

[In His suffering] the eyes of Jesus wandered over the multitude that had collected together to witness His death, and He saw at the foot of the cross John supporting Mary, the mother of Christ. She had returned to the terrible scene, not being able to longer remain away from her Son. The last lesson of Jesus was one of filial love. He looked upon the grief-stricken face of His mother, and then upon John; said He, addressing the former: "Woman, behold thy son!" Then, to the disciple: "Behold thy mother!" John well understood the words of Jesus, and the sacred trust which was committed to him. He immediately removed the mother of Christ from the fearful scene of Calvary. From that hour he cared for her as would a dutiful son, taking her to his own home. Oh, pitiful, loving Saviour! Amid all His physical pain, and mental anguish, He had a tender, thoughtful care for the mother who had borne Him. He had no money to leave her, by which to insure her future comfort, but He was enshrined in the heart of John, and He gave His mother unto the beloved disciple as a sacred legacy. This trust was to prove a great blessing to John, a constant reminder of His beloved Master.—3SP 160, 161 (1878).

MARY AND MARTHA
Luke 10:38-42; John 11

Jesus frequently stayed at the home of Mary and Martha, and their brother Lazarus. Martha was often cumbered with the cares of daily duties, while Mary sought first the words of Jesus.

Jesus had often found the rest that His weary human nature required at the house of Lazarus, in Bethany. His first visit there was when He and His disciples were weary from a toilsome journey on foot from Jericho to Jerusalem. They tarried as guests at the quiet home of Lazarus, and were ministered unto by his sisters, Martha and Mary.

Notwithstanding the fatigue of Jesus, He continued the instruction which He had been giving His disciples on the road, in reference to the qualifications necessary to fit men for the kingdom of heaven. The peace of Christ rested upon the home of the brother and sisters. Martha had been all anxiety to provide for the comfort of her guests, but Mary was charmed by the words of Jesus to His disciples, and, seeing a golden opportunity to become better acquainted with the doctrines of Christ, quietly entered the room where He was sitting, and, taking her place at the feet of Jesus, drank in eagerly every word that fell from His lips.—2SP 358 (1877).

As Christ gave His wonderful lessons, Mary sat at His feet, a reverent and devoted listener. On one occasion, Martha, perplexed with the care of preparing the meal, went to Christ, saying, "Lord, dost thou not care that my sister hath left me to serve alone? bid her therefore that she help me." This was the time of Christ's first visit to Bethany. The Saviour and His disciples had just made the toilsome journey on foot from Jericho. Martha was anxious to provide for their comfort, and in her anxiety she forgot the courtesy due to her Guest. Jesus answered her with mild and patient words, "Martha, Martha, thou art careful and troubled about many things: but one thing is needful: and Mary hath chosen that good part, which shall not be taken away from her." Mary was storing her mind with the precious words falling from the Saviour's lips, words that were more precious to her than earth's most costly jewels.

The "one thing" that Martha needed was a calm, devotional spirit, a deeper anxiety for knowledge concerning the future, immortal life, and the graces necessary for spiritual advancement. She needed less anxiety for the things which pass away, and more for those things which endure forever. Jesus would teach His children to seize every opportunity of gaining that knowledge which will make them wise unto salvation. The cause of Christ needs careful, energetic workers. There is a wide field for the Marthas, with their zeal in active religious work. But let them first sit with Mary at the feet of Jesus. Let diligence, promptness, and energy be sanctified by the grace of Christ; then the life will be an unconquerable power for good.—DA 525 (1898).

Like Mary, we need to sit at the feet of Jesus to learn of Him, having chosen that better part which will never be taken from us. Like Martha we need to be ever abounding in the work of the Lord. The higher Christian attainments can be reached only by being much on our knees in sincere prayer. . . . One fiber of the root of selfishness remaining in the soul will spring up when least expected, and thereby will many be defiled.—TMK 351 (1894).

In the inspired record we are told that "Jesus loved Martha, and her sister, and Lazarus," yet after He received the message [that Lazarus was sick], "he abode two days still in the same place where he was." Guided by divine wisdom, He did not go at once to His beloved friends. The message that came to Him did not meet with an immediate response. Mary and Martha did not say, "Lord, come at once and heal our brother." They had confidence in Jesus, believing that He would do what was best for them. At length He said to His disciples, "Our friend Lazarus sleepeth; but I go, that I may awake him out of sleep."—21MR 111 (1892).

When He [Jesus] reached Bethany He heard from several persons that Lazarus was dead, and had been buried four days. . . . Martha hastened to meet Him; she told Him of her brother's death, saying, "Lord, if thou hadst been here, my brother had not died." In her disappointment and grief she had not lost confidence in Jesus, and added, "But I know, that even now, whatsoever thou wilt ask of God, God will give it unto thee." Jesus encouraged her faith by declaring to her, "Thy brother shall rise again." . . .

When Jesus asked Martha: "Believest thou?" she answered by a confession of her faith: "Lord: I believe that thou art the Christ, the Son of God, which should come into the world." Thus Martha declared her belief in the Messiahship of Jesus, and that He was able to perform any work which it pleased Him to do. Jesus bade Martha call her sister, and the friends that had come to comfort the afflicted women. When Mary came she fell at the feet of Jesus, also crying, "Lord, if thou hadst been here, my brother had not died." At the sight of all this distress, Jesus "groaned in the spirit, and was troubled, and said, Where have ye laid him? They said unto him, Lord, come and see." Together they all proceeded to the grave of Lazarus, which was a cave with a stone upon it.—2SP 362, 363 (1877).

In all that He did, Christ was cooperating with His Father. Ever He had been careful to make it evident that He did not work independently; it was by faith and prayer that He wrought His miracles. Christ desired all to know His relationship with His Father. "Father," He said, "I thank thee that thou hast heard me. And I knew that thou hearest me always: but because of the people which stand by I said it, that they may believe that thou hast sent me." Here the disciples and the people were to be given the most convincing evidence in regard to the relationship existing between Christ and God. They were to be shown that Christ's claim was not a deception.

"And when he thus had spoken, he cried with a loud voice, Lazarus, come forth." His voice, clear and penetrating, pierces the ear of the dead. As He speaks, divinity flashes through humanity. In His face, which is lighted up by the glory of God, the people see the assurance of His power. Every eye is fastened on the entrance to the cave. Every ear is bent to catch the slightest sound. With intense and painful interest all wait for the test of Christ's divinity, the evidence that is to substantiate His claim to be the Son of God, or to extinguish the hope forever.

There is a stir in the silent tomb, and he who was dead stands at the door of the sepulcher. His movements are impeded by the grave-clothes in which he was laid away, and Christ says to the astonished spectators, "Loose him, and let him go." Again they are shown that the human worker is to cooperate with God. Humanity is to work for humanity. Lazarus is set free, and stands before the company, not as one emaciated from disease, and with feeble, tottering limbs, but as a man in the prime of life, and in the vigor of a noble manhood. His eyes beam with intelligence and with love for his Saviour. He casts himself in adoration at the feet of Jesus.—DA 536 (1898).

By the raising of Lazarus, many were led to believe in Jesus. It was God's plan that Lazarus should die and be laid in the tomb before the Saviour should arrive. The raising of Lazarus was Christ's crowning miracle, and because of it many glorified God.—21MR 111 (1892).

Simon* had been healed of the leprosy, and it was this that had drawn him to Jesus. He desired to show his gratitude, and at Christ's last visit to Bethany he made a feast for the Saviour and His disciples. . . . At the table the Saviour sat with Simon . . . on one side and Lazarus . . . on the other. Martha served at the table, but Mary was earnestly listening to every word from the lips of Jesus. In His mercy, Jesus had pardoned her sins, He had called forth her beloved brother from the grave, and Mary's heart was filled with gratitude. She had heard Jesus speak of His approaching death, and in her deep love and sorrow she had longed to show Him honor. At great personal sacrifice she had purchased an alabaster box of "ointment of spikenard, very costly," with which to anoint His body. But now many were declaring that He was about to be crowned king. Her grief was turned to joy, and she was eager to be first in honoring her Lord. Breaking her box of ointment, she poured its contents upon the head and feet of Jesus; then, as she knelt weeping, moistening them with her tears, she wiped His feet with her long, flowing hair. . . .

Judas looked upon this act with great displeasure. . . . He asked, "Why was not this ointment sold for three hundred pence, and given to the poor?" . . . The murmur passed round the table, "To what purpose is this waste? . . ." Mary heard the words of criticism. . . . She was about to shrink away, when the voice of her Lord was heard, "Let her alone; why trouble ye her?" . . . Lifting His voice above the murmur of criticism, He said, "She hath wrought a good work on me. For ye have the poor with you always, and whensoever ye will ye may do them good: but me ye have not always. She hath done what she could: she is come aforehand to anoint my body to the burying."—DA 557-560 (1898).

THE SAMARITAN WOMAN
John 4:5-42

The Jews and the Samaritans despised each other. One would never ask a favor of the other even if the need were great. And they would never address a woman unless she spoke first. When Jesus, a Jew, asked a Samaritan woman for a drink of water, it was an action unheard of. The ensuing dialog changed her life.

How thankful we should be that Christ took human nature upon Himself, and became subject to temptation, even as we are! Though He took humanity upon Himself, He was divine. All that is attributed to the Father Himself is attributed to Christ. His divinity was clothed with humanity; He was the Creator of heaven and earth; and yet while upon earth, He became weary, as men do, and sought rest from the continual pressure of labor. He who made the ocean, who controls the waters of the great deep, who opened the springs and channels of the earth, felt it necessary to rest at Jacob's well, and to ask a drink of water from a strange Samaritan woman.

When she questioned the propriety of His request—how it was that He, being a Jew, should ask water of one who was a Samaritan—He spoke words to her that revealed His divine character. He said: "If thou knewest the gift of God, and who it is that saith to thee, Give me to drink; thou wouldest have asked of him, and he would have given thee living water."

When the woman expressed surprise at this statement, He continued, "Whosoever drinketh of the water that I shall give him shall never thirst; but the water that I shall give him shall be in him a well of water springing up into everlasting life."—RH, May 19, 1896.

The woman looked upon Him with wondering attention; He had succeeded in arousing her interest and inspiring respect for Himself. She now perceived that it was not the water of Jacob's well to which Jesus alluded, for of this she used continually, drinking, and thirsting again. With remarkable faith she asked Him to give her the water of which He spoke, that she might not thirst nor come to draw from the well. . . .

Jesus now abruptly changed the subject of conversation, and bade her call her husband. The woman answered frankly that she had no husband. Jesus had now approached the desired point where He could convince her that He had the power to read her life history, although previously unacquainted with her. He addressed her thus: "Thou hast well said, I have no husband; for thou hast had five husbands; and he whom thou now hast is not thy husband; in that saidst thou truly."

Jesus had a double object in view; He wished to arouse her conscience as to the sin of her manner of life, as well as to prove to her that a sight wiser than human eyes had read the secrets of her life. But the woman, although not fully realizing the guilt of her manner of living, was greatly astonished that this stranger should possess such knowledge. With profound reverence she said, "Sir, I perceive that thou art a prophet.". . .

The words of truth that fell from the lips of the divine Teacher stirred the heart of His listener. Never had she heard such sentiments, either from the priests of her own people or the Jews. The impressive teachings of this stranger carried her mind back to the prophecies concerning the promised Christ; for the Samaritans as well as the Jews looked for His coming. "I know that Messias cometh," said she; "when he is come, he will tell us all things." Jesus answered, "I that speak unto thee am he."

Blessed woman of Samaria! She had felt during the conference as if in the presence of divinity; now she gladly acknowledged her Lord. She required of Him no miracle, as did the Jews, to prove His divine character. She accepted His assertion, feeling perfect confidence in His words, and not questioning the holy influence that emanated from Him.—2SP 141-145 (1877).

She went forth publishing the news: "Come, see a man, which told me all things that ever I did: is not this the Christ?" This woman's testimony converted many to a belief in Christ. Through her report many came to hear Him for themselves and believed because of His own word.—3T 217 (1885).

She proved herself a more effective missionary than His own disciples. The disciples saw nothing in Samaria to indicate that it was an encouraging field. Their thoughts were fixed upon a great work to be done in the future. They did not see that right around them was a harvest to be gathered. But through the woman whom they despised a whole cityful were brought to hear Jesus. She carried the light at once to her countrymen. This woman represents the working of a practical faith in Christ.—MH 102 (1905).

THE WOMAN WHO TOUCHED THE HEM OF JESUS' GARMENT
Mark 5:25-34
This woman had been ill for many year.. The physicians could not help her, but she believed that if she could touch Jesus she would be healed.

Open the door of your heart, and Christ, the heavenly guest, will come in. . . . You may have a nominal faith, just such a faith as the people had who crowded about Jesus in the streets of Judea, but this faith will not connect you with Him. You need a faith similar to the faith of the poor woman who had been diseased for many years. She had sought help from the physicians, but her disease grew worse and worse. She heard of Christ, and her faith went out to Him. She believed that if she could only touch the hem of His garment she would be made whole. Christ understood the longing of her heart; He understands the desire of every heart that is drawn out after Him, and He responds to it. This poor woman who yearned after help improved her first opportunity to come into the presence of Jesus. The multitude were all about Him, but she pressed through the crowd, until she could touch His garment, and that moment she was healed. Christ realized that virtue had gone out of Him. The woman had felt her desperate need, and her faith had made her whole. So it will be with every one of you who go in your need to Jesus and lay hold upon Him by living faith.

Christ asked who touched Him. His disciples were astonished that He should ask such a question when He was surrounded by a great multitude. They said, "Thou seest the multitude thronging thee, and sayest thou, Who touched me?" But Jesus knew that somebody had touched Him with no casual touch, but with the touch of faith. A longing soul had reached out to Him for help which no one but He could give. Jesus said, "I perceive that virtue is gone out of me." "And he looked round about to see her that had done this thing," and when the woman knew she was not hid, she acknowledged the good work that had been wrought in her. She told the story of her suffering and her hopeless condition, and her act of faith in touching His garment. He said unto her, "Daughter, thy faith hath made thee whole."—ST, June 10, 1889.

PETER'S MOTHER-IN-LAW
Matthew 8:14, 15

While the congregation in the synagogue were still spellbound with awe, Jesus withdrew to the home of Peter for a little rest. But here also a shadow had fallen. The mother of Peter's wife lay sick, stricken with a "great fever." Jesus rebuked the disease, and the sufferer arose, and ministered to the wants of the Master and His disciples.—DA 259 (1898).

THE CANAANITISH WOMAN
Matthew 15:22-28

She was a heathen woman who had faith that Jesus could heal her daughter.

"Behold, a Canaanitish woman came out from those borders, and cried, saying, Have mercy on me, O Lord, thou son of David; my daughter is grievously vexed with a devil." (Matt. 15:22, RV). The people of this district were of the old Canaanite race. They were idolaters, and were despised and hated by the Jews. To this class belonged the woman who now came to Jesus. She was a heathen, and was therefore excluded from the advantages which the Jews daily enjoyed. There were many Jews living among the Phoenicians, and the tidings of Christ's work had penetrated to this region. Some of the people had listened to His words and had witnessed His wonderful works.

This woman had heard of the prophet, who, it was reported, healed all manner of diseases. As she heard of His power, hope sprang up in her heart. Inspired by a mother's love, she determined to present her daughter's case to Him. It was her resolute purpose to bring her affliction to Jesus. He must heal her child. She had sought help from the heathen gods, but had obtained no relief. And at times she was tempted to think, What can this Jewish teacher do for me? But the word had come, He heals all manner of diseases, whether those who come to Him for help are rich or poor. She determined not to lose her only hope.

Christ knew this woman's situation. He knew that she was longing to see Him, and He placed Himself in her path. By ministering to her sorrow, He could give a living representation of the lesson He designed to teach. . . . The people who had been given every opportunity to understand the truth were without a knowledge of the needs of those around them. No effort was made to help souls in darkness. The partition wall which Jewish pride had erected shut even the disciples from sympathy with the heathen world. But these barriers were to be broken down.

Christ did not immediately reply to the woman's request. . . . But although Jesus did not reply, the woman did not lose faith. As He passed on, as if not hearing her, she followed Him, continuing her supplications. . . . The woman urged her case with increased earnestness, bowing at Christ's feet, and crying, "Lord, help me." . . . The Saviour is satisfied. He has tested her faith in Him. By His dealings with her, He has shown that she who has been regarded as an outcast from Israel is no longer an alien, but a child in God's household. As a child it is her privilege to share in the Father's gifts. Christ now grants her request, and finishes the lesson to the disciples. Turning to her with a look of pity and love, He says, "O woman, great is thy faith: be it unto thee even as thou wilt." From that hour her daughter became whole. The demon troubled her no more. The woman departed, acknowledging her Saviour, and happy in the granting of her prayer.—DA 399-402 (1898).

THE MOTHER OF JAMES AND JOHN
Mark 20:35-41

James and John presented by their mother a petition requesting that they might be permitted to occupy the highest positions of honor in Christ's kingdom. The Saviour answered, "Ye know not what ye ask." Mark 10:38. How little do many of us understand the true import of our prayers! Jesus knew the infinite sacrifice at which that glory must be purchased, when He, "for the joy that was set before him endured the cross, despising the shame." Hebrews 12:2. That joy was to see souls saved by His humiliation, His agony, and the shedding of His blood.—SL 56 (1883).

Christ did not reprove John and James and their mother for offering this request to sit upon His right hand and upon His left hand in the kingdom. In presenting the principles of love that should actuate them in their dealings one with another, He presents to the indignant disciples the instruction that He would have them practice in their daily lives. They were to take His life as an example, and follow in His steps.

The apostle presents this matter before us also in its true light, and says: "Let nothing be done through strife or vainglory; but in lowliness of mind let each esteem others better than themselves. Look not every man on his own things, but every man also on the things of others. Let this mind be in you, which was also in Christ Jesus; who, being in the form of God, thought it not robbery to be equal with God: but made himself of no reputation, and took upon him the form of a servant, and was made in the likeness of men; and being found in fashion as a man, he humbled himself, and became obedient unto death, even the death of the cross. Wherefore God also hath highly exalted him, and given him a name which is above every name."—ST, July 16, 1896.

THE WIDOW OF NAIN
Luke 7:11-15

Jesus gave her only son, who had died, back to the Widow of Nain.

Jesus knows the burden of every mother's heart. He who had a mother that struggled with poverty and privation sympathizes with every mother in her labors. He who made a long journey in order to relieve the anxious heart of a Canaanite woman will do as much for the mothers of today. He who gave back to the widow of Nain her only son, and who in His agony upon the cross remembered His own mother, is touched today by the mother's sorrow. In every grief and every need He will give comfort and help.—DA 512 (1898).

The Saviour raised the dead to life. One of these was the widow's son at Nain. The people were carrying him to the grave, when they met Jesus. He took the young man by the hand, lifted him up, and gave him alive to his mother. Then the company went back to their homes with shouts of rejoicing and praise to God.—SJ 79 (1896).

WOMEN AT THE CROSS
Luke 23:27-31; Mark 15:40-47

When Jesus was thought to be dying beneath the burden of the cross, many women, who, though not believers in Christ, were touched with pity for His sufferings, broke forth into a mournful wailing. When Jesus revived, He looked upon them with tender compassion. He knew they were not lamenting Him because He was a teacher sent from God, but from motives of common humanity. He looked upon the weeping women and said, "Daughters of Jerusalem, weep not for me, but weep for yourselves, and for your children."

Jesus did not despise their tears, but the sympathy which they expressed wakened a deeper chord of sympathy in His own heart for them. He forgot His own grief in contemplating the future fate of Jerusalem. Only a short time ago the people had cried out, "His blood be on us and on our children." How blindly had they invoked the doom they were soon to realize! Many of the very women who were weeping about Jesus were to perish with their children in the siege of Jerusalem.—3SP 151 (1878).

The women of Galilee had remained with the disciple John to see what disposition would be made of the body of Jesus, which was very precious to them, although their faith in Him as the promised Messiah had perished with Him. . . . The women were astonished to see Joseph and Nicodemus, both honored and wealthy councilors, as anxious and interested as themselves for the proper disposal of the body of Jesus.—3SP 174, 175 (1878).

WOMEN AT THE TOMB OF JESUS
Matthew 28; Mark 16; Luke 24; John 19, 20

While John was troubled about the burial of his Master, Joseph returned with Pilate's order for the body of Christ; and Nicodemus came bringing a costly mixture of myrrh and aloes . . . for His embalming. . . . The disciples were astonished to see these wealthy rulers as much interested as they themselves in the burial of their Lord. . . .

Gently and reverently they [Joseph and Nicodemus] removed with their own hands the body of Jesus from the cross. Their tears of sympathy fell fast as they looked upon His bruised and lacerated form. Joseph owned a new tomb, hewn in a rock. This he was reserving for himself; but it was near Calvary, and he now prepared it for Jesus. The body, together with the spices brought by Nicodemus, was carefully wrapped in a linen sheet, and the Redeemer was borne to the tomb. There the three disciples [John, Joseph, and Nicodemus] straightened the mangled limbs, and folded the bruised hands upon the pulseless breast. The Galilean women came to see that all had been done that could be done for the lifeless form of their beloved Teacher. Then they saw the heavy stone rolled against the entrance of the tomb, and the Saviour was left at rest. The women were last at the cross and last at the tomb of Christ. While the evening shades were gathering, Mary Magdalene and the other Marys lingered about the resting place of their Lord, shedding tears of sorrow over the fate of Him whom they loved. "And they returned, . . . and rested the sabbath day according to the commandment." Luke 23:56.—DA 773, 774 (1898).

"In the end of the Sabbath, as it began to dawn toward the first day of the week, came Mary Magdalene and the other Mary to see the sepulcher." Matthew 28:1. As they approached, they saw that the great stone was rolled away and that a light was shining about the tomb. The body of Jesus was not there, but soon they saw an angel.—2SAT 281 (1906).

The women had not all come to the tomb from the same direction. Mary Magdalene was the first to reach the place; and upon seeing that the stone was removed, she hurried away to tell the disciples. Meanwhile the other women came up. A light was shining about the tomb, but the body of Jesus was not there. As they lingered about the place, suddenly they saw that they were not alone. A young man clothed in shining garments was sitting by the tomb. It was the angel who had rolled away the stone. He had taken the guise of humanity that he might not alarm these friends of Jesus. Yet about him the light of the heavenly glory was still shining, and the women were afraid.

They turned to flee, but the angel's words stayed their steps. "Fear not ye," he said; "for I know that ye seek Jesus, which was crucified. He is not here: for he is risen, as he said. Come, see the place where the Lord lay. And go quickly, and tell his disciples that he is risen from the dead." Again they look into the tomb, and again they hear the wonderful news. Another angel in human form is there, and he says, "Why seek ye the living among the dead? He is not here, but is risen: remember how he spake unto you when he was yet in Galilee, saying, The Son of man must be delivered into the hands of sinful men, and be crucified, and the third day rise again."—DA 788, 789 (1898).

"Mary stood without at the sepulchre weeping: and as she wept, she stooped down, and looked into the sepulchre, and seeth two angels in white sitting, the one at the head, and the other at the feet, where the body of Jesus had lain. And they say unto her, Woman, why weepest thou? She said unto them, Because they have taken away my Lord, and I know not where they have laid him."

Feeling that she must find someone who will tell her what has been done with Jesus, Mary turns away even from the words of the angels. As she does so, another voice addresses her: "Woman, why weepest thou?" Through her tear-dimmed eyes, Mary sees one whom she supposes to be the gardener. "Sir," she says, "if thou have borne him hence, tell me where thou hast laid him, and I will take him away. Jesus saith unto her, Mary." At the familiar voice, she turns to Him. She knows now that it is no stranger who speaks. Before her she sees the living Saviour. She springs toward Him, as if to embrace His feet, saying, "Rabboni." But the Saviour raises His hand and says, "Touch me not; for I am not yet ascended to my Father: but go to my brethren, and say unto them, I ascend unto my Father, and your Father; and to my God, and your God."—YI, July 21, 1898.

"Go your way," the angels had said to the women, "tell his disciples and Peter that he goeth before you into Galilee: there shall ye see him, as he said unto you." . . .

[The message was repeated a second time:] "Tell his disciples and Peter that he goeth before you into Galilee: there shall ye see him." All the disciples had forsaken Jesus, and the call to meet Him again includes them all. He has not cast them off. When Mary Magdalene told them she had seen the Lord, she repeated the call to the meeting in Galilee. And a third time the message was sent to them. After He had ascended to the Father, Jesus appeared to the other women, saying, "All hail. And they came and held him by the feet, and worshipped Him. Then said Jesus unto them, Be not afraid: go tell my brethren that they go into Galilee, and there shall they see me."—DA 793 (1898).

WOMEN WHO FOLLOWED JESUS
Ellen White does not elaborate on the individuals who followed Jesus from place to place during His ministry. However, the following quotes give us a glimpse of some of the women who followed Him and supported His work with their material resources.

Their [James' and John's] mother was a follower of Christ, and had ministered to Him freely of her substance.—DA 548 (1898).

The record declares, "He went throughout every city and village, preaching and shewing the glad tidings of the kingdom of God: and the twelve were with him, *and certain women*, which had been healed of evil spirits and infirmities, Mary called Magdalene, out of whom went seven devils, and Joanna the wife of Chuza Herod's steward, and Susanna, and many others, which ministered unto him of their substance." Not only Christ, but His disciples also, labored in the cities and villages; and those who had been in the truth longer than the new converts, ministered unto Him of their substance.—RH, Feb. 3, 1891. (Italics supplied.)

Among the believers to whom the commission was given were

many from the humbler walks of life—men and women who had learned to love their Lord, and who had determined to follow His example of self-denying service. To these lowly ones of but limited talent, as well as to the disciples who had been with the Saviour during the years of His earthly ministry, was the commission given to go "into all the world, and preach the gospel to every creature." These humble followers of Jesus shared with the apostles their Lord's comforting assurance, "Lo, I am with you alway, even unto the end of the world."—RH, Mar. 24, 1910.

The women who had been Christ's humble followers while He lived would not leave Him until they saw Him laid in the tomb and a stone of great weight placed before the door, lest His enemies should seek to obtain His body. But they need not have feared; for I saw that the angelic host watched with untold interest in the resting place of Jesus, earnestly waiting for the command to act their part in liberating the King of glory from His prison house.—EW 180 (1882).

Mary then hastened with all speed to the disciples, and informed them that Jesus was not in the sepulcher where they had laid Him. While she was upon this errand, the other women, who waited for her at the sepulcher, made a more thorough examination of the interior, to satisfy themselves that their Lord was indeed gone. Suddenly they beheld a beautiful young man, clothed in shining garments, sitting by the sepulcher. It was the angel who had rolled away the stone, and who now assumed a character that would not terrify the *women who had been the friends of Christ, and assisted Him in His public ministry.* But notwithstanding the veiling of the brightness of the angel, the women were greatly amazed and terrified at the glory of the Lord which encircled him. They turned to flee from the sepulcher, but the heavenly messenger addressed them with soothing and comforting words: "Fear not ye: for I know that ye seek Jesus, which was crucified. He is not here: for he is risen, as he said. Come, see the place where the Lord lay. And go quickly, and tell his disciples that he is risen from the dead; and, behold, he goeth before you into Galilee; there shall ye see him: lo, I have told you."—3SP 199 (1878). (Italics supplied.)

DORCAS

Acts 9:36-42

Dorcas was a much-loved woman who had always done good and helped others, especially the poor. When she died, the believers sent for Peter, who was nearby in Lydda.

In Joppa there was a Dorcas, whose skillful fingers were more active than her tongue. She knew who needed comfortable clothing and who needed sympathy, and she freely ministered to the wants of both classes. And when Dorcas died, the church in Joppa realized their loss. It is no wonder that they mourned and lamented, nor that warm teardrops fell upon the inanimate clay. She was of so great value that by the power of God she was brought back from the land of the enemy, that her skill and energy might still be a blessing to others.—5T 304 (1885).

"And it came to pass in those days, that she was sick, and died." The church in Joppa realized their loss, and hearing that Peter was at Lydda, the believers sent messengers to him, "desiring him that he would not delay to come to them. Then Peter arose and went with them. When he was come, they brought him into the upper chamber: and all the widows stood by him weeping, and shewing the coats and garments which Dorcas made, while she was with them." In view of the life of service that Dorcas had lived, it is little wonder that they mourned. . . .

The apostle's heart was touched with sympathy as he beheld their sorrow. Then, directing that the weeping friends be sent from the room, he kneeled down and prayed fervently to God to restore Dorcas to life and health. Turning to the body, he said, "Tabitha, arise. And she opened her eyes: and when she saw Peter, she sat up." Dorcas had been of great service to the church, and God saw fit to bring her back from the land of the enemy.—AA 131, 132 (1911).

LYDIA

Acts 16:14, 15, 40

Lydia was a merchant woman from Thyatira who traded in expensive purple cloth. She also was a worshiper of God and extended her hospitality to the disciples.

Women of Note in the New Testament

The time had come for the gospel to be proclaimed beyond the confines of Asia Minor. . . . The call was imperative, admitting of no delay. . . . [Said Luke,] "We came with a straight course to Samothracia, and the next day to Neapolis; and from thence to Philippi, which is the chief city of that part of Macedonia, and a colony."

"On the Sabbath," Luke continues, "we went out of the city by a river side, where prayer was wont to be made; and we sat down, and spake unto the women which resorted thither. And a certain woman named Lydia, a seller of purple, of the city of Thyatira, which worshipped God, heard us: whose heart the Lord opened." Lydia received the truth gladly. She and her household were converted and baptized, and she entreated the apostles to make her house their home.—AA 211, 212 (1911).

God's Spirit can only enlighten the understanding of those who are willing to be enlightened. We read that God opened the ears of Lydia, so that she attended to the message spoken by Paul. To declare the whole counsel of God and all that was essential for Lydia to receive—this was the part Paul was to act in her conversion; and then the God of all grace exercised His power, leading the soul in the right way. God and the human agent cooperated, and the work was wholly successful.—6BC 1062 (1900).

Acting upon the instruction given by Christ, the apostles would not urge their presence where it was not desired. "They went out of the prison, and entered into the house of Lydia: and when they had seen the brethren, they comforted them, and departed."—AA 218 (1911).

PRISCILLA
Acts 18:1-4; 18-28

Priscilla and her husband, Aquila, were tentmakers. They were faithful in teaching others about Jesus Christ. Paul, also being a tentmaker, worked closely with them, teaching them more about Christ.

The envy and rage of the Jews against the Christians [in Rome] knew no bounds, and the unbelieving residents were constantly stirred up. They made complaints that the Christian Jews were disorderly, and dangerous to the public good. Constantly they were setting in motion something that would stir up strife. This caused the

Christians to be banished from Rome.—RH, Mar. 6, 1900.

Soon after his arrival at Corinth, Paul found "a certain Jew named Aquila, born in Pontus, lately come from Italy, with his wife Priscilla." These were "of the same craft" with himself. Banished by the decree of Claudius, which commanded all Jews to leave Rome, Aquila and Priscilla had come to Corinth, where they established a business as manufacturers of tents. Paul made inquiry concerning them, and learning that they feared God and were seeking to avoid the contaminating influences with which they were surrounded, "he abode with them, and wrought. . . . And he reasoned in the synagogue every sabbath, and persuaded the Jews and the Greeks." Acts 18:2-4.—AA 349, 350 (1911).

The apostle Paul was an able minister of the gospel, and yet he labored with his hands, doing the humble work of a tent-maker. By working with his hands he did not lessen his work of communicating to Aquila and Priscilla the great truth of the gospel of Christ. These two men and Priscilla labored with their hands, and Paul's designs in tent-making were ingenious. He brought fresh methods into his work also as he labored for the people, preaching the gospel of Jesus Christ. Many were brought to a knowledge of the truth by witnessing the faithful toiler making tents to support himself, that he might not be dependent upon anyone for food and raiment. While thus at work, he showed himself skillful, "not slothful in business; fervent in spirit; serving the Lord." And in preaching the Word, he was no less fervent and able in speech because of his business tact.—19MR 25 (1897).

Why did Paul thus connect mechanical labor with the preaching of the gospel? Was not the laborer worthy of his hire? Why did he not labor all his time in preaching? Why waste time and strength in making tents? But Paul did not regard the time spent in making tents lost by any means. As he worked with Aquila, he kept in touch with the great Teacher. He gave Aquila needed instruction in spiritual things, and he also educated the believers in unity. While working at his trade he gave an example in diligence and thoroughness. He was diligent in business, fervent in spirit, serving the Lord. He and Aquila and Priscilla had more than one prayer-and-praise meeting with those associated with them in tent-making. This was a testimony to the value of the truth they were presenting.—AU Gleaner, June 16, 1909.

Aquila and Priscilla were not called to give their whole time to the ministry of the gospel, yet these humble laborers were used by God to show Apollos the way of truth more perfectly. The Lord employs various instrumentalities for the accomplishment of His purpose, and while some with special talents are chosen to devote all their energies to the work of teaching and preaching the gospel, many others, upon whom human hands have never been laid in ordination, are called to act an important part in soul-saving.—AA 355 (1911).

After leaving Corinth, Paul's next scene of labor was Ephesus. He was on his way to Jerusalem to attend an approaching festival, and his stay at Ephesus was necessarily brief. He reasoned with the Jews in the synagogue, and so favorable was the impression made upon them that they entreated him to continue his labors among them. His plan to visit Jerusalem prevented him from tarrying then, but he promised to return to them, "if God will." Aquila and Priscilla had accompanied him to Ephesus, and he left them there to carry on the work that he had begun.—AA 269 (1911).

ANNA THE PROPHET

The spirit of prophecy was upon this man of God [Simeon], and while Joseph and Mary stood by, wondering at his words, he blessed them, and said unto Mary, "Behold, this child is set for the fall and rising again of many in Israel; and for a sign which shall be spoken against; (yea, a sword shall pierce through thy own soul also,) that the thoughts of many hearts may be revealed."

Anna also, a prophetess, came in and confirmed Simeon's testimony concerning Christ. As Simeon spoke, her face lighted up with the glory of God, and she poured out her heartfelt thanks that she had been permitted to behold Christ the Lord.—DA 55 (1898).

PILATE'S WIFE

Christ's appearance made a favorable impression upon Pilate. His better nature was roused. He had heard of Jesus and His works.

His wife had told him something of the wonderful deeds performed by the Galilean prophet, who cured the sick and raised the dead. Now this revived as a dream in Pilate's mind. He recalled rumors that had reached him from several sources, even from his own relatives. He resolved that he would ask the Jews for their charges against the prisoner.—RH, Nov. 7, 1899.

Pilate from the first was convicted that He was no common man, but an excellent character. He believed Him to be entirely innocent. The angels who were witnessing the whole scene noticed the convictions of Pilate, and marked his sympathy and compassion for Jesus; and to save him from engaging in the awful act of delivering Jesus to be crucified, an angel was sent to Pilate's wife, and gave her information through a dream that it was the Son of God in whose trial Pilate was engaged, and that He was an innocent sufferer. She immediately sent word to Pilate that she had suffered many things in a dream on account of Jesus, and warned him to have nothing to do with that holy man. The messenger bearing the communication pressed hastily through the crowd, and handed it to Pilate. As he read it he trembled and turned pale. He at once thought he would have nothing to do in the matter; that if they would have the blood of Jesus he would not give his influence to it, but would labor to deliver him. . . . If Pilate had followed his conviction, he would have had nothing to do with condemning Jesus.—1SG 54-56 (1858).

---

*Simon was the one who had led Mary into sin. He was her uncle. See Appendix A.

Bible Study and Prayer Essential

4

All who would be efficient workers must give much time to prayer. The communication between God and the soul must be kept open, that the workers may recognize the voice of their Captain. The Bible should be diligently studied. The truth of God, like gold, is not always lying right on the surface; it is to be obtained only by earnest thought and study. This study will not only store the mind with most valuable knowledge, but will strengthen and expand the mental powers, and will give a true estimate of eternal things. Let the divine precepts be brought into the daily life; let the life be fashioned after God's great standard of righteousness, and the whole character will be strengthened and ennobled.

—Gospel Workers, *p. 76*

STUDY THE WORD

The Great Lesson Book.—The Word is the great lesson book for the students in our schools. The Bible teaches the whole will of God concerning the sons and daughters of Adam. The Bible is the rule of life, teaching us of the character we must form for the future, immortal life. Our faith, our practice, may make us living epistles, known and read of all men. Men need not the dim light of tradition and custom to make the Scriptures comprehensible. It is just as sensible to suppose that the sun, shining in the heavens at noonday, needs the glimmerings of the torchlight of earth to increase its glory. The fables or the utterances of priests or of ministers are not needed to save the student from error. Consult the divine Oracle, and you have light. In the Bible every duty is made plain, every lesson is comprehensible, able to fit men with a preparation for eternal life.

The gift of Christ and the illumination of the Holy Spirit reveal to us the Father and the Son. The Word is exactly adapted to make men and women and youth wise unto salvation. In the Word is the science of salvation plainly revealed. "All scripture is given by inspiration of God, and is profitable for doctrine, for reproof, for correction, for instruction in righteousness: that the man of God may be perfect, thoroughly furnished unto all good works." "Search the scriptures," for therein is the counsel of God, the voice of God speaking to the soul.—FE 390, 391 (1895).

All to Reach High Standard of Excellence.—The Bible should be a book for study. The precious pearls of truth do not lie upon the surface, to be found by a careless, uninterested reader. Christ knew what was best for us, of whatever age, when He commanded us, "Search the scriptures; for in them ye think ye have eternal life: and they are they which testify of me." Jesus, the greatest teacher the world ever knew, would have men and women and children and youth reach the highest standard of excellence of character. He would have them become fully developed mentally, morally, and physically.—RH, Nov. 9, 1886.

Take Heed What and How We Hear.—From time to time we need unitedly to examine the reasons of our faith. It is essential that we study carefully the truths of God's Word; for we read that "some shall depart from the faith, giving heed to seducing spirits, and doctrines of devils [demons]." We are in grave danger when we lightly regard any truth; for then the mind is opened to error. We must take heed how and what we hear. We need not seek to understand the arguments that men offer in support of their theories, when it may be readily discerned that these theories are not in harmony with the Scriptures. Some who think that they have scientific knowledge are by their interpretations giving wrong ideas both of science and of the Bible. Let the Bible decide every question that is essential to man's salvation.—MM 96 (1904).

Important to Counsel With Best Friend, Jesus.—Take time to study the Bible, the Book of books. There never was a time when it was so important that the followers of Christ should study the Bible as now. Deceptive influences are upon all sides, and it is essential that you counsel with Jesus, your best friend. The wayfaring man may find the way of life through faith and obedience, through abiding in the sunshine of Christ's righteousness. But how shall we understand what is meant by these terms, if we do not understand the Bible? In the Word of God duty is made plain, and everything relating to the religious life is presented in a definite way. The whole plan of salvation is delineated, and the helps to the soul are pointed out. The way in which the believer may be complete in Christ is unfolded.—YI, May 18, 1893.

Cultivate a Taste for the Bible.—Unless the mind is used, it will cease to expand; unless the taste is cultivated to love the Bible, it will cease to relish the truths of God's Word. The student can see only to the depth of what he has explored, and he cannot appreciate that which lies beyond the compass of his own narrow boundaries. But his very ignorance will make him conceited, talkative, and boastful.

What can I say to you, young men and young women, to arouse you to vigor in your efforts to overcome obstacles? Mental effort will become easier and more satisfactory as you put yourselves to the task of understanding the deep things of God. You should each decide that you will not be a second-class student, that you will not allow others to think for you. You should say, "That which other minds have acquired in the sciences and in the Word of God, I will obtain for myself through painstaking effort." You can rally the mind's best powers, and with a sense of your accountability to God, you can do your best, and you will not cease to advance, and to conquer difficulties.

Do not settle down in slothful ease, making no special effort to accomplish your work. Make a choice of some part in the large vineyard of the Master, and do a work that will require the exercise of tact and talent. As much as possible, place yourselves in the society of those who are intellectual, who will be able to detect your mistakes, and to put you on your guard against indolence, pretension, and surface work. A blusterer will be recognized and set down for just what he is worth and no more.—RH, May 20, 1890.

Study of the Bible Develops the Intellect.—"Sanctify them through thy truth: thy word is truth." The Word of God should be made the great educating power. How shall students know the truth, except by a close, earnest, persevering study of the Word? Here is the grand stimulus, the hidden force which quickens the mental and physical powers, and directs the life into right channels. Here in the Word is wisdom, poetry, history, biography, and the most profound philosophy. Here is a study that quickens the mind into a vigorous and healthy life, and awakens it to the highest exercise. It is impossible to study the Bible with a humble, teachable spirit, without developing and strengthening the intellect. Those who become best acquainted with the wisdom and purpose of God as revealed in His Word become men and women of mental strength; and they may become efficient workers with the great Educator, Jesus Christ.—FE 432 (1896).

Bible Greatest of All Educators.—The one book that is essential for all to study is the Bible. Studied with reverence and godly fear, it is the greatest of all educators. In it there is no sophistry. Its pages are filled with truth. Would you gain a knowledge of God and Christ, whom He sent into the world to live and die for sinners? An earnest, diligent study of the Bible is necessary in order to gain this knowledge.—CH 369 (1903).

Women to Train the Mind.—Women professing godliness generally fail to train the mind. They leave it uncontrolled, to go where it will. This is a great mistake. Many seem to have no mental power. They have not educated the mind to think; and because they have not done this, they suppose they cannot. Meditation and prayer are necessary to a growth in grace.—2T 187 (1856).

Make the Mind a Storehouse of Truth.—Oh, what is our excuse, my sisters, that we do not devote all the time possible to searching the Scriptures, making the mind a storehouse of precious things, that we may present them to those who are not interested in the truth? Will our sisters arise to the emergency? Will they work for the Master?—6T 118 (1900).

Organize a Bible Society for Reading and Study.—If youth, and men and women of mature age, should organize a society where Bible reading and Bible study should be made the prominent theme, dwelling upon and searching out the prophecies, and studying the lessons of Christ, there would be strength in the society. There is no book from the perusal of which the mind is so much elevated and strengthened and expanded as the Bible. And there is nothing that will so endow with new vigor all our faculties as bringing them in contact with stupendous truths of the Word of God, and setting the mind to grasp and measure those truths.—2MR 244 (1900).

Regular Study Opens New Truths.—The teacher of the truth should advance in knowledge, growing in grace and in Christian experience, cultivating habits and practices which will do honor to God and to His Word. He should show others how to make a practical application of the Word. Every advance we make in sanctified ability, in varied studies, will help us to understand the Word of God; and the study of the Scriptures helps us in the study of the other branches essential in education.

After the first acquaintance with the Bible, the interest of the earnest seeker grows rapidly. The discipline gained by a regular study of the Word of God enables him to see a freshness and beauty in truth that he never before discerned. Reference to texts, when speaking, becomes natural and easy to a Bible student.—RH, Apr. 20, 1897.

PRAYER

Daily Prayer Essential to Growth.—If we would develop a character which God can accept, we must form correct habits in our religious life. Daily prayer is as essential to growth in grace, and even to spiritual life itself, as is temporal food to physical well-being. We should accustom ourselves to often lift the thoughts to God in prayer. If the mind wanders, we must bring it back; by persevering effort, habit will finally make it easy. We cannot for one moment separate ourselves from Christ with safety. We may have His presence to attend us at every step, but only by observing the conditions which He has Himself laid down.—RH, May 3, 1881.

Obtain Victory Over Self Through Prayer.—The Lord needs men and women who carry with them into the daily life the light of a godly example, men and women whose words and actions show that Christ is abiding in the heart, teaching, leading, and guiding. He needs men and women of prayer, who, by wrestling alone with God, obtain the victory over self, and then go forth to impart to others that which they have received from the Source of power. God accepts those who crucify self, and makes them vessels unto honor. They are in His hands as clay in the hands of the potter, and He works His will through them. Such men and women receive spiritual power. Christ lives in them, and the power of His Spirit attends their efforts. They realize that they are to live in this world the life that Jesus lived—a life free from all selfishness; and He enables them to bear witness for Him that draws souls to the cross of Calvary.—ST, Apr. 9, 1902.

Prayer Refreshes the Soul.—There are rich promises for us in the Word of God. The plan of salvation is ample. It is no narrow, limited provision that has been made for us. We are not obliged to trust in the evidence that we had a year or a month ago, but we may have the assurance today that Jesus lives, and is making intercession for us. We cannot do good to those around us while our own souls are destitute of spiritual life. Our ministers do not wrestle all night in prayer, as many godly ministers before us have done. They sit up bent over tables, writing lessons, or preparing articles to be read by thousands; they arrange facts in shape to convince the mind in regard to doctrine. All these things are essential; but how much God can do for us in sending light and convicting power to hearts in answer to the prayer of faith! The empty seats in our prayer meetings testify that Christians do not realize the claims of God upon them; they do not realize their duty to make these meetings interesting and successful. They go over a monotonous, wearisome round, and return to their home unrefreshed, unblessed.—RH, Apr. 22, 1884.

Communion With God Necessary.—Several times each day precious, golden moments should be consecrated to prayer and the study of the Scriptures, if it is only to commit a text to memory, that spiritual life may exist in the soul. The varied interests of the cause furnish us with food for reflection and inspiration for our prayers. Communion with God is highly essential for spiritual health, and here only may be obtained that wisdom and correct judgment so necessary in the performance of every duty.—4T 459 (1880).

Do Not Neglect Prayer.—Some, fearing they will suffer loss of earthly treasure, neglect prayer and the assembling of themselves together for the worship of God, that they may have more time to devote to their farms or their business. They show by their works which world they place the highest estimate upon. They sacrifice religious privileges, which are essential to their spiritual advancement, for the things of this life and fail to obtain a knowledge of the divine will. They come short of perfecting Christian character and do not meet the measurement of God. They make their temporal, worldly interests first, and rob God of the time which they should devote to His service. Such persons God marks, and they will receive a curse rather than a blessing.—2T 654 (1871).

All Who Seek Jesus Find Him.—Is there no time to pray? No time to tell the Lord, "Thou must keep me by Thine own power"? Leaving the Lord out of sight will not lessen the cares but multiply them. A Christian spirit is as essential in active business lines as is having the Spirit of God in the place where prayer is wont to be made. All any of us need is to seek the Lord, and the grace of the Christian will be evidenced. All who seek Him find Jesus a very present help in every time of need.—21MR 358 (1898).

Be a Conqueror Through Jesus.—Do not take your sorrows and difficulties to man. Present yourself to Him who is able to do "exceeding abundantly." He knows just how to help you. Do not turn from the loving, compassionate Redeemer to human friends, who, though they may give you the best they have, may lead you into wrong paths. Take all your troubles to Jesus.

He will receive and strengthen and comfort you. He is the great Healer of all maladies. His great heart of infinite love yearns over you. He sends you the message that you may recover yourself from the snare of the enemy. You may regain your self-respect. You may stand where you regard yourself, not as a failure, but as a conqueror, in and through the uplifting influence of the Spirit of God.—ST, Feb. 14, 1906.

Prayer Is the Life of the Soul.—It is just as convenient, just as essential, for us to pray three times a day as it was for Daniel. Prayer is the life of the soul, the foundation of spiritual growth. In your

Daughters of God

home, before your family, and before your workmen, you should testify to this truth. And when you are privileged to meet with your brethren in the church, tell them of the necessity of keeping open the channel of communication between God and the soul. Tell them that if they will find heart and voice to pray, God will find answers to their prayers. Tell them not to neglect their religious duties. Exhort the brethren to pray. We must seek if we would find, we must ask if we would receive, we must knock if we would have the door opened unto us.—ST, Feb. 10, 1890.

Women
as Teachers

5

uch of Ellen White's counsel regarding teachers is general; she speaks of both men and women being well qualified to teach our young people. We cite the following statements as applying equally to both genders.

Suitable Teachers Needed.—I dwell much upon this because suitable teachers are much needed, and men and women must be fitted up in the home and in the school to do a work of ministry of which they will not be ashamed. In too many families today there is too much self-indulgence and disobedience passed by without being corrected, or else there is manifested an overbearing, masterful spirit that creates the worst evils in the dispositions of children. Parents correct them at times in such an inconsiderate way that their lives are made miserable, and they lose all respect for father, mother, brothers, and sisters. The souls of the children, God's property, the lambs of the flock, are thus prepared for Satan to work his will upon them.—13MR 95 (1898).

Teachers to Study the Word of God.—To train the young to become true soldiers of the Lord Jesus Christ is the most noble work ever given to man. Only devout and consecrated men and women, who love children and can see in them souls to be saved for the Master, should be chosen as church school teachers. Teachers who study the Word of God as it should be studied will know something of the value of the souls under their care, and from them the children will receive a true Christian education.—CT 166 (1913).

Need an Experience in Obeying the Lord.—All who teach in our schools should have a close connection with God and a thorough understanding of His Word, that they may be able to bring divine wisdom and knowledge into the work of educating the youth for usefulness in this life and for the future, immortal life. They should be men and women who not only have a knowledge of the truth, but who are doers of the Word of God. "It is written" should be expressed in their words and by their lives. By their own practice they should teach simplicity and correct habits in everything. No man or woman should be connected with our schools as an educator who has not had an experience in obeying the Word of the Lord. —6T 152, 153 (1900).

Young Women to Learn to Teach Others.—We need unselfish, devoted [people] to act as educators. Young men and young women are to be brought to our schools to receive an education, that they may learn how to teach others to understand the Word of the Lord. We need ministerial laborers in every school to educate the children and youth in Bible lines, and the pastor has work to do for the teachers as well as the students. Our schools must be more like the schools of the prophets. We call upon teachers and all connected with the school to make self-sacrificing efforts. We call upon our sisters to work intelligently, devotedly, interestedly, to make the school a success. Let our churches help. God will bless all who cooperate with Him.—6MR 400 (1899).

Women to Be Qualified to Occupy Any Position.—The Lord designs that the school [Avondale] should also be a place where a training may be gained in women's work—cooking, housework, dressmaking, bookkeeping, correct reading, and pronunciation. They are to be qualified to take any post that may be offered—superintendents, Sabbath school teachers, Bible workers. They must be prepared to teach day schools for children.—Ev 475 (1898).

Personal Qualifications of the Teacher.—The principles and habits of the teacher should be considered of greater importance than even his literary qualifications. If the teacher is a sincere Christian, he will feel the necessity of having an equal interest in the physical, mental, moral, and spiritual education of his scholars. In order to exert the right influence, he should have perfect control over himself, and his own heart should be richly imbued with love for his pupils, which will be seen in his looks, words, and acts. He should have firmness of character, then he can mold the minds of his pupils, as well as to instruct them in the sciences.

The early education of the youth generally shapes their character for life. Those who deal with the young should be very careful to call out the qualities of the mind, that they may better know how to direct their powers, and that they may be exercised to the very best account.—HR, Sept. 1, 1872.

What the Teacher Should Be.—In the choice of a teacher for the children, great care should be shown. Church school teachers should be men and women who have a humble estimate of themselves, who are not filled with vain conceit. They should be faithful workers, filled with the true missionary spirit, workers who have learned to put their trust in God and to labor in His name. They should possess the attributes of Christ's character—patience, kindness, mercy, and love; and into the daily experience they should bring the Saviour's righteousness and peace. Then, working with fragrant influence, they will give evidence of what grace can do through human agents who make God their trust.—CT 150, 151 (1913).

ALL WHO TEACH TO HAVE A CLOSE CONNECTION WITH GOD

Teachers Have a Most Responsible Position.—Teachers are to do more for their students than to impart a knowledge of books. Their position as guide and instructor of the youth is most responsible, for to them is given the work of molding mind and character. Those who undertake this work should possess well-balanced, symmetrical characters. They should be refined in manner, neat in dress, careful in all their habits; and they should have that true Christian courtesy that wins confidence and respect. The teacher should be himself what he wishes his students to become.

Teachers are to watch over their students as the shepherd watches over the flock entrusted to his charge. They should care for souls as they that must give an account.—CT 65 (1897).

Strive to Reach Highest Possible Standard.—To know oneself is a great knowledge. The teacher who rightly estimates himself will let God mold and discipline his mind. And he will acknowledge the source of his power. . . . Self-knowledge leads to humility and to trust in God, but it does not take the place of efforts for self-improvement. He who realizes his own deficiencies will spare no pains to reach the highest possible standard of physical, mental, and moral excellence. No one should have a part in the training of youth who is satisfied with a lower standard.—CT 67 (1896).

SCHOOLS TO REFLECT THE ORDER OF HEAVEN

Teachers to Talk and Pray With Students.—Our teachers need to be converted men and women, who know what it means to wrestle with God, who will not be at rest until the hearts of the children are turned to love, praise, and glorify God. Who will be earnest workers for souls in our Sabbath schools? Who will take the youth separately, and talk and pray with them, and make personal appeals to them, beseeching them to yield their heart to Jesus, that they may be as a sweet savor to Christ? As we view the magnitude of the work, and see how little it is appreciated, we feel like groaning in spirit, and exclaiming, Who will accept these grave responsibilities, and watch for souls as they that must give an account?

We are Christ's representatives upon the earth. How do we fulfill our mission? Christ's representatives will be in daily communion with Him. Their words will be select, their speech seasoned with grace, their hearts filled with love, their efforts sincere, earnest, persevering, to save souls for whom Christ has died. Let all do their utmost to work for the salvation of the dear children and youth, and by and by they will listen with joy to the words of Jesus, "Well done, good and faithful servant; . . . enter thou into the joy of thy Lord." What is this joy? It is beholding the redeemed saints saved through their instrumentality, through the blood of Jesus Christ.—SSW, July 1, 1885.

"Nicest Work" Ever Given to Humans

Great Care to Be Taken to Call Forth Highest Mental Powers.—
It is the nicest work* ever assumed by men and women to deal with
youthful minds. The greatest care should be taken in the education of
youth to vary the manner of instruction so as to call forth the high
and noble powers of the mind. Parents, and teachers of schools, are
certainly disqualified to educate children properly if they have not
first learned the lessons of self-control, patience, forbearance, gentle-
ness, and love. What an important position for parents, guardians,
and teachers! There are very few who realize the most essential wants
of the mind, and how to direct the developing intellect, the growing
thoughts and feelings of youth.—HR, Sept. 1, 1872.

Teaching Most Important Work.—This work [teaching] is the
nicest, the most difficult, ever committed to human beings. It requires the most delicate tact, the finest susceptibility, a knowledge of
human nature, and a heaven-born faith and patience, willing to
work and watch and wait. It is a work than which nothing can be
more important.—Ed 292 (1903).

Teachers Are Truly Missionaries

Divine Touch Needed.—The teachers and students in our school
need the divine touch. If a missionary spirit was encouraged, even
though it took some hours from the program of study, if there was
more faith and spiritual zeal, more of the realization that God can do
more for teachers and students than He has done, because in the past
His way has been restricted, much of heaven's blessing would be
given. There are holy chords yet to be touched. Teachers as well as
students need to show greater teachableness.

Just in proportion as the true missionary spirit is brought into the
education and training of young men and young women, will they
be blessed. The students should begin to work in missionary lines
where there are those with whom they can communicate to learn
how to work. As they do this, they advance, and their intellect
grows. They are learning how to work when the school term is
ended. As they approach those who are interested, they work under
the greatest Teacher the world has ever known. It is as essential that

they should know how to communicate as that they should receive a knowledge of the truth. The practice of telling others about Christ, of reading and explaining His Word, will stamp that Word on the mind, and will make the truth their own.

"Thou shalt love the Lord thy God with all thy heart" [and] "thy neighbour as thyself." This is God's command. Jesus has given an additional requirement, "A new commandment I give unto you, That ye love one another; as I have loved you, that ye also love one another." We are not merely to love our neighbor as ourselves; we are to love one another as Christ has loved us. "As the Father hath loved me, so have I loved you," He declared. "Continue ye in my love. If ye keep my commandments, ye shall abide in my love; even as I have kept my Father's commandments, and abide in his love. These things have I spoken unto you, that my joy might remain in you, and that your joy might be full. This is my commandment, That ye love one another, as I have loved you."

The students and also the teachers in our school need to take time to become acquainted with the members of the community in which they live. The love that Christ manifested toward us we must cultivate for others. The truth will not long remain in the heart unless it works by love to save the souls ready to perish.

The Lord God of Israel would have us beware of human precision, of making a line on which everyone must tread. A different element must be brought into our schools. Wrong maxims and methods of teaching, which have been looked upon as wholly essential, have been followed. Those connected with our schools must penetrate deeper than their own habits or opinions, which have been idolized as complete authority. The greatest need of our teachers is to live hourly in conscious, loving communion with the principles of truth, righteousness, and mercy, for that is the atmosphere of heaven. There must not be so many studies and duties placed on the students that they will neglect to talk with the Lord Jesus, the great Teacher, and let into their hearts the softening, subduing influence of the Spirit that dwelt in Him.

It is essential to teach the students how to do missionary work, not only by pen and voice, but by practice in its various lines. There is around us a community that needs to be taught how to cook, how to treat the sick. By doing this line of work, we practice the truth as it is in Jesus. Teachers and students need to learn how to do this work. . . .

The teachers must draw from the deep, central source of all moral and intellectual power, asking the Lord to give them the mind that was in Christ Jesus, that every case that calls for sympathy and help, in physical as well as in spiritual lines, may receive their attention. The great Teacher cooperates with all the efforts made to relieve suffering humanity. Teach the students to make a practical application of the lessons they have received. As they witness human woe, and the deep poverty of those they are trying to help, they will be stirred with compassion. Their hearts will be softened and subdued by the deep, holy principles revealed in the Word of God. The great Physician cooperates with every effort made in behalf of suffering humanity, to give health to the body and light and restoration to the soul.

We must give the Lord a chance to do His work, His great work for the soul. Christ is our sufficiency. Each one of us must understand what it means to have the Word of God fulfilled in us. As Christ was in this world, so we are to be. If in this life we are like Him in character, we shall in heaven have His likeness. If there is no likeness between Christ and us in this world, there can be no friendship between Christ and us when He shall come in His glory, and all the holy angels with Him. As religious teachers, we are under obligation to God to teach the students how to engage in medical missionary work. Those who do this work have many opportunities to sow the seeds of truth in a way that will be successful. The heart full of gratitude to God can pray, Teach me Thy way, O Lord, lead me in a plain path, because of mine enemies, or rather, because of mine observers.—Ms 70, 1898.

SARAH PECK CALLED TO TEACH

Sarah Peck was one of Ellen White's most able helpers. She taught the Sanitarium, California, school before becoming one of Mrs. White's secretaries, having the reputation of being "an excellent teacher." After serving on the Elmshaven staff for some time, she was invited to teach again. It was with regret that Mrs. White consented to her leaving, but she felt that Sarah

Peck should be free to do whatever the Lord called her to do.

Dear Sister Peck: During our conversation this morning, I felt greatly perplexed to know what to say in reference to your work. I love you, and I want to see you in a position where you can best serve the Master.

I do not know what would be your own choice of work. Many of our people desire and urge you to enter the educational work. If you feel that this is your duty, I am willing to release you from my employ. I know of no one who is better fitted than yourself to undertake educational work. In regard to your connection with me, I cannot say very much, because you have in the past been called to so many other lines of work.

One thing I must say: If you choose to remain with me, the school work must be laid aside. If you prefer to labor in educational lines, then you must be free so that you can give your undivided attention to that work. I leave the matter entirely with you, that you may follow your own choice. I dare not decide for you. The great necessity for your efficiency as a teacher is the only consideration that leads me to be willing to release you. So many have spoken to me of your efficiency and talent as an educator that I dare not hold you. If at any time in the future you shall choose to connect with me again, you will not have become less efficient.

I write this that you may not be left in uncertainty. Seek the Lord for yourself. If you feel impressed that you prefer to remain with me, I have abundance of work that you can do. If it seems to be the will of God for you to remain with me, we must take hold of the work in earnest and not allow others to come in and give you a double burden to bear.

Now, my sister, I feel anxious that if you take up the school work, you shall not load yourself down with too many responsibilities. Make that your work, and carry it as you did the school in St. Helena. If I should act a part in the work at Redlands and Loma Linda, we may be more or less connected in preparing students for time and for eternity.

May the Lord bless you and give you much of His Holy Spirit wherever you may labor. If it be your lot to educate students, that they may impart to others the heavenly intelligence, I shall be pleased. I have always loved and respected you, and I have not been disappointed in you. The form of sound words is to be prized above every earthly thing. God is glorified by every word that leads to right action. I respect you highly and desire you to have every advantage possible, that you may make continual progression in the service of God.—Letter 265, 1905.

Ellen White here uses "nicest work" in the context of being the most important, the finest, most noble work that God calls people to do for Him.

Women
as Physicians

6

Let it be known this day in my work for suffering humanity that there is a God in Israel, and that I am Thy servant. Let it be seen that I am working, not according to my own impulse and wisdom, but according to Thy Word.
—Welfare Ministry, pp. 123, 124

Women to Receive Thorough Medical Training.—In a remarkable way God has brought into our possession some of the institutions through whose agency we are to accomplish the work of reformation to which as a people we are called. At this time every talent of every worker should be regarded as a sacred trust to be used in extending the work of reform. The Lord instructed me that our sisters who have received a training that has fitted them for positions of responsibility are to serve with faithfulness and discernment in their calling, using their influence wisely and, with their brethren in the faith, obtaining an experience that will fit them for still greater usefulness. . . .

In ancient times the Lord worked in a wonderful way through consecrated women who united in His work with men whom He had chosen to stand as His representatives. He used women to gain great and decisive victories. More than once, in times of emergency, He brought them to the front and worked through them for the salvation of many lives. . . .

Women as Physicians

There are many who have ability to stand with their husbands in sanitarium work, to give treatments to the sick, and to speak words of counsel and encouragement to others. There are those who should seek an education that will fit them to act the part of physicians.

In this line of service a positive work needs to be done. Women as well as men are to receive a thorough medical training. They should make a special study of diseases common to women, that they may understand how to treat them. It is considered most essential that men desiring to practice medicine shall receive the broad training necessary for the following of such a profession. It is just as essential that women receive such training and obtain their diplomas certifying their right to act as physicians.—SpT-B15 1, 2 (1911).

Larger Number of Female Physicians Needed.—In our medical institutions there ought always to be women of mature age and good experience who have been trained to give treatments to the lady patients. Women should be educated and qualified just as thoroughly as possible to become practitioners in the delicate diseases which afflict women, that their secret parts should not be exposed to the notice of men. There should be a much larger number of lady physicians, educated not only to act as trained nurses, but also as physicians. It is a most horrible practice, this revealing the secret parts of women to men, or men being treated by women.—SpT-B15 13, 14 (1911).

Husband and Wife Physicians Work Together Effectively.—In the medical missionary work to be done, women should give treatment to women. A man and his wife who are both physicians can accomplish great good by laboring together. The wife can visit other women, and when she finds suffering and disease, she can consult with her husband as to the best method of helping the sufferers. We should have more women physicians than we have. When women who are sick are treated and cared for by women, a door through which Satan tries to enter is closed against him. Many cases have been presented to me where Satan has entered through this door to ruin families. Let him not obtain any advantage upon any point.

I wish all to understand this matter. There should be in our sanitariums women physicians who can stand by their husbands, and who can do the examining of women patients, and give them treatment. Many more sensible, thoroughly converted women should become intelligent physicians.

I am instructed that our sanitariums must have women physicians as well as men physicians.—MM 140 (1910).

WOMEN TO TREAT WOMEN; MEN TO TREAT MEN

Women to Be Thoroughly Trained as Physicians.—Women physicians should utterly refuse to look upon the secret parts of men. Women should be thoroughly educated to work for women, and men to work for men. Let men know that they must go to their own sex, and not apply to lady physicians. It is an insult to women, and God looks upon these things of commonness with abhorrence. —SpT-B15 14 (1911).

Do Not Mix Cases.—Now, the Lord would have us pursue a course that can be an example to others. We are right in the last days. The women should take charge of the women, and the men take charge of the men whenever they are sick and privately sick. Do not in such cases mix up men and women. See that you remove temptations. I cannot tell you how many have come to me with their complaints, and wanted me to heal these difficulties, but I felt as though I was not prepared to do it. But recently the light has come to me that too great commonness has been practiced. It must be that the women will take charge of the women, and the men take charge of the men. Of course, there are some things in which they have to mingle. Women will have to do some things. But it is too great commonness that has been brought in, and this has been brought before me several times. But I felt as though I could not rein myself up to touch the point.—13MR 114 (1911).

Physician to Respect Delicacy of Patients.—The light given me of the Lord regarding this matter is that as far as possible lady physicians should care for lady patients, and gentlemen physicians have the care of gentlemen patients. Every physician should respect the delicacy of the patients. Any unnecessary exposure of ladies before male physicians is wrong. Its influence is detrimental.—SpT-B15 13 (1911).

Women as Physicians

CHILDBIRTH

Women to Take Charge in Childbirth.—The time has come now when there are to be—and there should have been long ago—sensible changes. Men have their appointment to take care of the men, and women are to take care of the women. But when it comes to bringing the men and women together in private practices of childbirth and such cases—to have them associated right together—I should say it is not right nor to be justified. Women had their appointed work in Bible times and these women took charge of the women, and there was a special understanding that was the way it should be. And that is the way it should be now in childbirth. Let the women be as thoroughly trained as the men, and let them take charge of these matters. I speak intelligently. I speak because I understand what I am speaking about, that there is too great a commonness.—13MR 113 (1911).

Not to Open Door of Temptation.—I have had this before me time and time again. I have put it in writing for fear I might be taken away. But I want to say that we must step up onto a higher plane of action, and if we will do this the Lord will let His blessing rest upon us. I have had so many letters from women and from men about their falling right under the temptations of the devil as they were brought in connection with the childbirth of women. I do not need to argue this because your own sense will tell you that we are in a world of temptation and trial. And we are to purify ourselves from every such thing. God help us. You have no need to have me dwell upon this any longer. The light given me is that we open the door to temptation and for transgression. Let us have just as much a duty to take the burden that rests upon the women for the women in childbirth as it is possible for us to do. This is the right as it is presented to me.—13MR 116 (1911).

In Bible Times Women Took Care of Women.—I have felt recently . . . that it should be so arranged that the women will have greater responsibilities. It is their privilege to be educated in some lines of work just as thoroughly as the men are educated. In Bible times the women always took charge of the women, and the Lord worked with them. I want to say there are many temptations presented to me by individuals [and] that I have kept my own counsel. I have not said anything, but it has been sins brought in by this commonness and the temptations that come in. Now, I know of some that have been tempted over matters. I know the women for myself. I know the women are clear, and they are not to be censured, only in one point, and that is to take their stand of propriety and not to mix and mingle right together, the men and the women taking charge.— 13MR 114 (1911).

Midwives to Take Responsibility.—I have written to you the instruction that has been given me regarding the special work to be done by the lady physicians in our sanitariums. It is the Lord's plan that men shall be trained to treat men, and women trained to treat women. In the confinement of women, midwives should take the responsibility of the case. In Bible times it was not considered a proper thing for men to act in this capacity; and it is not the will of God that men should do this work today. Very much evil has resulted from the practice of men treating women, and women treating men. It is a practice according to human devising, and not according to God's plan. Long has the evil been left to grow, but now we lift our voice in protest against that which is displeasing to God.—SpT-B17b 15, 16 (1911).

DR. PATIENCE BOURDEAU

Dr. Patience Bourdeau was the daughter of Elder D. T. Bourdeau. At this time she operated her own sanitarium in Grand Rapids, Michigan. She was superintendent of the Medical Department of the West Michigan Conference. She later married a Mr. Sisco and became known as Dr. Bourdeau-Sisco.

Dear Sister Patience: I have been having a long talk with my son W. C. White as to how we can best conduct the sanitarium at Washington, D.C. I told him that I had a conversation with your father in reference to your connecting with our sanitarium there. There is need of a lady physician's connecting with the institution at once. The experience that we have had during the past few days has decided us to secure a capable lady physician who can care for the women patients and be matron of the home, that the patients may receive prompt attention and that the helpers may be given the right kind of instruction, such as you can give. The young ladies connected with the institution should be taught to act their part intelligently.

I have much written upon the subject of gentlemen physicians giving the delicate treatments to lady patients. The light given me is that the influence exerted by this is not good, and that grave and serious consequences result from this generally established custom. I have been giving instruction on the point of lady patients coming under the examination of gentlemen physicians.

I shall advise that you be called to Washington as soon as possible, for this is a most important time for our work there. We need you as soon as someone can be secured to take your place.

After I reach home, I will write you again and send you copies of things I have already written.

An expensive building has been rented in Iowa Circle, Washington [D. C.]. It is a beautiful location for a sanitarium and has been fitted up for the giving of treatment, but it needs a house physician and a manager. We need you. We believe that you can help us in Washington. You can give the nurses the instruction that they need and can also give lectures in the parlor to the patients. Will you receive this invitation as prompted by the Lord? I have an assurance that you can do the work essential. Brother Hare is an excellent physician, but not a manager. We need someone who can plan and manage. You can help us out of our difficulty. Washington is a most important place, and a right representation of our work must be given by the sanitarium.

I shall be in St. Helena, California, next week. Write to me there, and please write also to Elder Daniells, Takoma Park, Washington, D.C.—Letter 177, 1905.

DR. JULIA A. WHITE

Dr. Julia Ann White graduated from the American Medical Missionary College of Chicago in 1900. She was associated with the Battle Creek Sanitarium until 1906, when she went to Loma Linda. She was the leading founder of the school of nursing at the Glendale Sanitarium and Hospital. She also founded the La Crescenta Clinic in California.

Dr. Julia A. White: Dear Sister: I write to urge you to connect with our sanitarium work at Loma Linda. In the providence of God, this property has passed into our hands. The securing of this sanitarium, thoroughly equipped and furnished, is one of the most wonderful providences that the Lord has opened before us. It is difficult to comprehend all that this transaction means to us.

The Lord has signified that the time has come for us to work Redlands, San Bernardino, Riverside, and the neighboring towns. I am filled with a solemn joy at the thought that these places are soon to be entered by our workers.

We need your services, my sister, just as soon as you can come. We are hoping that we may secure the services also of Dr. Holden. Sister Sarah Peck may undertake some of the lines of educational work. We are now anxious to see the work started, and we hope to see you just as soon as you can come.

I have recently spent two weeks at Loma Linda. I am sending you a booklet that will give you some idea of the property. The large main building is furnished in an expensive manner. There are also five cottages, one having nine rooms, the others four each. In some of these, the verandahs are so arranged that beds can be rolled out from the rooms. The grounds are beautifully laid out. There are concrete walks between all the buildings. These walks are bordered with flowers. There is a good orchard and ample grounds for gardens. There are many eucalyptus, pepper trees, and many other varieties of ornamental trees and shrubbery. Meetings can be held in the open air on the beautiful lawns. There is also another building that has been used as a bowling alley and billiard hall. This can be utilized as a meetinghouse.

We hope that you can see your way clear to connect with this sanitarium as lady physician. Your services will be greatly appreciated, and I hope that you may soon be on the ground.—Letter 291, 1905.

Women's Role in Soul-winning Ministry

∾

7

God's cause at this time is in special need of men and women who possess Christlike qualifications for service, executive ability, and a large capacity for work, who have kind, warm, sympathetic hearts, sound common sense, and unbiased judgment; who will carefully weigh matters before they approve or condemn, and who can fearlessly say No, or Yea and Amen; who, because they are sanctified by the Spirit of God, practice the words "All ye are brethren," striving constantly to uplift and restore fallen humanity.

—Manuscript Releases, *vol. 2, p. 88*

Christ Provided a Perfect Pattern for True Ministry.—Sunday, March 15, 1891. I attended the morning ministers' meeting. The blessing of the Lord came upon me, and I spoke in the demonstration of the Spirit of God and with power. There are those who are working out a great circle. The Lord has given Christ to the world for ministry. Merely to preach the Word is not ministry. The Lord desires His ministering servants to occupy a place worthy of the highest consideration. In the mind of God, the ministry of men and women existed before the world was created. He determined that His ministers should have a perfect exemplification of Himself and His purposes. No human career could do this work; for God gave Christ in humanity to work out His ideal of what humanity may become through entire obedience to His will and way.

God's character was revealed in the life of His Son. Christ not only held a theory of genuine ministry, but in His humanity He wrought out an illustration of the ministry that God approves. Perfection has marked out every feature of true ministry. Christ, the Son of the living God, did not live unto Himself, but unto God.—18MR 380 (1891).

Christians Are God's Helping Hands.—God's promises to the obedient are "good tidings of great joy." They are gladdening to the humble, contrite soul. The life of the true Christian is radiant with the bright beams of the Sun of Righteousness. If men and women would act as the Lord's helping hand, doing deeds of love and kindness, uplifting the oppressed, rescuing those ready to perish, the glory of the Lord would be their rereward. . . . They would call, and the Lord would answer, "Here am I." They would turn to the One close beside them, who has given them the promise, "Lo, I am with you alway, even unto the end of the world."—16MR 73, 74 (1901).

Women to Consecrate Their Time to Service of God.—Women who are willing to consecrate some of their time to the service of the Lord should be appointed to visit the sick, look after the young, and minister to the necessities of the poor. They should be set apart to this work by prayer and laying on of hands.* In some cases they will need to counsel with the church officers or the minister; but if they are devoted women, maintaining a vital connection with God, they will be a power for good in the church. This is another means of strengthening and building up the church. We need to branch out more in our methods of labor. Not a hand should be bound, not a soul discouraged, not a voice should be hushed; let every individual labor, privately or publicly, to help forward this grand work. Place the burdens upon men and women of the church, that they may grow by reason of the exercise, and thus become effective agents in the hand of the Lord for the enlightenment of those who sit in darkness.—RH, July 9, 1895.

Not Eloquence That Makes Work Acceptable.—God wants workers who can carry the truth to all classes, high and low, rich and poor. In this work women may act an important part. God grant that those who read these words may put forth earnest efforts to present an open door for consecrated women to enter the field. Those who in their life-work have not come into contact with the higher classes of society need not feel that they cannot do the work. It is not eloquence that makes their work acceptable. It is through the human and contrite that the Lord works. The dignified and self-sufficient cannot touch or help needy souls.—5MR 162 (1898).

WOMEN CAN REACH A CLASS THAT MEN CANNOT REACH

Women Can Do a Work Men Cannot Do in the Homes.—Discreet and humble women can do a good work in explaining the truth to the people in their homes. The Word of God thus explained will do its leavening work, and through its influence whole families will be converted. . . . In the home circle, at your neighbor's fireside, at the bedside of the sick, in a quiet way you may read the Scriptures and speak a word for Jesus and the truth. Precious seed may thus be sown that will spring up and bring forth fruit after many days.—9T 128, 129 (1909).

VISITING AND FOLLOW-UP WORK ESSENTIAL

Teach Others to Give Bible Studies.—The same interest is still manifested in the meetings in Stanmore [Australia]. During the coming week, there is to be a baptism. Since the camp meeting I have visited Stanmore often, and have spoken eight times on Sabbath and Sunday afternoons. The interest is wide and extended. Brother Wilson and wife, Brother Starr and wife, and Brother Haskell and wife are all working in the mission, educating workers to give Bible readings.—19MR 171 (1898).

Hold Smaller Meetings When Large Effort Is Finished.—The tent has been taken down, and Brother Colcord is holding meetings in a small hall connected with the house in which the mission family live. Brother and Sister James from Ballarat [Australia] have charge of the mission home. They both labor as they can to instruct the people. Sisters Wilson and Robertson have been and are doing a good work in Maitland [Australia]. The Lord sustains them, and they have many friends. In the past they have had to walk three and four miles to give their [Bible] readings, but now they have a horse and buggy.—KC 129 (1900).

Visitation Essential Part of Ministry.—Elder H used to live here [Adelaide, Australia] and preach to the people, but he was not a shepherd of the flock. He would tell the poor sheep that he would rather be horsewhipped than visit. He neglected personal labor, therefore pastoral work was not done in the church and its borders. The deacons and elders of the church have acted wisely and worked judiciously to keep the church in order, and we find the people in a much better condition than we had expected. We are happily disappointed. But when I look over the years and think of what might have been done if the man entrusted with the flock had been a faithful steward of God, watching for souls as one that must give an account, my heart is made sad. Had the preacher done the work of a pastor, a much larger number would now be rejoicing in the truth.—9MR 343, 344 (1892).

AN ARMY FOR THE LORD

A Well-trained Army.—Men and women are not to be spiritually dwarfed by a connection with the church, but strengthened, elevated, ennobled, prepared for the most sacred work ever committed to mortals. It is the Lord's purpose to have a well-trained army, ready to be called into action at a moment's notice. This army will be made up of well-disciplined men and women, who have placed themselves under influences that have prepared them for service.—RH, June 2, 1903.

To Encourage One Another in Faithful Service.—There is need of a great reformation in our ranks. The ministers who are drawing pay from the conference need to ask themselves the question "Am I a faithful worker? Am I a spiritual help to the church?" There are those who demand high wages for their labors, but who bring few souls into the truth to stand steadfast and true to its principles. It is time for our ministers to humble their hearts before the Lord, and bear a straight, convincing testimony to the people. It is time for them to labor earnestly to increase the membership of the churches, leading all to a thorough understanding of the truth for this time. The Lord wants living members in His church, men and women who will encourage one another in faithful service.—9MR 115 (1908).

For examples of the public ministry of Ellen White, see Appendix B.

---

*The article in which this statement appears is entitled "The Duty of the Minister and the People." It is a call for involvement of the laity in the church to become active and to share the burdens of the minister. See Appendix C.

The Labourer
Is Worthy
of His Hire

8

Lord, how shall I best serve and glorify Thy name in the earth? How shall I conduct my life to make Thy name a praise in the earth, and lead others to love, serve, and honor Thee? Let me only desire and choose Thy will. Let the words and example of my Redeemer be the light and strength of my heart. While I follow and trust in Him, He will not leave me to perish. He shall be my crown of rejoicing.

—Review and Herald, *Aug. 10, 1886*

God Has Settled the Question of Wages.—If women do the work that is not the most agreeable to many of those who labor in word and doctrine, and if their works testify that they are accomplishing a work that has been manifestly neglected, should not such labor be looked upon as being as rich in results as the work of the ordained ministers? Should it not command the hire of the laborer? . . .

This question is not for men to settle. The Lord has settled it. You are to do your duty to the women who labor in the gospel, whose work testifies that they are essential to carrying the truth into families. Their work is just the work that must be done, and should be encouraged. In many respects a woman can impart knowledge to her sisters that a man cannot. The cause would suffer great loss without this kind of labor by women. Again and again the Lord has shown me that women teachers are just as greatly needed to do the work to which He has appointed them as are men.—Ev 493 (1903).

Women to Receive Wages for Their Work.—There are ministers' wives—Sisters Starr, Haskell, Wilson, and Robinson—who have been devoted, earnest, whole-souled workers, giving Bible readings and praying with families, helping along by personal efforts just as successfully as their husbands. These women give their whole time, and are told that they receive nothing for their labors because their husbands receive wages. I tell them to go forward and all such decisions will be revised. The Word says, "The labourer is worthy of his hire." Luke 10:7. When any such decision as this is made, I will, in the name of the Lord, protest. I will feel it my duty to create a fund from my tithe money to pay these women who are accomplishing just as essential work as the ministers are doing, and this tithe I will reserve for work in the same line as that of the ministers, hunting for souls, fishing for souls.

I know that the faithful women should be paid wages as it is considered proportionate to the pay received by ministers. They carry the burden of souls and should not be treated unjustly. These sisters are giving their time to educating those newly come to the faith and hire their own work done and pay those who work for them. All these things must be adjusted and set in order and justice be done to all. Proofreaders in the office receive their wages; those who are working at housework receive their wages, two dollars and a half and three dollars a week. This I have had to pay and others have to pay. But ministers' wives, who carry a tremendous responsibility, devoting their entire time, have nothing for their labor.—12MR 160 (1898).

LETTER TO CAPT. HENRY NORMAN

Women Should Receive Suitable Pay for Their Work.—My Brother in Christ Jesus: I feel very grateful to my heavenly Father, who has answered our prayers in His own time and His own way. Often in our experience we have been brought into very strait places, but the Lord has answered our petitions, and has greatly blessed us. Again and again we have presented our case before the Lord, wrestling as did Jacob before he met his brother Esau. Some months ago the assurance was given me to call upon our brethren in America for help. The Lord said,

The Labourer Is Worthy of His Hire

"Continue to pray, continue to ask. I will move upon hearts, and means will come in the way I have appointed." Since receiving this communication from the Lord, I have felt no distrust. I have awakened in the night season with these words upon my lips: the gold and silver is the Lord's, and He will not fail us in our emergency.

How wonderful is the way of our Lord! It is His glory to impart to us the things we most need. In the night season I have seen the arm of Omnipotence outstretched to guide us, and lead us onward and still onward. "Go forward," the Lord said. "I understand the whole case, and I will send you help. Continue to pray. Have faith in Me: it is for My name's glory that you ask, and you shall receive. I will be honored before those who are watching critically for your financial failure. They shall see the truth triumph gloriously. And whatsoever ye ask in My name believing, ye shall receive."

I have often been instructed in cases of perplexity as to the path of duty. Where there is a sincere desire to do the will of God apart from all selfish, personal consideration, the Lord will hear and answer prayer.

If we rely upon the promises God has given in His Word, we may with assurance go forward in spite of discouraging appearances. The Lord will raise us up helpers in men whom He will move upon by His Spirit to impart to us in our necessity. Every lawful scheme for advancing the work of saving perishing souls will be a success. We are to see and acknowledge the working of God's special providence. The Lord authorizes us to pray, declaring that He will hear the prayers of those who trust, not in their finite wisdom, but in His infinite power. He will be honored by those who draw nigh to Him, who faithfully do His service. "Thou wilt keep him in perfect peace, whose mind is stayed on thee, because he trusted in thee." The Lord has made you a steward of means. I thank my heavenly Father for impressing you to identify your interests with the work of advancing His kingdom in our world. The safest rule of action is to abide closely by God's Word. The Christian is given the invitation to carry his burdens to God in prayer, and to fasten himself closely to Christ by the cords of living faith.

I have a request to make of you, my brother in Christ Jesus. Will you appropriate a certain sum to create a fund for the education of workers to give Bible readings in families after camp meetings have closed? During this time we can also hold meetings for the children on Sabbath and Sunday afternoons. This rule we have followed in our camp meetings here. There was not one Sabbathkeeper among the citizens of Newcastle when the tent was pitched there. Since then thousands have had an opportunity to hear the truth, and we know that many of them heard it gladly. They seemed to be hungry for the truth.

During the Newcastle camp meeting children's meetings were appointed. The best teachers were appointed, and during the week from one hundred to one hundred and twenty children came to the meetings each day. These were given precious lessons on the love of Christ and His willingness to save all who would come to Him. Between three and four hundred children came out to the meetings held on Sabbath and Sunday afternoons. The children behaved well, and when they returned to their homes they told their parents about the lessons they had learned. Some of these parents have received the truth.

Tent meetings have been continued in Newcastle since the camp meeting closed, and thirty-five have been converted and baptized. Many more are interested. Wonderful conversions have been witnessed among men who had not attended a religious meeting for years before coming to the tent. Smokers and liquor drinkers have seen themselves in the gospel mirror as transgressors of the law, and have in repentance received Christ as their personal Saviour. The ministers are astonished, for they see those who were smokers and beer drinkers no longer smoking and drinking, but changed and converted. This to them seems like a miracle.

A house has been hired for the ministers and their wives and those whom they are educating to give Bible readings from house to house. The people are invited to ask their friends and neighbors to these meetings, and opportunity is given for them to ask questions on the lessons given. These are occasions of deep interest. I have great confidence in this method of labor. The workers who are hunting and fishing for the souls of men and women labor hard from morning till night. Often their appointments are not over till ten o'clock.

Work has now been begun in Wallsend, a suburb of Newcastle,

ten miles from Newcastle, and in Maitland, a town twenty miles from Newcastle. This is a large field, and we shall employ workers who will give their whole time to the work. Elder Haskell and his wife are now laboring in Newcastle. They have tact and skill, and teach the truth both in public and from house to house. There will be other ministers there besides Elder Haskell and the Bible readers. No less than twelve workers are needed in this place, for it is a large field.

In the past I have appropriated means to sustain this kind of work, but my fund is now exhausted, for in this field the calls have been continual. Missionary work has been done in many cities.

The ministers' wives join their husbands in this work, and accomplish that which their husbands could not possibly do. In order to do the work, these sisters have to hire someone to do their housekeeping. It takes the very best talent to do this class of missionary work, and the women who do it should receive a suitable amount for their work. But because of the dearth of means, our sisters have received very little pay, yet they have faithfully worked on, without any definite provision being made for them. Less qualified workers, who are receiving instruction by precept and example, are paid one pound a week, out of which they pay their board. But as yet the ministers' wives have been paid nothing.

I wish to create a fund for the payment of these devoted women who are the most useful workers in giving Bible readings. I am also led to say that we must educate more workers to give Bible readings. I come right to the point. Will you consent to make me your steward, entrusting me with a certain amount to be invested in educating and sustaining workers, and also in helping to erect the humble meetinghouses we have to build? I have invested means in every house of worship save one which has been built by our people in Australia.

I think I have made the case plain. If you desire, I will send you a half-yearly statement of how your money has been invested.

I have been determined to advance the work here, and to do this I borrowed one thousand pounds from Africa. A few months ago this loan fell due, but it has been extended for one year at four and a half percent. I have also borrowed money from America at five and six percent. I am not pressed to pay this money, but when it is called for, it must be paid. Those who lent it to me felt that it would be safer in my possession than in the bank; but now some of them are in straitened circumstances. One or two are widows, and they must have their money sooner or later. I tell you this that you may know why I ask you to help me to raise this fund to keep workers in the field.—Letter 83, 1899.

When Spouses Work Together, Both Should Receive Remuneration.—Again and again I have repeated the instruction the Lord has given me concerning the opening of new fields, that our large cities might hear the truths of the third angel's message. . . .

The printed page cannot accomplish alone the work that the living minister can do. He can explain the Scriptures to the people, praying with them and appealing to them, and making effective the truths of the Bible. Not merely one or two men are called to do this work, but many men and women who have ability to preach and teach the Word. . . .

Let us send forth men and women to labor in faith and consecration for the giving of this last message of mercy to the world. When it is possible let the minister and his wife go forth together. The wife can often labor by the side of her husband, accomplishing a noble work. She can visit the homes of the people and help the women in these families in a way that her husband cannot. . . .

Elder Haskell and his wife have united their labors in the California Conference. Conditions here demanded the capabilities of both. Let none question the right of Sister Haskell to receive remuneration for her work. Dr. Kress and his wife are likewise capable of uniting in missionary effort. None would question the right of Sister Kress to receive a salary. Laboring thus, Brother and Sister Kress can accomplish more than if they labored separately.—12MR 165-167 (1909).

Injustice Done in Not Paying Women for Faithful Work.—The ministers are paid for their work, and this is well. And if the Lord gives the wife, as well as the husband, the burden of labor, and if she devotes her time and her strength to visiting from family to family, opening the Scriptures to them, although the hands of ordination have not been laid upon her, she is accomplishing a work that is in the line of ministry. Should her labors be counted as naught, and her husband's salary be no more than that of the servant of God whose wife does not give herself to the work, but remains at home to care for her family?

While I was in America, I was given light upon this subject. I was instructed that there are matters that need to be considered. Injustice has been done to women who labor just as devotedly as their husbands, and who are recognized by God as being as necessary to the work of ministry as their husbands. The method of paying men laborers and not their wives is a plan not after the Lord's order. Injustice is thus done. A mistake is made. The Lord does not favor this plan. This arrangement, if carried out in our conference, is liable to discourage our sisters from qualifying themselves for the work they should engage in.

A mistake is made when the burden of the work is left entirely upon the ministers. This plan was certainly arranged without the mind of God. Some women are now teaching young women to work successfully as visitors and Bible readers. Women who work in the cause of God should be given wages proportionate to the time they give to the work. God is a God of justice, and if the ministers receive a salary for their work, their wives, who devote themselves just as interestedly to the work as laborers together with God, should be paid in addition to the wages their husbands receive, notwithstanding that they may not ask this. As the devoted minister and his wife engage in the work, they should be paid wages proportionate to the wages of two distinct workers, that they may have means to use as they shall see fit in the cause of God. The Lord has put His Spirit upon them both. If the husband should die, and leave his wife, she is fitted to continue her work in the cause of God, and receive wages for the labor she performs.—5MR 29-31 (1898).

Let None Feel That Women Should Not Receive Just Wages.— Select women who will act an earnest part. The Lord will use intelligent women in the work of teaching. And let none feel that these women, who understand the Word, and who have ability to teach, should not receive remuneration for their labors. They should be paid as verily as are their husbands. There is a great work for women to do in the cause of present truth. Through the exercise of womanly tact and a wise use of their knowledge of Bible truth, they can remove difficulties that our brethren cannot meet. We need women workers to labor in connection with their husbands, and should encourage those who wish to engage in this line of missionary effort.—Ev 491 (1909).

Proper Compensation for Work of Women.—If a woman is appointed by the Lord to do a certain work, her work should be estimated according to its value. Some may think it good policy to allow persons to devote their time and labor to the work without compensation. But God does not sanction such arrangements. When self-denial is required because of a dearth of means, the burden is not to rest wholly upon a few persons. Let all unite in the sacrifice.—7T 207, 208 (1902).

Sacrificing Not to Be Limited to Faithful Women.—A great work is to be done in our world, and every talent is to be used in accordance with righteous principles. If a woman is appointed by the Lord to do a certain work, her work is to be estimated according to its value. Every laborer is to receive his or her just due.—Ev 491 (1898).

Wages to Be Paid to Women Doing Gospel Work.—I was solicited to visit Melbourne before the tent would have to be taken down, but on account of the severe heat they dared not make the request too urgent. Elder Robinson thought my testimony must be given, as it was greatly needed. He and his wife were left to bear the responsibility of the work, giving Bible readings, conducting the mission, and training several young men and women as workers. The work has rested heavily upon them. Sister Robinson has hired a girl to do her housework and is doing work every way as taxing as that of a minister. The women workers have not received pay, but this will be changed in due time. The cause is now hemmed in for want of means.—12MR 160 (1898).

Wages From Tithe to Be Determined by Situation.—Women, as well as men, are needed in the work that must be done. Those women who give themselves to the service of the Lord, who labor for the salvation of others by doing house-to-house work, which is as taxing as, and more taxing than standing before a congregation, should receive payment for their labor. If a man is worthy of his hire, so also is a woman.

The Labourer Is Worthy of His Hire

God has entrusted talents to His servants, and He expects them to see [understand] that mistakes can be . . . made. [But] make no mistake in neglecting to correct the error of giving ministers less than they should receive. When you see persons in necessity who have been placed in positions of trust, let God move upon your heart to set things right. The tithe should go to those who labor in word and doctrine, be they men or women.—1MR 263 (1899).*

---

*See Appendix D.

Neighborhood Ministry

9

We should feel it our special duty to work for those living in our neighborhood. Study how you can best help those who take no interest in religious things. As you visit your friends and neighbors, show an interest in their spiritual as well as in their temporal welfare. Speak to them of Christ as a sin-pardoning Saviour. Invite your neighbors to your home, and read with them from the precious Bible and from books that explain its truths. Invite them to unite with you in song and prayer. In these little gatherings, Christ Himself will be present, as He has promised, and hearts will be touched by His grace.

—The Ministry of Healing, *p. 152*

Women Needed in Various Branches of the Work.—In the various branches of the work of God's cause, there is a wide field in which our sisters may do good service for the Master. Many lines of missionary work are neglected. In the different churches, much work which is often left undone or done imperfectly, could be well accomplished by the help that our sisters, if properly instructed, can give. Through various lines of home missionary effort they can reach a class that is not reached by our ministers. Among the noble women who have had the moral courage to decide in favor of the truth for this time are many who have tact, perception, and good ability, and who may make successful workers. The labors of such Christian women are needed.—RH, Dec. 10, 1914.

Be Friends of the People.—If one member of Christ's household falls into temptation, the other members are to look after him with kindly interest, seeking to arrest the feet that are straying into false paths, and win him to a pure, holy life. This service God requires from every member of His church. . . .

This is home missionary work, and it is as helpful to those who do it as to those for whom it is done. The kindly interest we manifest in the home circle, the words of sympathy we speak to our brothers and sisters, fit us to work for the members of the Lord's household, with whom, if we remain loyal to Christ, we shall live through eternal ages. "Be thou faithful unto death," Christ says, "and I will give thee a crown of life." Then how carefully should the members of the Lord's family guard their brethren and sisters! Make yourself their friend. If they are poor and in need of food and clothing, minister to their temporal as well as their spiritual wants. Thus you will be a double blessing to them.—Ev 353 (1898).

Be a Friend to the Family in Need.—The sisters can do much to reach the heart and make it tender. Wherever you are, my sisters, work in simplicity. If you are in a home where there are children, show an interest in them. Let them see that you love them. If one is sick, offer to give him treatment; help the careworn, anxious mother to relieve her suffering child.—RH, Nov. 11, 1902.

ALL TO HAVE A PART IN THE WORK OF GOD

Our Sisters Can Do Much.—Our sisters are doing comparatively nothing, when they might do very much. Christ is searching the life and character for fruit, and He finds many professed Christians, like the fruitless fig tree, bearing nothing but leaves. The sisters can work efficiently in obtaining subscribers for our periodicals, in this way bringing the light before many minds. The distribution of tracts, and the work of Christian canvassers and colporteurs, can be done as well by our sisters as by our brethren.

Satan is busy in this department of his work, scattering literature which is debasing the morals and poisoning the minds of the young. Infidel publications are scattered broadcast throughout the land.

Why should not every member of the church be as deeply interested in sending forth publications that will elevate the minds of the people, and bring the truth directly before them? These papers and tracts are for the light of the world, and have often been instrumental in converting souls. Our publications are now sowing the gospel seed, and are instrumental in bringing as many souls to Christ as the preached word. Whole churches have been raised up as the result of their circulation.

In this work every disciple of Christ can act a part. Let the leaflets and tracts, the papers and books, go in every direction. Carry with you, wherever you go, a package of select tracts, which you can hand out as you have opportunity. Sell what you can, and lend or give them away as the case may seem to require. Important results will follow.—RH, June 10, 1880.

Be Sure We Are Working for Jesus.—Our sisters are not excused from taking a part in the work of God. Everyone who has tasted of the powers of the world to come has earnest work to do in some capacity in the Lord's vineyard. Our sisters may manage to keep busy with their fingers constantly employed in manufacturing little dainty articles to beautify their homes, or to present to their friends. Great quantities of this kind of material may be brought and laid upon the foundation stone; but will Jesus look upon all this variety of dainty work as a living sacrifice to Himself? Will He pronounce the commendation upon the workers, "I know thy works, . . . and how thou . . . for my name's sake hast laboured"?—RH, May 31, 1887.

All Can Do Something at Home.—Our sisters have been too willing to excuse themselves from bearing responsibilities which require thought and close application of the mind; yet this is the very discipline they need to perfect Christian experience. They may be workers in the missionary field, having a personal interest in the distribution of tracts and papers which correctly represent our faith. All cannot go abroad to labor, but all can do something at home. . . .

We should, as Christians, have an abiding sense that our time, our strength and ability, have been purchased with an infinite price. We are not our own to use our moments in gratifying our fancy and our pride. As children of the light we should diffuse light to others.

Neighborhood Ministry

It should be our study how we may best glorify God, how we can work to save and bless souls for whom Christ died. In working to bless others we shall be gathering strength and courage to our own souls, and shall receive the approval of God. Hundreds of our sisters might be at work today if they would. . . .

Those who are now doing nothing should go to work. Let each sister who claims to be a child of God feel indeed a responsibility to help all within her reach. The noblest of all attainments may be gained through practical self-denial and benevolence for others' good.—RH, Dec. 12, 1878.

Sow Beside All Waters.—If our sisters would spend their God-given time in earnest prayer to God, and the study of His Word, He would impart to them heavenly wisdom, that they might know how to labor through the grace given them of God, to save the souls of those around them. Our sisters might begin with missionary work in their own households; then they would know how to work intelligently for their neighbors. If they would become interested in this kind of work, they might be sowing the seeds of truth. We must sow beside all waters, though we know not which will prosper, this or that. This kind of work pays; for its results are as lasting as eternity. It is represented as bringing to the foundation, gold, silver, and precious stones—materials which are not consumable and perishable, but as enduring as eternity. The first work for us individually is a personal consecration to God.—RH, Nov. 6, 1888.

Coworkers With God

Pray for Personal Friends.—God will do for us greater things than we can ask or think, if we will only confide in and trust Him fully. Shall we believe, shall we move forward in faith, in hope, in courage, clinging with firm grasp to the Mighty One? . . . Let all those who profess the present truth carry out its pure and holy principles in their lives. If our sisters would only feel that they can do very much, if they will consecrate themselves to God, they could be a great help. If they would talk and labor in heavenly wisdom among those with whom they are acquainted, they could do a good work.

If they would talk less upon unimportant matters and pray more earnestly, and take the cases of their personal friends, who are not in the truth, to Jesus, pleading with Him to enlighten their minds, their prayers might do much good; they certainly will if offered in faith. Our sisters may be coworkers with God. They may be able, when this life here shall close, to look back upon their lives not as a barren desert, but upon buds, flowers, and fruit as the result of their life's toil.—7MR 40, 41 (1874).

LET THE YOUTH BE TRAINED TO SERVE OTHERS

Organize for Service.—Young men and young women, cannot you form companies, and, as soldiers of Christ, enlist in the work, putting all your tact and skill and talent into the Master's service, that you may save souls from ruin? Let there be companies organized in every church to do this work. . . . Will the young men and young women who really love Jesus organize themselves as workers, not only for those who profess to be Sabbathkeepers, but for those who are not of our faith?—ST, May 29, 1893.

Instruct in Practical Methods of Doing Missionary Work.—That which is needed now for the upbuilding of our churches is the nice work of wise laborers to discern and develop talent in the church that can be educated for the Master's service. Those who shall labor in visiting the churches should give them instruction in the Bible reading and missionary work. Let there be a class for the training of the youth who are willing to work if they are taught how. Young men and women should be educated to become workers at home, in their own neighborhoods, and in the church.—RH, May 15, 1888.

Youth Can Hold Meetings.—Before I presented these matters [holding meetings in Australia] to the students of the Avondale school, a few had been diligently engaged in missionary effort, visiting families, distributing reading matter, and holding Bible readings in places from one to five miles away; but many of the students here, as in most other schools, were acting upon the theory that it was wisest to learn all they could while in school, and wait till after school closed before undertaking any active missionary effort. . . .

As we studied what would be for the best interests of the New South Wales churches, and for those students in the school who had

had an experience in working for Christ, it was thought best to encourage persons of some experience to leave the school, and spend the week in visiting in the churches, in helping to conduct the meetings, and uniting with the workers in these churches in earnest work for those needing help. Seven were thus sent out from Cooranbong, besides Elder Haskell, who spent the week with the Stanmore church, upon which he has bestowed so much efficient and loving labor.

When this matter was first considered, by some it seemed a serious thing to lose one week out of the school term. It had cost much to reach the school, and apparently this was the last opportunity for attendance, and each lesson was very precious. But after consideration, the service was accepted cheerfully; the cross was lifted, and as it was lifted, it lifted the bearer. None of the workers settled down to have an easy time, but they moved rapidly from place to place. They met a hearty reception. They found lonely souls hungry for spiritual encouragement; as they watered others, their own souls were watered. When these workers returned to the school, they were full of joy and courage. Their faith had developed with labor, and they were ready to cheer and help their fellows.

Just then there was throughout the colony a visitation of the influenza, in a severe form. It appeared first in the cities, and then worked its way through the country. As might be expected, the school was one of the last places visited. There were many sick all around us; and the students who are in the class of practical nursing freely offered to go, when needed, and care for the sick. So they were sent out, two and two, to give treatments, and to nurse those who were very feeble.

These experiences prepared their hearts to appreciate and receive instruction regarding the value of missionary effort as a part of their education. As this subject was presented in the school and in the church, during the week of prayer, students and teachers sought to act upon the suggestions, and opportunities for labor were found in all directions. Sabbath and Sunday afternoons, from sixteen to twenty students are engaged in holding prayer meetings, Bible readings, young people's meetings, and preaching services, in from six to ten different places. One result of this work we already see—the workers are greatly blessed. Other results may be seen in the future.—RH, Oct. 4, 1898.

Daughters of God

A MISSIONARY LETTER TO MARIA CHASE

Maria Chase was James White's niece, the daughter of his sister Mary.

Dear Niece Maria: I have a desire to write you a few lines. I have not lost my interest for you although I have become very much discouraged in regard to your case. As the prospect of your becoming a Christian has seemed to lessen, I have felt a painful anxiety in regard to your future course and prospects.

I do not know as I fully understand your present state of mind and I may not be as prepared to help you as though I did. I should know better how to address you if I knew that you sincerely desired to become a humble Christian. I have thought that perhaps you desired this but that on account of your late failure to carry out your purposes to become a Christian you have become discouraged. [You may have] thought that the confidence of others in you was so much shaken that they could not have faith in efforts you might make in the future.

But, Maria, if the Christian life has charms in it for you, and you see the sinfulness of sin and your lost condition out of Christ, I advise you to commence again in earnest. In meekness seek the Lord. You may be very distrustful of yourself, for you have reason to be. But God is true, and I advise you for your soul's sake to try again and earnestly seek to become a follower of Christ. This work no other can do for you. It is a solemn work between God and your own soul, which must bear the test of the Almighty.

Let me entreat of you to seek for those things which make for your peace. You have all your life been anxiously, worriedly seeking for earthly pleasure and worldly enjoyments to satisfy the longing mind; but a thorn has been found in every earthly, worldly pleasure. With you it has been disappointment upon disappointment, and life has been a failure. You have not filled the purpose on earth which God designed you should. Your mind has been allowed to dwell upon frivolity, fashion, and show. Appearance has been the altar whereon you have sacrificed soberness of thought—high and elevated considerations and eternal interests which are as much higher and more valuable than earthly considerations as the heavens are higher than the earth.

Satan has strewed the broad and downward road with tempting flowers, but those who are allured to death in this road learn by experience that these pleasing flowers wither as soon as grasped. They yield no rich perfume, but a disagreeable, sickening odor.

Maria, do you intend to devote to God the little time that is allowed you and secure your happiness here and salvation hereafter? I beg of you to take hold of the work in earnest. No longer worship your personal appearance, which cannot bring you into favor with God in the least. God prizes moral worth. Says Peter, "Whose adorning let it not be that outward adorning of plaiting the hair, and of wearing of gold, or of putting on of apparel; but let it be the hidden man of the heart, in that which is not corruptible, even the ornament of a meek and quiet spirit, which is in the sight of God of great price." 1 Peter 3:3, 4.

Seek for this meek and quiet spirit. Get rid of this spirit which controls [you] to a great extent. Overcome this desire for change, and seek meekness, seek righteousness. I believe that God will yet be gracious unto you, if you turn to Him with your whole heart, and make it your first and primary business to learn of Christ. Learn how to serve Him. Study the Bible, beseeching God to enlighten your mind to understand its sacred teachings, which you have so long neglected and despised. Turn your attention to the words of life. "Search the scriptures."

All your life long your heart has been in rebellion against God. You have trampled upon His offered mercy, choosing the pleasing things of the world and the service of Satan rather than the service of Christ. Yet Jesus in unbounded mercy still invites you to choose Him as your Saviour and become a child of God, an heir of glory. You can choose life and salvation if you will, or you can choose to worship self and devote your precious hours of probation to making your person attractive to please the eye of the worldling and the sensualist, to receive flattery from lying lips, and at last reap that harvest which you have been sowing—corruption. The poor mortal body which has been your idol, your god, will be cut down like the grass and wither as the green herb. Oh, Maria, how heartsick it has made me to see your mind almost wholly taken up with your own person, your dress, your appearance. Your mind seemed to be on a constant stretch to improve your appearance.

The Word of God exhorts us to study to show ourselves

approved unto God. How much has this important lesson been studied? You have coveted the approval and the praise of those who are lovers of pleasure and the enemies of God while you have had no elevated desires and determination of purpose to seek, above everything else, to show yourself approved unto God. [It is] He who grants you life and every good thing which you have enjoyed.

I leave these hastily written lines with you, praying that they may do you good. Again I beseech you to make a business of seeking the Lord. Pray much. Weep and pray. Humble yourself before God, relying alone upon the merits of a crucified and risen Saviour, One who maketh intercessions for just such sin-polluted souls as yours. If others do not help you as you think they ought to, do not be discouraged. With you it is a case of life or death. Angels of God are watching with interest to see whether you will be overcome by Satan, or [whether you] yourself [will] be an overcomer and through the efficacy of the blood of Christ bruise Satan under your feet. Will you choose Christ as your portion forever?

Pray, Maria, earnestly, that God will reveal to you yourself the sin and corruption of your own heart. Let this desire be ever with you, for it is important for you to see yourself as a sinner in order for you to feel the necessity of pardon through the blood of Christ. Let your second prayer be, "Lord, reveal to me Thyself, Thy mercy, and the value of Thy blood." Lay hold on everlasting life. You have proved the worthlessness of earthly things, and it has been perfectly astonishing to me that you yet seemed to manifest so little interest in becoming a Christian. But I can understand it now. Your personal appearance is your idol. God cannot dwell in your heart or thoughts where self rules supreme. Your good appearance Satan means to use to your own destruction and, if he succeeds, it will prove to be the greatest curse that ever came upon you.

What is show and appearance merely? What are good looks alone without moral worth or true goodness of heart and nobleness of mind? They are a mere outside gloss, which pleases a certain class of minds, but which will perish in the day of God, leaving only sinful, corrupt deformity. Seek heaven, seek true humility, and God will then direct your path.—Letter 2, 1865.

Temperance
Work

10

*M*rs. *White was remarkable for her broad definition of temperance: "True temperance teaches us to dispense entirely with everything hurtful, and to use judiciously that which is healthful."—Te 138. However, in this section we are dealing with temperance reform primarily in reference to the use of alcohol. Ellen White was a much-sought-after speaker on temperance. She had a great burden for this subject, and it was often her topic as she spoke in large public meetings. The principles set forth here can be well applied to any substance abuse.*

Use Influence for Temperance.—The advocates of temperance fail to do their whole duty unless they exert their influence by precept and example—by voice and pen and vote—in favor of prohibition and total abstinence.—RH, Nov. 8, 1881.

A Part of the Third Angel's Message.—In our work more attention should be given to the temperance reform. Every duty that calls for reform involves repentance, faith, and obedience. It means the uplifting of the soul to a new and nobler life. Thus every true reform has its place in the work of the third angel's message. Especially does the temperance reform demand our attention and support. At our camp meetings we should call attention to this work and make it a living issue. We should present to the people the principles of true temperance and call for signers to the temperance pledge. Careful attention should be given to those who are enslaved by evil habits. We must lead them to the cross of Christ.

In other churches there are Christians who are standing in defense of the principles of temperance. We should seek to come near to these workers and make a way for them to stand shoulder to shoulder with us. We should call upon great and good men to second our efforts to save that which is lost. . . .

Only eternity will reveal what has been accomplished by this kind of ministry—how many souls, sick with doubt, and tired of worldliness and unrest, have been brought to the Great Physician, who longs to save to the uttermost all who come unto Him. Christ is a risen Saviour, and there is healing in His wings.—6T 110, 111 (1900).

Lose No Opportunity to Unite With Temperance Work.—I am sorry that there has not been a more lively interest among our people of late years to magnify this branch of the Lord's work. We cannot afford to lose one opportunity to unite with the temperance work in any place. Although the cause of temperance in foreign countries does not always advance as rapidly as we could wish, yet in some places decided success has attended the efforts of those who engaged in it. In Europe we found the people sound on this question. On one occasion, when I accepted an invitation to speak to a large audience on the subject of temperance, the people did me the honor of draping above the pulpit the American flag. My words were received with the deepest attention, and at the close of my talk a hearty vote of thanks was accorded me. I have never, in all my work on this question, had to accept one word of disrespect.—Te 225, 226 (1907).

Youth Can Be a Great Force for Temperance.—There is no class of persons capable of accomplishing more in the warfare against intemperance than are God-fearing youth. In this age the young men in our cities should unite as an army, firmly and decidedly to set themselves against every form of selfish, health-destroying indulgence. What a power they might be for good! How many they might save from becoming demoralized in the halls and gardens fitted up with music and other attractions to allure the youth! Intemperance and profanity and licentiousness are sisters. Let every God-fearing youth gird on the armor and press to the front. Put your names on every temperance pledge presented. Thus you lend your influence in favor of sign-ing the pledge, and induce others to sign it. Let no weak excuse deter you from taking this step. Work for the good of your own souls and for the good of others.—YI, July 16, 1903.

Support Temperance.—The temperance question is to receive de-cided support from God's people. Intemperance is striving for the mastery; self-indulgence is increasing, and the publications treating on health reform are greatly needed. Literature bearing on this point is the helping hand of the gospel, leading souls to search the Bible for a better understanding of the truth. The note of warning against the great evil of intemperance should be sounded; and, that this may be done, every Sabbathkeeper should study and practice the instruction contained in our health periodicals and our health books. And they should do more than this: they should make earnest efforts to circu-late these publications among their neighbors.—PUR, Nov. 20, 1902.

OUR RELATIONSHIP TO THE WOMAN'S CHRISTIAN TEMPERANCE UNION

Ellen White was especially appreciative of the work of the WCTU. She urged cooperation between our workers and theirs in this worthy cause. This principle of cooperation could be carried through in other areas of hu-manitarian work.

To Unite With Other Women in Temperance Work.—The Woman's Christian Temperance Union is an organization with whose efforts for the spread of temperance principles we can heartily unite. The light has been given me that we are not to stand aloof from them, but, while there is to be no sacrifice of principle on our part, as far as possible we are to unite with them in laboring for temperance reforms. . . . We are to work with them when we can, and we can assuredly do this on the question of utterly closing the saloon.—RH, June 18, 1908.

Work With the Woman's Christian Temperance Union.—We need at this time to show a decided interest in the work of the Woman's Christian Temperance Union. None who claim to have a part in the work of God should lose interest in the grand object of this organization in temperance lines. It would be a good thing if at our camp meetings we should invite the members of the WCTU to take part in our exercises. This would help them to become acquainted with the reasons of our faith, and open the way for us to unite with them in the temperance work. If we do this, we shall come to see that the temperance question means more than many of us have supposed. In some matters, the workers of the WCTU are far in advance of our leaders. The Lord has in that organization precious souls, who can be a great help to us in our efforts to advance the temperance movement. And the education our people have had in Bible truth and in a knowledge of the requirements of the law of Jehovah will enable our sisters to impart to these noble temperance advocates that which will be for their spiritual welfare. Thus a union and sympathy will be created where in the past there has sometimes existed prejudice and misunderstanding.—RH, Oct. 15, 1914.

MRS. S.M.I. HENRY,
LEADER OF THE WOMAN'S CHRISTIAN TEMPERANCE UNION

Mrs. S.M.I. Henry, leader of the Woman's Christian Temperance Union, was converted to Adventism while she was a patient at the Battle Creek Sanitarium and while Mrs. White was living in Australia. The two became fast friends through correspondence, although they never had the privilege of meeting in person. The following extracts from letters to Mrs. Henry show the relation that may be sustained with the Woman's Christian Temperance Union by Seventh-day Adventist women of ability.

I would be very much pleased could I be seated by your side and converse with you in regard to the incidents of your experience. I have an earnest desire to meet you. It is not impossible that, even in this life, we shall see each other face to face. When I learn of the gracious dealings of God with you, I feel very grateful to my heavenly Father that the light of the truth for this time is shining into the chambers of your mind and into the soul temple. Across the broad waters of the Pacific, we can clasp hands in faith and sweet fellowship. I rejoice with you in every opportunity you have of reaching the people. I praise the Lord that He has wrought for you, that the Great Physician who has never lost a case, has healed you, and given you access to the people, that you may set before many your experience of the loving-kindness of a gracious Redeemer.—7MR 155 (1898).

I thank the Lord with heart, and soul, and voice that you have been a prominent and influential member of the Woman's Christian Temperance Union. In the providence of God you have been led to the light, to obtain a knowledge of the truth. . . . This light and knowledge you need to bring into your work, as you associate with women whose hearts are softened by the Spirit of God, and who are searching for the truth as for hidden treasure. For twenty years I have seen that the light would come to the women workers in temperance lines. But with sadness I have discerned that many of them are becoming politicians, and that against God. They enter into questions and debates and theories that they have no need to touch. Christ said, "I am the light of the world; he that followeth me shall not walk in darkness, but shall have the light of life."

The Lord, I fully believe, is leading you that you may keep the principles of temperance clear and distinct, in all their purity in connection with the truth for these last days. They that do His will shall know of the doctrine. The Lord designs that women shall learn of Him meekness and lowliness of heart, and cooperate with the greatest Teacher the world has ever known. When this is done, there will be no strife for the supremacy, no pride of opinion; for it will be realized that mind, and voice, and every jot of ability, are only lent talents, given by God to be used in His work, to accumulate for Him, and to be returned to the Giver with all the increase. We are expected to grow in capability, in influence, and in power, ever looking unto Jesus. And by beholding, we shall be changed into His likeness.

The woman's work is a power in our world, but it is lost when, with the Word of God before her, she sees a "thus saith the Lord" and refuses to obey. The great and difficult thing for the soul to do is to part with its own supposed works of merit. It is not an easy matter to understand what it means to refuse self the best place of honor in the service of God. All unconsciously we act out the attributes of our own character and the bias of our own mind in the very presence of God, in our prayer and worship, in our service, and fail to see that we are absolutely dependent upon the leading of the Holy Spirit. Self is expected to do a work that is simply out of its power to do. This is the great peril of women's work in Christian temperance lines.

The Lord does not bid you separate from the Woman's Christian

Temperance Union. They need all the light you can give them. You are not to learn of them but of Jesus Christ. Flash all the light possible into their pathway. You can agree with them on the ground of the pure, elevating principles that first brought into existence the Woman's Christian Temperance Union. "Behold," said Christ, "I send you forth as lambs among wolves." If He sends His disciples on such a mission, will He not work through you to open the Scriptures to those who are in error? Cherish the fragrance of that love that Christ has revealed for fallen humanity, and by precept and example teach the truth as it is in Jesus.

The Holy Spirit alone is able to develop in the human heart that which is acceptable in the sight of God. The Lord has given you capabilities and talents to be preserved uncorrupted in their simplicity. Through Jesus Christ you may do a good work. As souls shall be converted to the truth, have them unite with you in teaching these women who are willing to be taught, to live and labor intelligently and unitedly.—LLM 232, 233 (from letter 118, 1898; written Dec. 1, 1898).

I am so glad, my sister, that you did not sever your connection with the Woman's Christian Temperance Union. You may have to sever this connection, but not yet, not yet. Hold your place. Speak the words given you by God, and the Lord will certainly work with you. You may see many things you do not approve of, but do not fail nor be discouraged. I hope and pray that you may be clothed daily with the righteousness of Christ.—LLM 233 (from letter 54, 1899; written Mar. 24, 1899).

I hope, my sister, that you will have an influence in the Woman's Christian Temperance Association to draw *many* precious souls to the standard of truth. The Lord is drawing many to an examination of the truth, and you need not fail nor be discouraged. Sow beside all waters. These are good waters in which you can sow the seeds of truth, even if you do not dwell publicly upon the prominent features of our faith. It would not be wise to be too definite. The oil of grace revealed in your conscious and unconscious influence will make known that you have the light of life. This will shine forth to others in your direct, positive testimony upon subjects

Temperance Work

on which you can all agree, and this will have a telling influence.—
LLM 234 (from letter 96, 1899; written June 21, 1899).

I was greatly pleased with your letter, in which you gave me the
history of your experience with the WCTU. When I read it, I said,
"Thank the Lord. That is seed-sowing which is of value." I am
pleased, so much pleased. The Lord has certainly opened your way.
Keep it open, if possible. A work can be accomplished by you.
Preserve your strength for such efforts. Attend important gatherings
when you can. These occasions will be very trying seasons, but when
the Lord gives His loved ones a special work to do, He sends His angels to be round about them.

There are very many precious souls whom the Lord would have
reached by the light of truth. Labor is to be put forth to help them to
understand the Scriptures. I have felt an intense interest in the
WCTU workers. These heroic women know what it means to have
an individuality of their own. I desire so much that they shall triumph with the redeemed around the great white throne. My prayers
shall be in your behalf that you may be given special opportunities
to attend their large gatherings, and that your voice may be heard in
defense of the truth.

I dare not give you advice in this important matter. You are on
the ground and Christ is on the ground. Be assured that He will
work with you and through you and by you.

It ought to be a great encouragement to you in your work to
think of the compassion and tender love of God for those who are
seeking and praying for light. We should hold convocations for
prayer to ask the Lord to open the way that the truth may enter the
stronghold where Satan has set up his throne, and dispel the shadow
which he has cast athwart the pathway of those he is seeking to deceive and to destroy. We have the promise or rather, the assurance,
"The effectual fervent prayer of a righteous man availeth much."—
LLM 234 (from letter 231, 1899; written December 1899).

The work you are doing to help our sisters feel their individual
accountability to God is a good and necessary work. Long has it been
neglected; but when this work has been laid out in clear lines, simple and definite, we may expect that the essential duties of the home,

instead of being neglected, will be done much more intelligently. The Lord would ever have us urge upon those who do not understand, the worth of the human soul. . . .

Christ our Saviour appreciated the excellency of the soul. Our sisters have generally a very hard time, with their increasing families and their unappreciated trials. I have so longed for women who could be educators to help them to arise from their discouragement, and to feel that they could do a work for the Lord. And this effort is bringing rays of sunshine into their lives, and is being reflected upon the hearts of others. God will bless you, and all who shall unite with you, in this grand work. . . .

If we can, my sister, we should speak often to our sisters, and lead them in the place of saying "Go." Lead them to do as we should do—to feel as we should feel, a strong and abiding perception of the value of the human soul. We are learners that we may be teachers. This idea must be imprinted in the mind of every church member.

We believe fully in church organization, but in nothing that is to prescribe the precise way in which we must work; for all minds are not reached by the same methods. Nothing is to be allowed to keep the working servant of God from his fellowman. The individual believer is to labor for the individual sinner. . . .

Teach this, my sister. You have many ways opened before you. Address the crowd whenever you can; hold every jot of influence you can by any association that can be made the means of introducing the leaven to the meal. Every man and every woman has a work to do for the Master. Personal consecration and sanctification to God will accomplish, through the most simple methods, more than the most imposing display. . . .

Teach our sisters that every day the question is to be, Lord, what wilt thou have me to do this day? Each vessel consecrated to God will daily have the holy oil emptied into it, that it may be emptied out into other vessels. Every day we may be advancing in the Christian character, waiting and watching for opportunities to do the will and work of God. Every word uttered, every work performed in Christ's lines, will have an enduring preeminence. Speak the words that are given you of God, and the Lord will certainly work with you. Do not fail nor be discouraged, although you may see many things which you do not approve. I hope and pray that you may be clothed with the righteousness of Christ daily.—RH, May 9, 1899 (written to Mrs. S.M.I. Henry Mar. 25, 1899).

SEEDS OF TRUTH CAN BE SOWN IN WCTU
Only Eternity Will Reveal Accomplishments.—I would not have any of our people so narrow that they should say to Sister Henry, Sever your connection with the Woman's Christian Temperance Union. Sister Henry can sow the seeds of truth in this society. Not that she needs to give all the knowledge she has obtained on subjects that are objectionable. She can tell the glad tidings of salvation. Then when hearts have become warmed by the Holy Spirit's working, and the walls of prejudice begin to give way, she can present the truth point by point. This work for the WCTU has a wearying and discouraging side, and we should unite in helping our sister. Only eternity will reveal what has been accomplished by this kind of ministry, how many souls, sick with doubt, and tired of worldliness and unrest, have been brought to the Great Physician, who longs to save to the uttermost all who will come unto Him. Christ is a risen Saviour, and there is healing in His wings.—7MR 165 (1899).

DEATH OF MRS. S.M.I. HENRY
BRINGS A REAL LOSS TO THE CAUSE OF GOD
Mrs. Henry Had a Work to Do Among WCTU Members.—I feel very sad in regard to Sister Henry's death. The light given me by the Lord was that He had a work for her to do among the WCTU, and that her strength must not be absorbed among our people. She could do for the WCTU that which no other one in our ranks could do, and she must not allow our people to lead her to use her God-given capabilities upon them. The Lord would go before her in her work.—7MR 167 (1900).

Work Through Women of Influence in Tenderness and Love.—Do not represent truth and the situation of things as so formidable that those belonging to the WCTU will turn away in despair. There are vital truths upon which they have had very little light. They should be dealt with in tenderness, in love, and with respect for their good work. . . . Withhold your condemnation till you and our people have done all that can be done to reach them, not by the learned arguments of ministers, but through women of influence working as Sister Henry worked.—1MR 125 (1900).

Excellence of the Soul.—Sister Henry's whole soul was enlisted in the work of reform, and her influence was a savor of life unto life. Her personal labors we shall greatly miss. She has borne her testimony unfalteringly, yet judiciously. When convicted of the truth, her soul was glad, and without seeking to make excuse she came thankfully to the gospel feast. She rejoiced in the privilege of receiving precious truth, which makes the soul wise unto salvation, and in gratitude to God for His rich favors she felt herself under obligation to impart to others. As she had freely received, she freely gave. Faithfully did she testify to the truth. And she did this, not merely as a duty, as the work appointed her, but as a great privilege. It was her joy to make His ways known upon the earth, and His saving health among all whom her influence could reach. She was a true missionary, a gospel worker, and in heaven's record her name is written as a laborer together with God. How many souls will be saved through her precious service in drawing with Christ we cannot know. The seed she has sown will continue to reproduce itself, and will show a glorious yield in the day of harvest.—RH, Apr. 3, 1900.

For further information on the life of Mrs. S.M.I. Henry, see her biography, Whirlwind of the Lord, *by Margaret Rossiter White.*

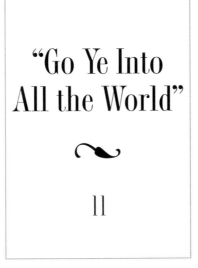

"Go Ye Into All the World"

11

Today the word "missionary" has been largely replaced by "inter-division worker," "expatriate worker," or other similar expressions. The spirit and sense of "missionary" is used to indicate those who teach others about Jesus and His love, whether they go to a foreign country, or into their own community.

Women to Be Educated to Missionary Labor.—There is hard work to be done in dislodging error and false doctrine from the head, that Bible truth and Bible religion may find a place in the heart. It was as a means ordained of God to educate young men and women for the various departments of missionary labor that colleges were established among us. It was God's will that they send forth not merely a few, but many laborers. But Satan, determined to overthrow this purpose, has often secured the very ones whom God would qualify for places of usefulness in His work. There are many who would work if urged into service, and who would save their souls by thus working. The church should feel her great responsibility in shutting up the light of truth and restraining the grace of God within her own narrow limits, when money and influence should be freely employed in bringing competent persons into the missionary field.—RH, July 17, 1883.

Women of Different Nationalities to Be Educated.—Missions are being established; and if the converting power of the truth comes to our youth, we shall see them pressing into the ranks of the workers. Had they been educated from the beginning of their religious experience to be true to their faith, fervent in piety, and in sympathy with Christ's longing for the salvation of souls, we would have hundreds of missionaries where we have one today. In every mission established, there should be a school for the education of laborers. The very best German, French, and Scandinavian* talent should be enlisted in the work of educating promising young men and women of these different nationalities. This essential matter has been greatly neglected. In the office at Battle Creek, at Basel, and at Christiana [now Oslo], there is pressing need of translators in these different languages. . . . We want a hundred workers where there is one.

The heavy responsibilities should not rest upon one man in any branch of the work. Two or three should be fitted to share the burden, so that if one should be called to another post of duty, another may come in to supply his place. Provision has not been made half as extensively as it should have been, against any and every emergency. A fund should be raised to educate for missionary work those who will give themselves unreservedly to God and the cause, and who will labor not for large wages, but for the love of Christ, to save souls for whom He died.—RH, Oct. 12, 1886.

A Liberal Education to Be Provided.—As a people who claim to have advanced light, we are to devise ways and means by which to bring forth a corps of educated workmen for the various departments of the work of God. We need a well-disciplined, cultivated class of young men and women in the sanitarium, in the medical missionary work, in the office of publication, in the conferences of different states, and in the field at large. We need young men and women who have a high intellectual culture, in order that they may do the best work for the Lord. We have done something toward reaching this standard, but still we are far behind that which the Lord has designed.—RH, Apr. 28, 1896.

Women to Work in the Great Cities of the World.—London has been presented to me again and again as a place in which a great work is to be done, and I have tried to present this before our people. I spent two years in Europe, going over the field three times. And each time I went, I saw improvement in the work, and the last time a decided improvement was manifest. And oh, what a burning desire filled my heart to see this great field, London especially, worked as it should be. Why have not workers been sent there, men and women who could have planned for the advancement of the work? I have wondered why our people, those who are not ordained ministers, but who have a connection with God, who understand the Scriptures, do not open the Word to others. If they would engage in this work, great blessing would come to their own souls. God wants His people to work. To every man—and that means every woman, also—He has given His work, and this work each one is to perform according to his several ability.—GCB, Apr. 22, 1901.

LITERATURE WORK

Literature Evangelism a Noble Work.—Canvassing for our literature is a missionary work, and should be carried on from a missionary standpoint. Those selected as canvassers should be men and women who feel the burden of service, whose object is not to get gain, but to do the very work that needs to be done to enlighten the world. All our service is to be done to the glory of God, to give the light of truth to those who are in darkness. Selfish principles, love of gain, dignity, or position, should not be once named among us.— AUCR, May 1, 1901.

Important to Get Our Literature Before the Public.—If there is one work more important than another, it is that of getting our publications before the public, thus leading them to search the Scriptures. Missionary work—introducing our publications into families, conversing, and praying with and for them—is a good work and one which will educate men and women to do pastoral labor.—4T 390 (1880).

SPECIAL WORK FOR THE OLD AND NEGLECTED

About a mile and a half from the [Hinsdale] Sanitarium we saw the soldiers' home, where there are located hundreds of veterans and their wives. Special missionary work should be carried forward at this home. Let men who fear the Lord seek to redeem the time, and take up a work that has been neglected for these old people.

Christ has purchased their souls with the price of His own blood. For this field there should be selected discreet men and women who will not fail nor be discouraged. And let no one belittle their efforts, for the Lord will be with those who labor with Him in self-denial and self-sacrifice. This work is as important as is the work in the foreign countries.—4MR 377 (1909).

TRUE MISSIONARY SPIRIT ESSENTIAL

The Steward family apparently left the church for a time, but were "reclaimed." Mary Steward became an efficient and valued proofreader and copy editor at the Review and Herald. After Ellen White returned from Australia, Mary was employed for several years as one of her helpers. She points out many character defects that kept Mary from becoming a missionary. Perhaps it was this letter, written in 1891, that helped Mary Steward to a closer walk with Jesus.

Dear Sister Mary Steward: While I have been earnestly praying to the Lord to understand my duty in regard to going to Australia, and as to whom we shall take with us, the Lord has plainly made known to me that you are not the proper one to be that help to me that I need in the work He has given me to do. You cannot enter into the spirit of the work in a new and untried missionary field. These words were repeated, "Spiritual things are spiritually discerned." The character of everyone brought in connection with the light that the Lord communicates to His people will be proved and tested. If there is not expansion and development, and an increase of faith and holiness consistent with the light shining upon their pathway . . . there will be a blindness that will not see and discern the deep things of God. With those who appreciate the light God has given, there will be a freshness and power and growth in grace, and light will be diffused to others.

There is need of a missionary, self-sacrificing, self-denying spirit with all who connect with the work God has given me to do, else my influence will not be what God designs it shall be. And unless you are advancing in the knowledge and love of God, you cannot maintain even the light that you now have. If the light does not shine more and more, it will grow dim and flicker away in darkness. Every work will be mingled and tainted with self. God will not accept it. It is impossible for me, or any connected with me, to be channels of light and bear the duties and responsibilities that this work involves unless they are growing in grace and the knowledge of Jesus Christ. All connected with me and the solemn work God has given me to do must represent the character of that work. [They must] be an example to others in humility and Christlike character, in faithfulness, in cross-bearing, in prompt and vigorous action, in unswerving fidelity to the sanctifying influence of truth, and in sacrifices and labors to bless others. In order to do this there must be an ever-growing Christian experience. Faith must be strong, consecration complete; sympathy, tenderness, and love must pervade the soul. They must be patient in tribulation and Christlike in conversation, and even the thoughts [must be] brought into captivity to Jesus Christ.

You have an experience before you to gain. You cannot be self-centered and be prepared for whatever work or responsibility, however difficult or dangerous, which is in Christ's line. Your eye must be single to the glory of God, and then your profiting [growth] will appear unto all. You need to employ every means of grace [so] that your love to God, and to all with whom you associate, may be pure and Christlike. Then you will approve the things that are excellent and be filled with the fruits of righteousness which are by Jesus Christ unto the glory and praise of God. Your Christian life must take on a different mold, else you will never see the kingdom of heaven.

There are many represented to me in the church who seem just like drowning men engaged in a desperate struggle to keep their heads above water. They have not in their religious life ever died to self. Self is their idol; they worship at its shrine. Weakness and a fluctuating experience open the way for Satan's temptations and they will be easily overcome. A faithful waiting upon the Lord will renew their strength. Trials of faith will come, but love, patience, and constancy will be weighed by the golden scales of the heavenly sanctuary.

You must learn in the school of Christ meekness and lowliness of heart, and be trained, disciplined, and educated for usefulness and for immortality. May these words have the right effect upon your mind. I have an interest in you. Let nothing attract or amuse or divert your mind from the earnest work before you. It is for your present and eternal interest to see that this state of things does not continue. Let it not be said of you in the future, as it was of the Hebrew Christians, "For when for the time ye ought to be teachers, ye have need that we teach you again which be the first principles of the oracles of God; and are become such as have need of milk, and not of strong meat" (Hebrews 5:12). You need good home religion. Bring all the pleasantness and sunlight into your home life, in every word, in every action. Use diligently all the gifts of heaven in precious light given of God, and put this light to a practical use. Then the Lord will make a larger display of His mercy and goodness. Achieve a destiny on earth worthy of heaven.—Letter 26a, 1891.

MISSIONARIES MUST BE COMMITTED TO THE WORK

The following letter was written to Elder and Mrs. I. J. Van Horn, who had gone to Oregon as missionaries. Adelia Patton had lived in the White home for several years prior to her marriage to Isaac Van Horn, and was like a daughter to them. Elder and Mrs. White had high hopes and expectations that, working together, the Van Horns would make a mighty missionary team. Their hopes were short-lived.

My Dear Children, ever near and dear to me: It is with pain I now address you. When you went to your field of labor in Oregon it was with the idea that your wife and yourself would work in the interest of the cause of God. This I was shown was the will of God concerning you.

But you changed this order of things by your own course. God did not order it thus. Had you both devoted your powers, the ability that God had given you, to do the work with an eye single to His glory, you would have done only that which it was your duty to do. The importance of self-sacrificing labor in this cause and work of God should be ever felt in a higher sense than it is. If it was felt, then there would be a self-sacrificing spirit manifested. The love and pity for souls for whom Christ has died would call the thoughts away from selfish desires and selfish plans.

The love for Him who died for man will exercise a constraining power over our imagination, our purposes, and all our plans. We shall not plan for our pleasure, to gratify our wishes, but lay ourselves on the altar of God a willing sacrifice for the Lord to use us to His glory. The mind of Jesus Christ must be in us, controlling every thought, every purpose of our lives. This is the attitude in which we should ever keep our souls before God. This we will do if we realize the worth of souls and if the truth as it is in Jesus is stamped upon the soul. This work was given you—to be missionaries for God.

Satan lays his plans to defeat the purpose of God. He helps you to plan for yourselves, which plan he knows will succeed in hedging you both about with difficulties, not only robbing God of the labors of Adelia, but in a large degree of Brother Van Horn also. The care of children will so preoccupy the mind that Christ and His work will be neglected. The strongest earthly affection would be awakened, the mother for her children, which would make the work of God all secondary; and thus Satan would obstruct the path of usefulness the Lord had pointed out.

Oh, could you both have seen that the truth, the truth of God, the salvation of souls, is something stronger, deeper, and more constraining than even the love of a mother for her sons! No selfishness must come in to mar the work of God. Self-denial may be agonizing to the flesh, but the better portion, religion, must take the helm. Truth and love for Christ must occupy the citadel of the soul. There is God enthroned, there is conscience obeyed, and God would have given you a place in His house better than of sons and of daughters.

The Lord has given Adelia superior talents. Exercised in the work of winning souls to Jesus, they would have been wholly successful. The plain, sweet, elevating manner of teaching would have brought many sons and daughters to Jesus Christ. The light would flash from the throne of God to her mind and be reflected upon others.

But the enemy took the field and his suggestions were followed. You entered upon a work which God could not and did not approve. A way was contrived by the enemy to strike at you both and block your way. Adelia was a timid soul, feeling pain deeply, easily discouraged. That imagination which, if devoted to and exercised upon the truth, would have become a power for God, was now to be used as a hindrance, easily excited in a wrong direction to forebode evil, to see things in a distorted light, to feel that there is danger when there is none, to distrust God, to distrust her husband.

She had her own ideas about managing her case. No one would be accepted but her husband. There was but little faith and but little trust in God. Satan could control her feelings so as to make it a necessity for her husband to be with her and for her to feel aggrieved if he was not a present help. Imagination made light sufferings seem at times very earnest and acute. The minds of both were preoccupied in their new experience. The work in the conference was woefully neglected. The minister's labor was but little after the pulpit effort. Sometimes there was greater neglect than others, and Satan had things very much his own way. Neither of you have a sense of your neglect of duty. The very time you were so fully preoccupied with your own troubles, which you had brought about yourselves, was the time when the right kind of labor would have brought a harvest of souls to Jesus Christ.

It is really not wise to have children now. Time is short, the perils of the last days are upon us, and the little children will be largely swept off before this. If men and women who can work for God would consider that while they are pleasing themselves in having little children and caring for them, they might be at work teaching the way of salvation to large numbers and bringing many sons and daughters to Christ, great would be their reward in the kingdom of God.

Adelia, my heart is pained because you have made a failure, because you have robbed God. You are naturally fearful, borrowing trouble. You could not have rest or peace of mind separated from your children; and the worrying disposition you have closes up the way for your work. And this is not all: the work is greatly neglected.—Letter 48, 1876.

Only three people groups are mentioned, but the principle would follow that all groups need to be represented.

Self-respect

12

LOVING OTHERS, LOVING ONESELF

Many women struggle with feelings of self-worth and value in God's sight. As in other portions of this book, the passages used may not have been written specificall for or to women, but they are applicable to them in their search for an understanding of how God views them as His creation and how they should view themselves and others.

Developing Self-respect.—If we wish to do good to souls, our success with these souls will be in proportion to their belief in our belief in, and appreciation of, them. Respect shown to the struggling human soul is the sure means through Christ Jesus of the restoration of the self-respect the man has lost. Our advancing ideas of what he may become are a help we cannot ourselves fully appreciate.—FE 281 (1893).

We Should Respect Ourselves.—The Lord has given every one of us a sense of self-respect, and this must not be opposed too abruptly. God wants us to respect ourselves. In our families and in the church, we too often seek to destroy self-respect. Do not do it. Do not do it in our schools. Do not do it in our offices. The Lord has said that every one of these institutions is to be educational in character. The students and workers will follow the example set by those who have charge over them. The teacher is to be a pattern to the learner. If he wants the youth to respect him, he must respect them.—GCB, Apr. 25, 1901.

Not Pleasing to God to Demerit Oneself.—It is the privilege of everyone to so live that God will approve and bless him. You may be hourly in communion with Heaven; it is not the will of your heavenly Father that you should ever be under condemnation and darkness. It is not pleasing to God that you should demerit yourself. You should cultivate self-respect by living so that you will be approved by your own conscience, and before men and angels. It is not an evidence of true humility that you go with your head bowed down, and your heart filled with thoughts of self. It is your privilege to go to Jesus and be cleansed, and to stand before the law without shame and remorse. "There is therefore now no condemnation to them which are in Christ Jesus, who walk not after the flesh, but after the Spirit." While we should not think of ourselves more highly than we ought, the Word of God does not condemn a proper self-respect. As sons and daughters of God, we should have a conscious dignity of character, in which pride and self-importance have no part.—RH, Mar. 27, 1888.

Counsel to One Who Had Lost Self-respect.—Jesus loves you, and He has given me a message for you. His great heart of infinite tenderness yearns over you. He sends you the message that you may recover yourself from the snare of the enemy. You may regain your self-respect. You may stand where you regard yourself, not as a failure, but as a conqueror, in and through the uplifting influence of the Spirit of God. Take hold of the hand of Christ, and do not let it go.—MM 43 (1903).

Bitter Words Result in Loss of Self-respect.—What harm is wrought in the family circle by the utterance of impatient words; for the impatient utterance of one leads another to retort in the same spirit and manner. Then come words of retaliation, words of self-justification, and it is by such words that a heavy, galling yoke is manufactured for your neck; for all these bitter words will come back in a baleful harvest to your soul. Those who indulge in such language will experience shame, loss of self-respect, loss of self-confidence, and will have bitter remorse and regret that they allowed themselves to lose self-control and speak in this way. How much better would it be if words of this character were never spoken! How much better to have the oil of grace in the heart, to be able to pass by all provocation, and bear all things with Christlike meekness and forbearance.—RH, May 19, 1891.

Self-respect, Humility, and Efficiency in God's Work.—In doing the work of God you will be placed in a variety of circumstances which will require self-possession and self-control, but which will qualify you to adapt yourself to circumstances and the peculiarities of the situation. Then you can act yourself unembarrassed. You should not place too low an estimate upon your ability to act your part in the various callings of practical life. Where you are aware of deficiencies, go to work at once to remedy those defects. Do not trust to others to supply your deficiencies, while you go on indifferently, as though it were a matter of course that your peculiar organization must ever remain so. Apply yourself earnestly to cure these defects, that you may be perfect in Christ Jesus, wanting in nothing.—3T 505 (1885).

Respect and Love One Another.—If we keep uppermost in our minds the unkind and unjust acts of others we shall find it impossible to love them as Christ has loved us; but if our thoughts dwell upon the wondrous love and pity of Christ for us, the same spirit will flow out to others. We should love and respect one another, notwithstanding the faults and imperfections that we cannot help seeing. Humility and self-distrust should be cultivated, and a patient tenderness with the faults of others. This will kill out all narrowing selfishness and make us largehearted and generous.—SC 121 (1892).

Christians Have a Positive Duty to Cultivate Respect for Themselves.—It should be the fixed purpose of the youth to aim high in all their plans for their life-work. They should adopt for their government in all things the standard which God's Word presents. This is the Christian's positive duty, and it should be also his positive pleasure. Cultivate respect for yourself because you are Christ's purchased possession. Success in the formation of right habits, advancement in that which is noble and just, will give you an influence that all will appreciate and value. Live for something besides self. If your motives are pure and unselfish, if you are ever looking for work to do, if you are always on the alert to show kindly attentions and do courteous deeds, you are unconsciously building your own monument. This is the work God calls upon all children and youth to do. Do good, if you would be cherished in the memory of others. Live to be a blessing to all with whom you come in contact, wherever your lot may be cast. Let the children and youth awake to their opportunities. By kindness and love, by self-sacrificing deeds, let them write their names in the hearts of those with whom they associate.—YI, Feb. 7, 1901.

Duty of All to Respect Self.—We must have a better and deeper teaching than man can give us. There must be a deep conviction in our own souls that forms and ceremonies are as nothing without Christ. He is the Alpha and Omega. Truth is the only panoply for the covering of any soul. Our convictions need daily to be reinforced by humble, sincere prayer and reading of the Word. While we each have an individuality, while we each should hold our convictions firmly, we must hold them as God's truth and in the strength which God imparts. If we do not, they will be wrung from our grasp.

We need to be self-reliant; it is the duty of all to respect self; but we are to remember that we are God's property, that we are bought with a price, body, soul, and spirit. We must guard the living machinery, and keep it in the very best condition, that we may glorify God. It is to be daily oiled by His grace, to run at His touch, without friction. To trust in ourselves, to become boastful as if we had created and redeemed ourselves, is to dishonor God. Human wisdom, aside from God, will prove itself to be foolishness, and will bring confusion and perplexity. We need to have on the whole armor of God. The holy influence of a Saviour's loving protection is our sure defense. There is but One who can prove a safeguard against the schemes of Satan.—1888 Materials 1626 (1896).

Respect Self, for You Are Bought With a Price.—This feeling of guiltiness must be laid at the foot of the cross of Calvary. The sense of sinfulness has poisoned the springs of life and of true happiness. Now Jesus says, "Lay it all on Me; I will take your sins. I will give you peace. Banish no longer your self-respect, for I have bought you with the price of My own blood. You are Mine. Your weakened will I will strengthen; your remorse for sin I will remove."—9MR 305 (1896).

A LETTER OF ENCOURAGEMENT

*Written to Martha Bourdeau, a woman afflicted with feelings of self-doubt, despondency, worthlessness, and discouragement.**

Dear Sister Martha: We came here [Tramelan, Switzerland] last Friday, and the Lord has given me some precious tokens for good. I spoke with much freedom to our brothers and sisters from Malachi 4:16. The Lord spoke to hearts. Abel Guenin, who has been discouraged for a long time and had taken no part in the meetings, broke down and confessed his wrong, his indifference, and his discouragements. Said he would no longer remain in the place he was then in. He would come into harmony with the church and do his duty in the fear of God. The tears ran down his face while he talked. His mother, [who] has taken no part with the church and has been much prejudiced against anyone from America, spoke for the first time. She bore a good testimony.

A young man, a baker employed by Oscar Roth, made a humble confession. The Spirit of the Lord was indeed in our meeting. A sweet melting power was there. After meeting, we had a praying season in Brother Roth's house for the son of Brother Guenin. I prayed while Brother John Vuilleumier interpreted. The blessing of the Lord came in and the young man with tears running down his face shook hands with his sisters and confessed his wrongs. It was a precious season indeed. . . .

My mind goes to you, Martha, in Torre Pellice [Italy], and I believe that yourself and husband should attend the meeting of the conference. We want to see you, and we want to see you trusting fully in the precious Saviour. He loves you. He gave His life for you because He valued your soul. I had a dream not long since. I was going through a garden, and you were by my side. You kept saying, "Look at this unsightly shrub, this deformed tree, that poor stunted rosebush. This makes me feel bad, for they seem to represent my life and the relation I stand in before God." I thought a stately form walked just before us, and he said, "Gather the roses and the lilies and the pinks, and leave the thistles and unsightly shrubs, and bruise not the soul that Christ has in His choice keeping."

I awoke; I slept again and the same dream was repeated. And I awoke and slept and the third time it was repeated. Now I want you to consider this and put away your distrust, your worrying, your fears. Look away from yourself to Jesus; look away from your husband to Jesus. God has spoken to you words of encouragement; grasp them, act upon them, walk by faith, and not by sight. "Faith is the substance of things hoped for, the evidence of things not seen." Hebrews 11:1.

Jesus holds His hand beneath you. Jesus will not suffer the enemy to overcome you. Jesus will give you the victory. He has the virtue; He has the righteousness. You may look to yourself to find it and may well despair in doing this because it is not there. Jesus has it. It is yours by faith because you love God and keep His commandments.

Do not listen to Satan's lies, but recount God's promises. Gather the roses and the lilies and the pinks. Talk of the promises of God. Talk faith. Trust in God, for He is your only hope. He is my only hope. I have tremendous battles with Satan's temptations to discouragements, but I will not yield an inch. I will not give Satan an advantage over my body or my mind.

If you look to yourself, you will see only weakness. There is no Saviour there. You will find Jesus away from yourself. You must look and live; [look] to Him who became sin for us, that we might be cleansed from sin and receive of Christ's righteousness.

Now, Martha, do not look to yourself but away to Jesus. Talk of His love, talk of His goodness, talk of His power, for He will not suffer you to be tempted above that you are able to bear. But in Christ is our righteousness. Jesus makes up our deficiencies because He sees we cannot do it ourselves. While praying for you I see a soft light encompassing a hand stretched out to save you. God's words are our credentials. We stand upon them. We love the truth. We love Jesus. Feelings are no evidence of God's displeasure.

Your life is precious in the sight of God. He has a work for you to do. It is not unfolded to you now, but just walk on trustingly without a single word, because this would grieve the dear Jesus and show that you were afraid to trust Him. Lay your hand in His; He is reaching over the battlements of heaven [for it] to be laid confidingly in His. Oh, what love, what tender love has Jesus manifested in our behalf. The Bible promises are the pinks and the roses and the lilies in the garden of the Lord.

Oh, how many walk a dark path, looking to the objectionable, unlovely things on either side of them, when a step higher are the flowers. They think they have no right to say they are children of God and lay hold on the promises set before them in the gospel, because they do not have the evidence of their acceptance with God. They go through painful struggles, afflicting their souls, as did Martin Luther to cast himself upon Christ's righteousness.

There are many who think they can come to Jesus only in the way the child did who was possessed of the demon that threw him down and tore him as he was being led to the Saviour. You are not of the kind that should have any such conflicts and trials. Richard Baxter was distressed because he did not have such agonizing, humiliating views of himself as he thought he ought to have. But this was explained to his satisfaction at last and peace came to his heart.

There is no requirement for you to take on a burden for yourself, for you are Christ's property. He has you in His hand. His everlasting arms are about you. Your life has not been a life of sinfulness in the common acceptance of the term. You have a conscientious fear to do wrong, a principle in your heart to choose the right, and now you want to turn your face away from the briers and thorns to the flowers.

Let the eye be fixed on the Son of Righteousness. Do not make your dear, loving, heavenly Father a tyrant; but see His tenderness, His pity, His large, broad love, and His great compassion. His love exceeds that of a mother for her child. The mother may forget, yet will not I forget thee, saith the Lord. Oh, my dear, Jesus wants you to trust Him. May His blessing rest upon you in a rich measure is my earnest prayer.

You were born with an inheritance of discouragement, and you need constantly to be encouraging a hopeful state of feelings. You received from both father and mother a peculiar conscientiousness and also inherited from your mother a disposition to demerit self rather than to exalt self. A word moves you while a heavy judgment only is sufficient to move another of a different temperament. Were you situated where you knew you were helping others, however hard the load, however taxing the labor, you would do everything with cheerfulness and distress yourself that you did nothing.

Samuel, who served God from his childhood, needed a very different discipline than one who had a set, stubborn, selfish will. Your childhood was not marked with grossness, although there were the errors of humanity in it. The whole matter has been laid open before me. I know you far better than you know yourself. God will help you to triumph over Satan if you will simply trust Jesus to fight these stern battles that you are wholly unable to fight in your finite strength.

You love Jesus and He loves you. Now just patiently trust in Him, saying over and over, Lord, I am Thine. Cast yourself heartily on Christ. It is not joy that is the evidence that you are a Christian. Your evidence is in a Thus saith the Lord. By faith, I lay you, my dear sister, on the bosom of Jesus Christ.

Read the following lines [from "Jesus, Lover of My Soul"] and appropriate the sentiment as your own:

> "Other refuge have I none,
>   Hangs my helpless soul on Thee;
> Leave, O leave me not alone!
>   Still support and comfort me;
> All my trust on Thee is stayed,
>   All my help from Thee I bring;
> Cover my defenseless head
>   With the shadow of Thy wing.
>
> Plenteous grace with Thee is found—
>   Grace to pardon all my sin;
> Let the healing streams abound,
>   Make and keep me pure within;
> Thou of life the Fountain art,
>   Freely let me take of Thee;
> Spring Thou up within my heart,
>   Rise to all eternity."

I made two copies of the enclosed, one to send to you; but it was

Self-respect

too poor, I thought, to be read, so laid it by and did not send it New Year's as I intended. I think you can read it holding it up to the light.—Letter 35, 1887.

---

*Martha Bourdeau was the younger sister of George I. Butler, a prominent leader in the Seventh-day Adventist Church. She was first married to William Andrews, brother of J. N. Andrews. They had three children, among whom was Edith Andrews, who would soon die of tuberculosis. A. C. Bourdeau went to Europe in 1884, and Martha, now a widow, married him. They labored together in Italy.

The Influence of Christian Women

13

You may be dignified without vain self-confidence; you may be condescending and yielding without sacrificing self-respect or individual independence, and your life may be of great influence with those in the higher as well as the lower walks of life.

—Testimonies, *vol. 3, p. 506*

Wonderful Mission of Women.—Seventh-day Adventists are not in any way to belittle woman's work.—GW 453 (1898).

Wonderful is the mission of the wives and mothers and the younger women workers. If they will, they can exert an influence for good to all around them. By modesty in dress and circumspect deportment they may bear witness to the truth in its simplicity. They may let their light so shine before all that others will see their good works and glorify their Father which is in heaven. A truly converted woman will exert a powerful, transforming influence for good. Connected with her husband, she may aid him in his work and become the means of encouragement and blessing to him. When the will and way are brought into subjection to the Spirit of God, there is no limit to the good that can be accomplished.—WM 157 (1908).

Abstain From Appearance of Evil.—There are those who do not feel that it is a religious duty to discipline the mind to dwell upon cheerful subjects, that they may reflect light rather than darkness and gloom. This class of minds will either be engaged in seeking their own pleasure, in frivolous conversation, laughing and joking, keeping the mind continually elated with a round of amusements; or they will be depressed, having great trials and mental conflicts, which they think but few have ever experienced or can understand. These persons may profess Christianity, but they deceive their own souls. They have not the genuine article. The religion of Jesus Christ is first pure, then peaceable, full of righteousness and good fruits. Many have fallen into the sad error which is so prevalent in this degenerate age, especially with females. They are too fond of the other sex. They love their society. Their attentions are to them flattering, and they encourage, or permit, a familiarity which does not always accord with the exhortation of the apostle, to "abstain from all appearance of evil."—RH, Mar. 12, 1872.

No Time for Corrupt Impulses.—Our probation is short at best. We have no time to spend in indulging corrupt impulses. The familiarity of married men with married women and young girls is disgusting in the sight of God and holy angels. The forwardness of young girls in placing themselves in the company of young men, hanging around where they are at work, entering into conversation with them, talking common, idle talk, is belittling to womanhood. It lowers them, even in the estimation of those who themselves do such things.—TSB 245 (1888).

Proper Use of One's Talents.—All have not the same work. There are distinct and individual duties for each to perform; yet with these varied duties there may be a beautiful harmony, binding the work of all together in perfect fitness. Our heavenly Father requires of none to whom He has given but one talent, the improvement of five. But if the one be wisely used, the possessor will soon have gained more, and may continually increase her power of influence and sphere of usefulness by making the best use of the talents which God has given her. Her individuality may be distinctly preserved, and yet she be part of the great whole in advancing the work of reform so greatly needed.

Woman, if she wisely improves her time and her faculties, relying upon God for wisdom and strength, may stand on an equality with her husband as adviser, counselor, companion, and coworker, and yet lose none of her womanly grace or modesty. She may elevate her own character, and just as she does this she is elevating and ennobling the characters of her family and exerting a powerful though unconscious influence upon others around her.—HR, June 1, 1880.

Reaching One's Full Potential.—Why should not women cultivate the intellect? Why should they not answer the purpose of God in their existence? Why may they not understand their own powers, and realizing that these powers are given of God, strive to make use of them to the fullest extent in doing good to others, in advancing the work of reform, of truth and real goodness, in the world? Satan knows that women have a power of influence for good or for evil; therefore he seeks to enlist them in his cause. . . .

Sisters and mothers, we have a higher aim, a more noble work, than to study the latest fashion, and form garments with needless adorning to meet the standard of this modern Moloch. We may become its slave, and sacrifice upon its altars our own and the present and future happiness of our children. But what do we gain in the end? We have sown to the flesh; we shall reap corruption. Our works cannot bear the inspection of God. We shall see at last how many souls might have been blessed and redeemed from darkness and error by our influence, which, instead, encouraged them in pride and outward display, to the neglect of the inward adorning.—HR, June 1, 1880.

To Act a Part in the Closing Work.—Our sisters, the youth, the middle-aged, and those of advanced years, may act a part in the closing work for this time; and in doing this as they have opportunity, they will obtain an experience of the highest value to themselves. In forgetfulness of self, they will grow in grace. By training the mind in this direction, they will learn how to bear burdens for Jesus.—RH, Jan. 2, 1879.

A Transforming Influence.—Great is the work and mission of women, especially those who are wives and mothers. They can be a blessing to all around them. They can have a powerful influence for good if they will let their light so shine that others may be led to glorify our heavenly Father. Women may have a transforming influence if they will only consent to yield their way and their will to God, and let Him control their mind, affections, and being. They can have an influence which will tend to refine and elevate those with whom they associate. But this class are generally unconscious of the power they possess. They exert an unconscious influence which seems to work out naturally from a sanctified life, a renewed heart. It is the fruit that grows naturally upon the good tree of divine planting. Self is forgotten, merged in the life of Christ. To be rich in good works is as natural as their breath. They live to do others good and yet are ready to say: We are unprofitable servants.—2T 465 (1870).

INFLUENCE OF THE CHRISTIAN WOMAN'S DRESS

Inward Beauty More Desirable Than Outward Display.—God would be pleased to see our sisters clad in neat, simple apparel and earnestly engaged in the work of the Lord. They are not deficient in ability, and if they would put to a right use the talents they already have, their efficiency would be greatly increased. If the time they now spend in needless work were devoted to searching the Word of God and explaining it to others, their own minds would be enriched with gems of truth, and they would be strengthened and ennobled by the effort made to understand the reasons of our faith. Were our sisters conscientious Bible Christians, seeking to improve every opportunity to enlighten others, we should see scores of souls embracing the truth through their self-sacrificing endeavors alone.

Sisters, in the day when the accounts of all are balanced, will you feel a pleasure in reviewing your life, or will you feel that the beauty of the outward man was sought, while the inward beauty of the soul was almost entirely neglected?—4T 629, 630 (1885).

Bring Manner of Dress Into Conformity With the Bible.—My sisters, if you would bring your manner of dressing into conformity with the rules given in the Bible, you would have an abundance with which to help your poorer sisters. You would have not only means, but time. Often this is most needed. There are many whom you might help with your suggestions, your tact and skill. Show them how to dress simply and yet tastefully. Many a woman remains away from the house of God because her shabby, ill-fitting garments are in such striking contrast to the dress of others. Many a sensitive spirit cherishes a sense of bitter humiliation and injustice because of this contrast. And because of it many are led to doubt the reality of religion and to harden their hearts against the gospel.—MH 207 (1905).

Outward Appearance an Index to the Heart.—I saw that the outside appearance is an index to the heart. When the exterior is hung with ribbons, collars, and needless things, it plainly shows that the love for all this is in the heart; unless such persons are cleansed from their corruption, they can never see God, for only the pure in heart will see Him.—1T 136 (1856).

While the outward adorning beautifies only the mortal body, the ornament of meekness adorns the soul, and connects finite man with the infinite God. This is the ornament of God's own choice. . . . Angels of heaven will register as best adorned, those who put on the Lord Jesus Christ, and walk with Him in meekness and lowliness of mind.—RH, Jan. 18, 1881.

The Christian Woman Is Modest at All Times

∾

14

*T*he lives of those who are connected with God are fragrant with deeds of love and goodness. The sweet savor of Christ surrounds them; their influence is to elevate and bless. They are fruitful trees. Men and women of this stamp of character will render practical service in thoughtful deeds of kindness, and earnest, systematic labor.

—Review and Herald, *Aug. 24, 1886*

Be Reserved and Modest.—Let not those who profess the religion of Christ descend to trifling conversation, to unbecoming familiarity with women of any class, whether married or single. Let them keep their proper places with all dignity. At the same time they should be sociable, kind, and courteous to all. Young ladies should be reserved and modest. They should give no occasion for their good to be evil spoken of. . . . Those who give evidence that their thoughts run in a low channel, whose conversation tends to corrupt rather than to elevate, should be removed at once from any connection with the institution, for they will surely demoralize others.—CH 294 (1885).

Manifest Less Boldness.—From the light which the Lord has given me, our sisters should pursue a very different course. They should be more reserved, manifest less boldness, and encourage in themselves "shamefacedness and sobriety." Both brethren and sisters indulge in too much jovial talk when in each other's society. Women professing godliness indulge in much jesting, joking, and laughing. This is unbecoming and grieves the Spirit of God. These exhibitions reveal a lack of true Christian refinement. They do not strengthen the soul in God, but bring great darkness; they drive away the pure, refined, heavenly angels and bring those who engage in these wrongs down to a low level.—2T 455 (1870).

A Guard to Virtue.—Cherish the precious, priceless gem of modesty. This will guard virtue. . . . I feel impelled by the Spirit of the Lord to urge my sisters who profess godliness to cherish modesty of deportment and a becoming reserve. . . . I have inquired: When will the youthful sisters act with propriety? I know there will be no decided change for the better until parents feel the importance of greater carefulness in educating their children correctly. Teach them to act with reserve and modesty.—2T 458, 459 (1870).

Influence of Debasing Books and Pictures.—Many of the young are eager for books. They read everything they can obtain. Exciting love stories and impure pictures have a corrupting influence. Novels are eagerly perused by many, and, as the result, their imagination becomes defiled. In the [railroad] cars photographs of females in a state of nudity are frequently circulated for sale. These disgusting pictures are also found in daguerrean saloons [photo shops] and are hung upon the walls of those who deal in engravings. This is an age when corruption is teeming everywhere. The lust of the eye and corrupt passions are aroused by beholding and by reading. The heart is corrupted through the imagination. The mind takes pleasure in contemplating scenes which awaken the lower and baser passions. These vile images, seen through defiled imagination, corrupt the morals and prepare the deluded, infatuated beings to give loose rein to lustful passions. Then follow sins and crimes which drag beings formed in the image of God down to a level with the beasts, sinking them at last in perdition.—2T 410 (1870).

Satan Is Successful in Bewitching Minds of the Youth.—The corrupting doctrine which has prevailed, that, as viewed from a health standpoint, the sexes must mingle together, has done its mischievous work. When parents and guardians manifest one tithe of the shrewdness which Satan possesses, then can this association of sexes be nearer harmless. As it is, Satan is most successful in his effort to bewitch the minds of the youth; and the mingling of boys and girls only increases the evil twentyfold. Let boys and girls be kept employed in useful labor. If they are tired, they will have less inclination to corrupt their own bodies. There is nothing to be hoped for in the case of the young, unless there is an entire change in the minds of those who are older. Vice is stamped upon the features of boys and girls, and yet what is done to stay the progress of this evil? Boys and young men are allowed and encouraged to take liberties by immodest advances of girls and young women. May God arouse fathers and mothers to work earnestly to change this terrible state of things is my prayer.—2T 482, 483 (1870).

GIVE A GOOD EXAMPLE IN DRESS

Fannie Bolton was employed for a time by Ellen White as one of her helpers. The following is a portion of a letter written to her in 1894.

I have a word to say upon another point. Our sisters who have come from America have an account to render before God of their example in dress; in this matter they have not been approved of God as His missionaries. We need to be converted—soul, body, and spirit. Shall we by our example lead to pride, to selfish indulgence and selfish expenditure of means in dress that testifies that we are not the doers of the Word? The principles were presented before me, which are not as God would have them. I am not called upon to specify, but to warn you to take heed.

The spirit that characterizes your work, Fannie, is not discerned by many—yourself or others. They cannot see the true inwardness of these matters, but it manifests itself on certain occasions. Although you are full of activity and zeal and stir and push, there is so much of one-sided, impulsive, ill-developed movements that the results are of the same order as the working. God's chosen vessels will work under the guidance of the Holy Spirit. You have worked largely under the sustaining influence of the self-satisfaction you have cherished, feeling that you were doing a large work. But winnow the wheat from the chaff and there will be very few kernels of pure grain. But many judge from outward appearance, not from the spirit and real results.

We are living in an age represented as being like that before the Flood. All who now plead for souls should in their dress and deportment carry the modesty and marks of the Lord Jesus. They must wait, watch, and pray for the Holy Spirit to be abundantly bestowed. We must take in the idea of Christianity; in conversation and in dress we must represent the truth. A decided guard must be placed upon the human agents in regard to the impressions they are making upon others in deportment and in dress. The Bible is our guide; study its teachings with a purpose to obey, and you need make no mistakes.

Our dress should be in strict accordance with the character of our holy faith. [1 Timothy 2:9, 10; 1 Peter 3:3-5 quoted.] There is need of putting more of the Bible precept into the dress, as well as the inward adorning into the character.

Fannie, wherever you go, wherever you may be, you need to study that the colors and material and style of your dress should be adapted to, and correspond with, your age and to the faith you profess. You remember I made the remark to Elder Olsen that when at Preston you were destitute of suitable clothing and felt too poor to supply yourself with what you should have. The remarks you made showed that you did not understand me. I want to be understood now.

You need comfortable underclothing, which you must have in order to have health. But I certainly do not, in all respects, approve of your style of dress. I felt rather sad and ashamed when you stood upon the platform before the large crowd under the tent, with that light, large-figured dress. It was not appropriate for the occasion. Your judgment in the matter of dress may be much improved. I hope you will not consult your dressmaker but [consult] those who are of sensible minds and who will not flatter you or have any guile in their mouths as to suitable clothing that will make a proper impression upon the minds of both believers and unbelievers. We who claim to be in the light, and who take prominent positions to instruct others in children's meetings, need to be severely plain, yet tidy and tasteful, in dress; we should not give a semblance of excuse to any for patterning after the worldly, changing fashions of this corrupt age.

The Christian Woman Is Modest at All Times

Those who dress after the order given in the Bible can, with appropriate words, help others to reach a proper standard.

Do not come to me to ask how you shall dress. If our sisters have the Spirit of God abiding as a living principle in the heart, they will not in a single instance give occasion for any to turn aside the counsels of God by quoting the ministers' wives or those engaged in giving Bible readings. Ever have your dress of good, durable material, and modest colors; let it be made plainly, without adornment. You certainly need to improve in your style of dress.—Letter 7, 1894. (Printed in entirety in *The Fannie Bolton Story*, available at the Ellen G. White Estate.)

LETTER OF COUNSEL TO ADDIE WALLING

Addie Walling was the grandniece of Ellen White, the granddaughter of her sister, Caroline. James and Ellen White took Addie and her sister, May, into their home when they were young children and reared them as their own.

To Addie Walling: Brother Whitney returns today on his way to Basle, Switzerland. Edith Andrews is steadily failing. I think this climate is better than Basle for my lungs. There has been much labor brought upon me through the lovesick sentimentalism of the workers in the office. I hope, my dear girl, you will keep free of this. You will gain the confidence of all whom you respect if you are reserved and do not encourage the attentions and the society of young men. If I had time, I would write you some things I have had to meet here and in every place where I have been. Edith, poor child, is not fit to die. She has attracted attention to herself and had a few favorites and neglected those who were worthy and good because they did not just meet her taste. These few she lavished her affections upon—[they] thought her perfection, and have petted her, and she petted them and [they] idolized one another. So, you see, God was left out of the question. This sentimentalism has injured the usefulness of excellent young men in the office and unfitted young girls for their work.

I talked very plainly with Edith, and she does not seem to sense her condition. I have written to her, and I think she will now see her mistakes. She has had no experience in genuine religion, but has everything to do now in her feeble condition to know Christ and the power of His grace. Oh, that she had learned this while in health.

I do hope you will not be deceived, Addie, as this poor child is. I hope you will be an earnest, true Christian day by day, seeking God in prayer. Do not be so busy you cannot give time to read the Bible and seek the grace of God in humble prayer. Follow no one's example or custom in dress or in actions. If they lead to indifference and worldliness, do not express vanity in dress, but dress becomingly, neatly; but seek earnestly to be meek and lowly of heart and be obtaining a rich experience in the things of God. Learn to overcome vanity which exists in the heart that is not sanctified through the truth. Do not be forward, but be retiring and modest.

You will now be looked to by many and criticized to see how you will come forth from Sister White's teachings. Do not misrepresent me, but seek to give influence by your course of action. Ever be true, open, sincere, and frank. All affectation despise. Keep yourself aloof from young men. Let them know that there is one girl who will not be crazy and bewildered at their first notice and attentions. I want you to be prepared to travel with me and help me, if I want you.

You see those who have married cease their improvement and settle down to a dwarfed life. Be not afraid to tell me your whole mind and to seek counsel, and I will give you all the help I can. But above everything else, preserve self-control and a self-possession and womanly ways without appearing to know everything. Do not claim to know too much. Be modest in conversation, for people will be disgusted if a young girl talks as if she knew a great deal. You may evidence your wisdom by works, but do not do this by words and self-praise. Be cautious, discreet, and humble.

We want to learn daily in the school of Christ. Now, my dear daughter, I have written you much more than I expected to write, but I may not get a chance to write very soon again.

I am glad you do not live in Italy, at least in this valley, for women and girls have a hard lot. They work very hard, and fourteen hours per day, and obtain less than twenty cents per day. We need missionaries all through this valley. There are men who live high, who are paid as missionaries, but who do nothing in missionary work. They eat and drink and have a good time. They are supported by societies from England.—Letter 28, 1885.

Balance
in the Life

15

Although Ellen White used the word "intemperance" in some of her writings, in today's language a preferable word might be "imbalance" or lack of balance in the life. The principles found in the following general counsel can be applied to any aspect of our lives, from recognizing our limitations in accepting extra responsibilities, to living a simpler lifestyle in order to ease the stress and strain of modern living, and finding time for the things that matter most. Again, most of this was written to men, but the principles apply equally.

BALANCE NECESSARY IN EVERY PHASE OF LIFE

Balance Is a Principle of the Religious Life.—Temperance in all things of this life is to be taught and practiced. Temperance in eating, drinking, sleeping, and dressing is one of the grand principles of the religious life. Truth brought into the sanctuary of the soul will guide in the treatment of the body. Nothing that concerns the health of the human agent is to be regarded with indifference. Our eternal welfare depends upon the use we make during this life of our time, strength, and influence.—6T 375 (1900).

Lack of Balance Exhausts Vital Forces.—Intemperance in eating and drinking, intemperance in labor, intemperance in almost everything, exists on every hand. Those who make great exertions to accomplish just so much work in a given time, and continue to labor when their judgment tells them they should rest, are never gainers. They are living on borrowed capital. They are expending the vital force which they will need at a future time. And when the energy they have so recklessly used is demanded, they fail for want of it. The physical strength is gone, the mental powers fail. They realize that they have met with a loss, but do not know what it is. Their time of need has come, but their physical resources are exhausted. Everyone who violates the laws of health must sometime be a sufferer to a greater or lesser degree. God has provided us with constitutional force, which will be needed at different periods of our life. If we recklessly exhaust this force by continual overtaxation, we shall sometime be losers. Our usefulness will be lessened, if not our life itself destroyed.

As a rule, the labor of the day should not be prolonged into the evening. If all the hours of the day are well improved, the work extended into the evening is so much extra, and the overtaxed system will suffer from the burden imposed upon it. I have been shown that those who do this often lose much more than they gain, for their energies are exhausted and they labor on nervous excitement. They may not realize any immediate injury, but they are surely undermining their constitution.—CH 99 (1890).

Caution Concerning Overwork.—Remember that man must preserve his God-given talent of intelligence by keeping the physical machinery in harmonious action. Daily physical exercise is necessary to the enjoyment of health. It is not work but *over*work, without periods of rest, that breaks people down, endangering the life forces. Those who overwork soon reach the place where they work in a hopeless way.

The work done to the Lord is done in cheerfulness and with courage. God wants us to bring spirit and life and hopefulness into our work. Brain workers should give due attention to every part of the human machinery, equalizing the taxation. Physical and mental effort, wisely combined, will keep the whole man in a condition that makes him acceptable to God. . . .

Bring into the day's work hopefulness, courage, and amiability. Do not overwork. Better far leave undone some of the things planned for the day's work than to undo oneself and become overtaxed, losing the courage necessary for the performance of the tasks of the next day. Do not today violate the laws of nature, lest you lose your strength for the day to follow.—2MCP 375, 376 (1903).

Proper Periods of Rest Needful.—There is danger that the women connected with the work will be required to labor too hard without proper periods of rest. Such severe taxation should not be brought upon the workers. Some will not injure themselves, but others, who are conscientious, will certainly overwork. Periods of rest are necessary for all, especially women.—Ev 494 (1896).

Well-balanced Minds.—All the powers of the mind should be called into use and developed, in order for men and women to have well-balanced minds. The world is full of one-sided men and women, who have become such because one set of their faculties was cultivated, while others were dwarfed from inaction. The education of most youth is a failure. They overstudy, while they neglect that which pertains to practical business life. Men and women become parents without considering their responsibilities, and their offspring sink lower in the scale of human deficiency than they themselves. Thus the race is fast degenerating.—CH 179 (1872).

Wise Improvement of Talents a Blessing.—There must be no burying of our talents in the earth, to corrode through inaction. A persistent indulgence of self, a refusal to exercise our God-given abilities, will ensure our eternal separation from God, the loss of an eternity of bliss. These gifts are bestowed upon us in accordance with our ability to use them, and the wise improvement of each will prove a blessing to us, and will bring glory to God. Every gift gratefully received is a link in the chain which binds us to heaven.—ST, Aug. 18, 1898.

BALANCE IN TIME MANAGEMENT NECESSARY

Must Give Strict Account of Our Time.—Our time belongs to God. Every moment is His, and we are under the most solemn obligation to improve it to His glory. Of no talent He has given will He require a more strict account than of our time.—COL 342 (1900).

Balance Watching and Working for the Coming of the Lord.—When we give ourselves unreservedly to the Lord, the simple, commonplace duties of home life will be seen in their true importance, and we shall perform them in accordance with the will of God. We are to be vigilant, watching for the coming of the Son of man; and we must also be diligent; working as well as waiting is required; there must be a union of the two. This will balance the Christian character, making it well developed, symmetrical. We should not feel that we are to neglect everything else, and give ourselves up to meditation, study, or prayer; neither are we to be full of bustle and hurry and work, to the neglect of personal piety. Waiting and watching and working are to be blended. "Not slothful in business; fervent in spirit; serving the Lord."—RH, Sept. 15, 1891.

SELF-IMPROVEMENT

Do Not Neglect Opportunities for Improvement.—If the worker has consecrated himself fully to God and is diligent in prayer for strength and heavenly wisdom, the grace of Christ will be his teacher, and he will overcome his defects and become more and more intelligent in the things of God. But let none take license from this to be indolent, to squander time and opportunities, and neglect the training that is essential in order to become efficient. The Lord is not pleased with those who, having had opportunities to obtain knowledge, neglect to improve the privileges placed within their reach.—CT 510 (1893).

"Little Things" Make Life a Success.—It is conscientious attention to what the world terms "little things" that makes life a success. Little deeds of charity, little acts of self-denial, speaking simple words of helpfulness, watching against little sins—this is Christianity. A grateful acknowledgment of daily blessings, a wise improvement of daily opportunities, a diligent cultivation of entrusted talents—this is what the Master calls for.—YI, Jan. 17, 1901.

LETTER TO A SELF-CENTERED WOMAN

The following letter was written to Mrs. Sidney Brownsberger, a miserable woman whose life was unbalanced because of her selfishness and lack of self-control.

Dear Sister Brownsberger: I have written some things for you while the camp meeting was in session, but as I repeated to you some of these things, I did not write them. But again my mind is burdened. I feel the deepest pity and sympathy for you because you think you know all about yourself. [You] will take a fixed position that no one understands you and that you are peculiar in temperament and disposition. You must acknowledge that the Lord is better acquainted with you than you are with yourself. At the time of the camp meeting I felt intensely that you should be blessed and comforted and strengthened, which would give you happiness, peace, and true Christian enjoyment daily.

In order for this to be the case, I knew you must have clearer views of yourself and of your duties than you had ever had hitherto in your life. I knew that you must be a truly converted woman, and this is the very thing you have argued against, as though no change could take place with you—you must remain just as you were. Now this is all a delusion. Unless a very great change shall take place with you, unless you overcome self and selfishness, unless these peculiar traits of character which you have cherished are overcome, you will have a defective, spotted character which will find no place in Christ's pure and perfect and holy kingdom. The work is before you and me, and all who win eternal life must overcome every fault, every error, every defect in character.

Do you have a sense that you are selfish, that your thoughts are allowed to center upon self? You must have things your own way, and unless you do, you are perfectly miserable. Your husband is more attentive to you than most men to their wives. He has done the very things for you which you should in no case have had him do, that you yourself could and should have done as your part of the work; but because they were not as pleasant, not as agreeable, you have been glad to have him do them, when it would have been for your good to do these things for yourself. I now fear greatly for you.

Your present condition will be made by you an excuse for you to lay your weight very heavily upon your husband. Your marked traits of character will appear; your thoughts and sympathies will be centered on yourself, not because in your peculiar situation you suffer more than a large class of women, but because you think more upon the matter; your imagination will be active, and you will forget that others pass through the same without a complaint, without sympathy, without conveniences.

You have, my sister, but little self-control and do not exercise the strong will you possess to hold in control your own thoughts and your own feelings. You give way to your feelings when things do not go to suit you; you have, in short, hysterics. Is this necessary? I saw it was not, but [that] your condition utterly forbids anything of the kind. You need to hold your feelings with a firm will and never allow these nervous spasms to get the victory over you. You may ask, How can I do this? By thoughtful self-control. Your feelings fret terribly if things do not go according to your mind. You are not thinking how much perplexity and anxiety and distress you bring upon your husband, and you throw your whole weight upon him as though it was your privilege and duty, when it is the education you need to be self-sufficient and unselfish, to look upon and regard others as well as yourself. This lesson you must learn.

You need not have one of the spasms. You are educating yourself [so] that they will become a fearful reality, second nature; and when the pains of childbirth shall come, these will come upon you and the conditions that produce them will be beyond your control. But you can now control these conditions and need not have them any more than I need to be thus afflicted. It rests with yourself whether you will be a happy or unhappy woman.

You should be what God would have you—a self-reliant woman. I tell you now in the fear of God that you must be less self-caring. You seem to think no inconvenience or taxation must come upon you, but many women no stronger than yourself, to whom the common duties of domestic life are fully as distasteful as to you, bravely take up these duties and bear them uncomplainingly because it is given them as their work. Deeds of kindness, charity, and love to others will make you one with Christ and take your mind from yourself.

The prejudice of education is yours, but you cannot enjoy wholeness of character, which is true sanctification, unless you steadily and earnestly discipline yourself. It will not be a debasement to you to do many things in domestic life you do not now touch. God wants you to feel the responsibility of being a comfort and blessing to your husband as well as to expect him to be a comfort and blessing to you.

Get your mind off yourself; be uncomplaining; be cheerful. There is no reason you should not be cheerful, no reason gratitude should not dwell in your heart although you are in the situation you are. It is no disgrace to have children, and the mother by her own course of action may determine the health and disposition of her children.

I entreat of you to hide in Jesus, to be His own true child, walking in love and obedience to all His requirements, exemplifying in your life the character of Jesus—tender and thoughtful of others, considering them just as good and just as deserving as yourself of conveniences and comforts and happiness. This you have not done. Self has been put first, and others' pleasure, taste, and happiness have come second. Now, this is not as it should be, although it is natural.

If she is ever to enter heaven, there is a work Florida must do for herself that no one can do for her. What kind of a heaven would it be to you if you could enter there with all these peculiarities which you earnestly argue against the possibility of overcoming? Will it be necessary for the Lord to remove your husband by death, to send adversity upon you in removing your children, to deprive you of blessings which you now have in order to call you to your true senses and refine and polish you [so] that you will become self-forgetful, patient, unmurmuring, and thankful? I write to you now because I have been shown the many excuses pregnant women make for the perversity of temper, which is all the temptation of Satan. God will give grace if you pursue the course of a Bible Christian.

You will feel bad, I know, over this letter, but I dare not withhold it. Your work now is to love God supremely and your neighbor as yourself. Be just as considerate and thoughtful in regard to your neighbor as you are in regard to yourself. We must not be so wrapped in self that we fail to put ourselves in the position of others and fail to make their case our own. There are others just as sensitive as you are, just as refined in taste, and who have excellent intellect, who dislike the disagreeable little duties of life which somebody must do. Share these responsibilities with them and forget Florida in the interest you take in others' happiness. Do what you can to lighten the burden of others in any capacity, and do not be wrapped up in selfishness.

This you may feel is severe, but it is just as God has presented the case to me, and for some reason I feel His Spirit moving upon me to rise at three o'clock in the morning and write it. You may through faith in Christ become strong, self-reliant, and useful. But I tell you, Florida, in the name of Jesus, you need not have one of these nervous spasms which call for so great extra labor and bring such fear, such anxiety and true distress, upon your husband. He cannot endure everything; he is mortal, as well as you are. God claims the talents He has lent him. He cannot make a success in his work and have health and vigor of mind unless you, his wife, shall take up your lifework and help him as only a wife can. You can be the greatest load a man can carry, or you can be a blessing. It is in your power to break down and destroy the courage of your husband by your own ways and your own actions, or you may strengthen and build him up. Let Jesus into the soul temple to preside there, and all things will then be after the order of God.

I do not write you because I do not love you. I write because I love you. You are the purchase of the blood of Christ. I want that you should perfect Christian character. The great respect which you cherish for self creates a moral deformity. You will never perfect Christian character until you think less of self and have a better opinion of others. You should not try to excuse yourself from coming in contact with obstacles and overcoming them. You will become strong in spiritual sinew and muscle by lifting responsibilities. You argue your own feebleness too much and shun the very things which will give you strength.

Religion is an active, working principle, and furnishes a stamina sufficient for the stern realities of life. Religion even has power to restrain and control self, to overcome sharp hereditary tendencies. It has a true transforming power upon life, modulating the character. Christ was a worker; He toiled for a livelihood, working in the carpenter's shop. Thus He ennobled and dignified even common labor. Now, my sister, intelligence and education are never designed to make ordinary labor disgusting and disinteresting or distasteful. Even the most common duties of domestic life may be elevated and dignified.

Balance in the Life

Religion ever imparts power to its possessor to restrain, control, and balance the character and intellect and emotions. It has a power to persuade, entreat, and command with divine authority all the ability and affections. Religion—oh, I wish we all understood its workings! It lays us under the weightiest obligations. As we connect ourselves with Christ we solemnly pledge ourselves to walk as Christ walked. Whether we eat or drink or whatsoever we do, all must be done with self out of sight and God's glory in view. Every act of ours has its influence upon others, therefore every thought and every motive is to be under the control of the Spirit of God.

Our notions, our peculiarities, are wholly human and must not be humored or indulged. Self is to be crucified, not now and then, but daily, and the physical, mental, and spiritual must be subordinate to the will of God. The glory of God, the perfection of Christian character, is to be the aim, the purpose of our life. Christ's followers must imitate Christ in disposition. The Pattern is given us to copy, and no excuse will be accepted of God as a reason for not meeting the divine standard, however contrary it may be to our own nature, our own selfish desires and inclinations. Like Christ is the watchword, not like your father or your mother, but like Jesus Christ—hid in Christ, clothed with Christ's righteousness, imbued with the Spirit of Christ.

All the peculiarities given us as an inheritance or acquired by indulgence or through erroneous education must be thoroughly overcome, decidedly resisted. Love of esteem and pride of opinion, all must be brought to the sacrifice. They must be overcome. There is no compromise to be made with the enemy of righteousness.

The conflict will be hard and wearisome, but Jesus is our helper; in Him and through Him we must conquer, however severe the process. God requires no less of you than this. Every one of His children must be like Christ, who lived not to please Himself. Symmetry of character we must have in order to stand before the Son of man. The grace of God is waiting your demand upon it. If you ask Him, He will give you grace and strength as you need it.

That which you term sensitiveness is pride that will not bear contradiction. Self must be disciplined, guarded, and controlled. The most becoming dignity you can possess is the Christian self-control that will endure provocation. The religion of Christ will bind and restrain every unholy passion, will stimulate to energy, to self-discipline and industry even in the matters of homely, everyday life, leading us to learn economy, tact, self-denial, and to endure even privation without a murmur. The Spirit of Christ in the heart will be revealed in the character, will develop noble qualities and powers. "My grace is sufficient," says Christ.

Your wishes, your will, will be often crossed, but you should not be discouraged. Jesus loves you and He wants you to be happy even in this life and to be a light in the world. I wish you could see, and our people could see, what they may be and what they may become. God will work with your efforts. Tests will come to us daily in trials and disappointments, and the true character is developed. Those who cannot endure the vexations and crosses of life will utterly fail when the sterner trials shall open upon them. Jesus wants you to be happy, but you cannot be happy in having your own way and following the impulse of your own heart.

God wants you and your husband to set an example to others worthy of imitation. You can do this, or He would never require it of you. Your help is in God.—Letter 25, 1882.

Health, Exercise, and Healthful Living

16

The knowledge that man is to be a temple for God, a habitation for the revealing of His glory, should be the highest incentive to the care and development of our physical powers. Fearfully and wonderfully has the Creator wrought in the human frame, and He bids us make it our study, understand its needs, and act our part in preserving it from harm and defilement.

—The Ministry of Healing, *p. 271*

Exercise Makes Sleep Sweeter, Steps Livelier.—Females neglect to exercise their limbs in walking. Riding cannot take the place of walking. Many who are very feeble can walk if they only think so. They have not the disposition, and you will hear them plead, "Oh! I cannot walk. It puts me out of breath; I have a pain in my side, a pain in my back." Dear sisters, I wish you did not have these infirmities. But I know that yielding to them, and giving up to an inactive life, will not free you from them. Try to exercise moderately at first. Have rules to govern you. Walk! Yes, walk! If you possibly can, walk! Try it a short distance at first, you who think walking is impossible. You will no doubt become weary. Your side may ache, your back give you pain, but this should not frighten you. Your limbs may feel weak. And no wonder when you have not used them much more than as if you had no limbs. . . .

If you would only walk, and possess a perseverance in the matter, you could accomplish much in the direction of recovery. Your sleep would be sweeter. At every trial, go a little farther. Do not go dragging yourself along as though weights were attached to your limbs. . . . Let the motion of your arms assist you in walking. Walk with a cheerful mind. And as you walk, look at the beauties of nature, listen to the sweet songsters whose melody warbles forth in praises to their Creator. Be inspired by their happy gratitude. See all that you can that is beautiful, and good, and joyful, and let it enliven your steps, and live in your thoughts through the day.

Continue this exercise, and let no one dissuade you from it. Use the limbs God has given you, and look to Him for strength to use them. You may pray for strength day after day, and yet realize no change until you exercise the strength you already have. Give the Lord a chance to do something for you, by beginning the work for yourself. Every day you will realize a change for the better, notwithstanding you feel a sense of weariness. Sleep will bring you all right again, and you can increase your effort, until you, who cannot now walk a few rods from your boarding place, or from home to church, may walk one mile, and perhaps two, without injury.

As I have labored to impress upon females the necessity of walking, some have received my ideas, and determined to carry them out at once. And [at] the first effort they walked perhaps half a mile, became exhausted and really suffered so much that they decided that walking was not best for them. These went to an extreme. They could not bear so much walking at first without injury. Some are ever disposed to go to extremes. They can never come up to the mark, and then be content to stop. They go beyond. They fail to make the best use of the reason Heaven has granted them.—HR, July 1, 1868.

EXERCISE ESSENTIAL
The following is a portion of a letter written to Edith Andrews, niece of J. N. Andrews.

Attention to health is one of our most important duties. We owe this to ourselves, to society, and to God. Young men and young women are proverbially careless in regard to their health. Hundreds

Health, Exercise, and Healthful Living

die in early life, not because of a dispensation of providence, but because of a dispensation of carelessness. Many girls go half clad in cold weather. Others choose to sit reading or writing when they should be taking physical exercise. God gave them organs for use. The living machinery is not to be allowed to rust from inaction. To keep all the powers of the body equally taxed will require self-restraint. The lives of many who have suffered premature death might have been prolonged to old age had they acted intelligently.

Disease and death have become common because of the unpardonable ignorance of those who ought to know better.

Exercise is indispensable to the health of every organ. If one set of muscles is used to the neglect of others, the living machinery is not being worked intelligently.

When physical exercise is taken, the circulation is quickened. The heart receives blood faster and sends it to the lungs faster. The lungs work more vigorously, furnishing a greater amount of blood, which is sent with stronger power through the entire being. Exercise gives new life and strength to every part of the body.

The nerves gain or lose strength in accordance with the way in which they are treated. If used too long and too severely, they are overtaxed and weakened. If used properly, they gain strength.

In order to have health, equilibrium of action must be maintained. The mind must harmonize with this, or the benefits are not realized. If physical exercise is regarded as drudgery, the mind takes no interest in the exercise of the different parts of the body. The mind must be interested in the exercise of the muscles.

In the education of the youth, physical exercise must be combined with mental taxation.

Young girls who have health never know how to appreciate its value. If their employment is sedentary, they have a distaste for other branches of labor. They complain of great weariness if they take exercise. This should be to them a convincing fact that they need to train their muscles.—Letter 6, 1885.

Laws of Health to Be Strictly Obeyed.—A great amount of suffering might be saved if all would labor to prevent disease by strictly obeying the laws of health. Strict habits of cleanliness should be observed. Many, while well, will not take the trouble to keep in a healthy condition. They neglect personal cleanliness, and are not careful to keep their clothing pure. Impurities are constantly and imperceptibly passing from the body, through the pores; and if the surface of the skin is not kept in a healthy condition, the system is burdened with impure matter.

If the clothing worn is not often washed and frequently aired, it becomes filthy with impurities, which are thrown off from the body by sensible and insensible perspiration. And if the garments worn are not frequently cleansed from these impurities, the pores of the skin absorb again the waste matter thrown off. The impurities of the body, if not allowed to escape, are taken back into the blood and forced upon the internal organs.

Nature, to relieve herself of poisonous impurities, makes an effort to free the system. This effort produces fevers and what is termed disease. But even then, if those who are afflicted would assist nature in her efforts by the use of pure, soft water, much suffering would be prevented. But many, instead of doing this, and seeking to remove the poisonous matter from the system, take a more deadly poison into the system, to remove a poison already there.—RH, Dec. 12, 1899.

True Remedies for Health.—Pure air, sunlight, abstemiousness, rest, exercise, proper diet, the use of water, trust in divine power—these are the true remedies. Every person should have a knowledge of nature's remedial agencies and how to apply them. It is essential both to understand the principles involved in the treatment of the sick and to have a practical training that will enable one rightly to use this knowledge.—MH 127 (1905).

The Influence of Fresh Air.—Air, air, the precious boon of heaven which all may have, will bless you with its invigorating influence if you will not refuse it entrance. Welcome it, cultivate a love for it, and it will prove a precious soother of the nerves. Air must be in constant circulation to be kept pure. The influence of pure, fresh air is to cause the blood to circulate healthfully through the system. It refreshes the body and tends to render it strong and healthy, while at the same time its influence is decidedly felt upon the mind, imparting a degree of composure and serenity. It excites the appetite, and renders the digestion of food more perfect, and induces sound and sweet sleep.—1T 702 (1868).

Sunlight a Necessity.—There are but few who realize that, in order to enjoy health and cheerfulness, they must have an abundance of sunlight, pure air, and physical exercise. . . .

No room in the house should be considered furnished and adorned without the cheering, enlivening light and sunshine, which are Heaven's own free gift to man. . . .—HR, Apr. 1, 1871.

Pure Water One of Heaven's Blessings

Free Use of Water.—In health and in sickness, pure water is one of heaven's choicest blessings. Its proper use promotes health. It is the beverage which God provided to quench the thirst of animals and man. Drunk freely, it helps to supply the necessities of the system and assists nature to resist disease. The external application of water is one of the easiest and most satisfactory ways of regulating the circulation of the blood.—MH 237 (1905).

Pure water to drink and fresh air to breathe, . . . invigorate the vital organs, purify the blood, and help nature in her task of overcoming the bad conditions of the system.—RH, Dec. 5, 1899.

Ellen White Insisted on Following
Health Principles in Her Home

This letter was written from Reno, Nevada, to Brother and Sister Lock-wood, Marian Davis, Fannie Bolton, and May Walling, who remained at home. Mrs. White was attending a camp meeting there.

We arrived here in good condition this morning a little before seven o'clock. We find it would have been exactly as well for us if we had waited one day longer. There are preparations going on for our tent. A board floor is laid, and they are now looking for a carpet for the floor.

The sister that worked for Sister Leinenger has decided to come to my house or go to St. Helena. She is disappointed in her visit and wants to return, so I think she had better come. I can give her twelve dollars per month now, and when I shall return, or when there are more responsibilities and more work to do, then I will increase her wages.

When we found out I could not have her, I altered my plans materially, and that leaves but a small family at St. Helena and a small [one] at Healdsburg which May could manage; but if May should have a place to work and learn a trade, she needs clothing made for her. She has the material, and I want her dresses made respectably. The black dress I brought from Europe is to be finished and others are to be made, and if Fannie has not employed a seamstress, let this girl do the sewing. If she cannot cut, let another seamstress cut; but tell them it is my positive orders that sleeves and waist be made loose and not so tight that there will be compression anywhere. Every muscle must be left free to do its work without having to strain the cloth to use the arms freely.

This pinching is the fashion, but none of it must be done in my house, for I have some regard for the health of my workers. Give the lungs ample room to exercise, the heart ample room to do its work without one particle of pinching. The standard of fashion I do not respect, and will not have these new inventions practiced. I want to stand out clear and free from everything that will be the least detrimental to breathing or to perfect freedom of action. Let this sister have the sewing from Fannie to do. If she cannot cut and fit, she can work with one who does cut and fit. And I am decided that these close, skin-tight sleeves cannot be wise or healthful, and whether it be fashionable or unfashionable, I advise that they not be made after the tight order. Read this to the ones who do my sewing.

I would be pleased to have May's clothing prepared, that she may go anywhere that it shall be necessary to learn a trade or go to St. Helena in time. I want her to be fitted with good clothing. She needs a good sack [short jacket] of some kind made. There is that beaver sack in the trunk. May can have a cloak from that. Again, I give positive orders that it shall be made roomy and not so tight that she cannot get it on or off without tugging and pulling. Now, if this girl at Brother Leinenger's can sew, May can do the work and get her sewing done. . . .

If she [May] does her work systematically and considers in the morning and jots down upon paper just what she intends to do in the orderly accomplishment of her work, she will not lose time but can take up one thing after another. The dishes are not to be left, to do any other part of the work. Attend to the kitchen work first. Then the beds have had a chance to air and may be made up. . . .

It is a very bad habit to let the work drag and drive one. Drive the work, and then you will not become discouraged. It is a bad plan to give way to impulse. If you see a book you would like to read and sit down in the midst of your work and read during the precious hours of the day when there is work that needs to be done, then the work is neglected. Make it [a] habit not to sit up after nine o'clock. Every light should be extinguished. This turning night into day is a wretched, health-destroying habit, and this reading much by brain workers, up to the sleeping hours, is very injurious to health. It calls the blood to the brain and then there is restlessness and wakefulness, and the precious sleep that should rest the body does not come when desired.

It is needful to take care of the body and to study its needs and preserve it from unnecessary exposure. It is a sin to be ignorant of how to care for the wants of this habitation God has given us. Especially should brain workers begin to be soothed and not in any way excited as they draw nigh their hours for sleep. Let the blood be attracted from the brain by some kind of exercise, if need be. Let not the brain be taxed even to read, and, of course, not to put forth literary effort. You shall, Marian and Fannie, have one or two hours, as will best please you, in the daytime, and you will not feel so starved for intellectual food that you will partake of it in the night hours. God designed that the night shall be given to sleep.

Well, enough upon this point, I am sure. If we are not aroused to obey the laws God has established in our being, we need not expect that the Lord will work a miracle to counteract our own wrong course of action. We must put reason to work and do our utmost to learn what we must do [in order] not to form habits to pursue a certain course because we are inclined to do this, but to break up every habit that is the least injurious to health, for this God requires of us. Then we may ask God in faith to help us and He will do it.

Especially do I feel concerned for Fannie. I want her to recover from this nervousness and wakefulness, and in order to do this she must take time to rest the brain, that the nerves may not be completely out of tune, like our old organ. When Fannie takes herself in hand, then she will see ways that she can improve her health. I feel so sorry for Fannie. She has a good frame, large bones, and should have good, sound nerves and muscles; and the reason she has not is because she has abused her brain and nerve power by overtaxation, keeping herself upon a strain, keyed up, when reason should take the reins and hold her in obedience to the laws of God which control the human system. I wish Fannie could hear the lectures given now upon health at the [Rural Health] Retreat. She needs her mind and conscience stirred up on these things, and needs to use every power God has bestowed upon her to get well, that she may use these powers as God's entrusted gifts, that she may have healthful powers to exercise in all her work.

Fannie, you need some physical exercise indoors and out each day. If you get tired, it will relieve the brain. What this exercise shall be, I leave you to determine. You can plan it yourself. Use your tact and powers of brain to devise what you will do daily in the line of physical exercise. And I want you to get waked up to this matter. Do not be a creature of impulse, but just bring yourself to regular rules and order. Take yourself in hand, bring yourself to time, and when the Lord sees you are doing what you can for yourself to keep in health, He will do on His part that which you cannot do.

I now commit the keeping of your souls and bodies to your enlightened conscience, and to the power of God, which will work with your intelligent efforts to be well, that you may render to God better service because it is not a sickly, diseased offering.

I want that May Walling should feel that she must take care of her health and fence against colds and needless exposure. I want you all there to keep in health, as a solemn duty that is devolving upon you. You must not be creatures of circumstances or impulse, but of sound reason. You must all study from cause to effect. I do not want one of you to overwork, but I want you to so systematize your work that you will be able to accomplish that which you do without friction and constant wear. God wants you to do this, and He will help you to do it; only be true to yourself.

Wake up in the mornings; set your hour to rise early, and bring yourself to it; then retire at an early hour, and you will see that you will overcome many painful disorders which distress the mind, cause gloomy feelings, discouragement, and unhappy friction, and disqualify you for doing anything without great taxation.

I hope and pray that these words may not prove to be idle tales to you, but that you will act upon them. May, especially, must consider what she has to do and then not be slow and heartless, but do her work promptly and with cheerfulness as if doing it for Jesus Christ.—Letter 76, 1888.

Marriage, Home, Family

17

The measure of your Christianity is gauged by the character of your home life. The grace of Christ enables its possessors to make the home a happy place full of peace and rest.

—Signs of the Times, *Nov. 14, 1892*

MARRIAGE

God's Original Design.—God celebrated the first marriage. Thus the institution has for its originator the Creator of the universe. "Marriage is honourable" (Hebrews 13:4); it was one of the first gifts of God to man, and it is one of the two institutions that, after the Fall, Adam brought with him beyond the gates of Paradise. When the divine principles are recognized and obeyed in this relation, marriage is a blessing; it guards the purity and happiness of the race, it provides for man's social needs, it elevates the physical, the intellectual, and the moral nature.—PP 46 (1890).

Marriage a Sacred Institution.—Marriage has received Christ's blessing, and it is to be regarded as a sacred institution. True religion is not to counterwork the Lord's plans. God ordained that man and woman should be united in holy wedlock, to raise up families that, crowned with honor, would be symbols of the family in heaven.

And at the beginning of His public ministry Christ gave His decided sanction to the institution that had been sanctioned in Eden. Thus He declared to all that He will not refuse His presence on marriage occasions, and that marriage, when joined with purity and holiness, truth and righteousness, is one of the greatest blessings ever given to the human family.—ST, Aug. 30, 1899.

Each Has Individual Responsibilities.—The two who unite their interest in life will have distinct characteristics and individual responsibilities. Each one will have his or her work, but women are not to be valued by the amount of work they can do as are beasts of burden. The wife is to grace the family circle as a wife and companion to a wise husband. At every step she should inquire "Is this the standard of true womanhood?" and "How shall I make my influence Christlike in my home?" The husband should let his wife know that he appreciates her work.

The wife is to respect her husband. The husband is to love and cherish his wife; and as their marriage vow unites them as one, so their belief in Christ should make them one in Him. What can be more pleasing to God than to see those who enter into the marriage relation seek together to learn of Jesus and to become more and more imbued with His Spirit?—AH 114 (1899).

Wife to Be Treated Tenderly.—Yours can yet be a happy family. Your wife needs your help. She is like a clinging vine; she wants to lean upon your strength. You can help her and lead her along. You should never censure her. Never reprove her if her efforts are not what you think they should be. Rather encourage her by words of tenderness and love. You can help your wife to preserve her dignity and self-respect. Never praise the work or acts of others before her to make her feel her deficiencies. You have been harsh and unfeeling in this respect. You have shown greater courtesy to your hired help than to her and have placed them ahead of her in the house.—2T 305 (1869).

Wife Cheerfully to Help Husband Maintain Dignity.—I have also been shown that there is often a great failure on the part of the wife. She does not put forth strong efforts to control her own spirit and make home happy. There is often fretfulness and unnecessary complaining on her part. The husband comes home from his labor weary and perplexed, and meets a clouded brow instead of cheerful, encouraging words. He is but human, and his affections become weaned from his wife, he loses the love of his home, his pathway is darkened, and his courage destroyed. He yields his self-respect and that dignity which God requires him to maintain.—1T 307 (1862).

Love for Christ, Love for Each Other.—Neither the husband nor the wife should merge his or her individuality in that of the other. Each has a personal relation to God. Of Him each is to ask, "What is right?" "What is wrong?" "How may I best fulfill life's purpose?" Let the wealth of your affection flow forth to Him who gave His life for you. Make Christ first and last and best in everything. As your love for Him becomes deeper and stronger, your love for each other will be purified and strengthened.

The spirit that Christ manifests toward us is the spirit that husband and wife are to manifest toward each other. "As Christ also hath loved us," "walk in love." "As the church is subject unto Christ, so let the wives be to their own husbands in everything. Husbands, love your wives, even as Christ also loved the church, and gave himself for it."

Neither the husband nor the wife should attempt to exercise over the other an arbitrary control. Do not try to compel each other to yield to your wishes. You cannot do this and retain each other's love. Be kind, patient and forbearing, considerate and courteous. By the grace of God you can succeed in making each other happy, as in your marriage vow you promised to do.—RH, Dec. 10, 1908.*

TAKE CARE IN CHOOSING A LIFE COMPANION

Unwise Marriage Can Ruin Usefulness.—If those who are contemplating marriage would not have miserable, unhappy reflections after marriage, they must make it a subject of serious, earnest reflection now. This step taken unwisely is one of the most effective means of ruining the usefulness of young men and women. Life becomes a burden, a curse. No one can so effectually ruin a woman's happiness and usefulness, and make life a heartsickening burden, as her own husband; and no one can do one hundredth part as much to chill the hopes and aspirations of a man, to paralyze his energies and ruin his influence and prospects, as his own wife. It is from the marriage hour that many men and women date their success or failure in this life, and their hopes of the future life.—RH, Feb. 2, 1886.

Is He Worthy?—Before giving her hand in marriage, every woman should inquire whether he with whom she is about to unite her destiny is worthy. What has been his past record? Is his life pure? Is the love which he expresses of a noble, elevated character, or is it a mere emotional fondness? Has he the traits of character that will make her happy? Can she find true peace and joy in his affection? Will she be allowed to preserve her individuality, or must her judgment and conscience be surrendered to the control of her husband? As a disciple of Christ, she is not her own; she has been bought with a price. Can she honor the Saviour's claims as supreme? Will body and soul, thoughts and purposes, be preserved pure and holy? These questions have a vital bearing upon the well-being of every woman who enters the marriage relation.—5T 362 (1885).

Wife to Keep Her Own Identity.—A woman that will submit to be ever dictated to in the smallest matters of domestic life, who will yield up her identity, will never be of much use or blessing in the world, and will not answer the purpose of God in her existence. She is a mere machine to be guided by another's will and another's mind. God has given each one, men and women, an identity, an individuality, that they must act in the fear of God for themselves.—TSB 25 (1885).

WHEN PROBLEMS ARISE

Christ Our Help in Time of Trouble.—*The following letter was written to Mrs. Philip Wessels on March 7, 1897. Portions of it appear in* The Adventist Home. *It is hoped that this letter will be an encouragement to those who face similar circumstances.*

Dear Sister Philip Wessels: I will pen a few lines to you this morning. I hope and pray that you will not lose faith, or become discouraged. We all have our individuality; this cannot be submerged in another. You have a soul to save or to lose. The Lord will be to you a present help in every time of trouble. He would have you stand at your post of duty, relying wholly upon Him who has loved us and died for us.

You now have a double responsibility, because your husband has turned his face away from Jesus. As a mother, your work is to bring your children to the Master. When Christ was upon earth, and the mothers brought their children to Him, the disciples were about to send them away, but Jesus rebuked the disciples, saying, "Suffer the little children to come unto me, and forbid them not: for of such is the kingdom of heaven."

I know it must be a great grief for you to stand alone, as far as the doing of the Word is concerned. But how knowest thou, Oh wife, but that your consistent life of faith and obedience may win back your husband to the truth. Let the dear children be brought to Jesus. In simple language speak the words of truth to them. Sing to them pleasant, attractive songs, which reveal the love of Christ. Bring your children to Jesus, for He loves little children.

Keep cheerful. Do not forget that you have a Comforter, the Holy Spirit, which Christ has appointed. You are never alone. If you will listen to the voice that now speaks to you, if you will respond without delay to the knocking at the door of your heart, "Come in, Lord Jesus, that I may sup with Thee, and Thee with me," the heavenly Guest will enter. When this element, which is all divine, abides with you, there is peace and rest. It is the kingdom of heaven come nigh unto you.

Let every hour be one of trust and prayer and faith. You may expect trials. We must all be purified from dross, and made white and tried. In the time of trial, seek to bring every thought into captivity to Jesus Christ. One foe after another may come in unexpected ways, but dismiss the temptations of the enemy. In this way, we go on from grace to grace, from strength to strength, obtaining one spiritual victory after another.

Hold fast to Christ, and He will give you His strong arm to lean upon. There is a crown of life for the overcomer.

Close union with Christ means to do the words of Christ. He calls this union a continuance of His love. Then the heart is in harmony with God. Treasure up the promises, doing every little duty faithfully, as unto God. "If ye keep my commandments, ye shall abide in my love." Here is compliance and dependence.

You have a strong Helper, and while you trust in your surety, you are safe. The sapless twig, grafted into the living vine, partakes of the same nourishment [as] the vine, and becomes a branch. The closest possible relation between the sinner and the Saviour is seen when the sinner is a doer of the Word of God. Then the heart, the will, the mind, are in close union with Christ. By faith, finite, feeble, helpless humanity joins its feebleness to His strength. Such a union—[showing] entire confidence and love—our helplessness and dependence demands.

Christ died a shameful death that He might bring us unto God. When the soul is persuaded that Christ is able to save to the uttermost all who come unto Him, when it resigns itself entirely to Him as an all-sufficient Saviour, when it clings to the promises made and believes fully in Jesus, it is pronounced by God [as] one with Christ. A soul that depends on Christ with the simplicity that a child depends upon its mother is justified, for it becomes one with the Substitute, who was justification and redemption. Herein is love, that the heart and will are knit together in Christ Jesus.

What saith our Saviour? "I will not leave you comfortless: I will come to you." "He that hath my commandments, and keepeth them, he it is that loveth me: and he that loveth me shall be loved of my Father; and I will love him, and will manifest myself to him." When trials overshadow the soul, remember the words of Christ, remember that He is an unseen presence in the person of the Holy Spirit, and He will be the peace and comfort given you, manifesting to you that He is with you, the Sun of Righteousness, chasing away your darkness. "If a man love me," Christ said, "he will keep my words: and my Father will love him, and we will come unto him, and make our abode with him." Be of good cheer; light will come, and your soul will rejoice greatly in the Lord.—Letter 124, 1897.

HOLD FAST UNDER TRYING CIRCUMSTANCES

Again, on October 5, 1898, Mrs. White wrote to Sister Wessels, encouraging her to have faith and to stay close to the Lord.

Dear Sister Philip Wessels: I feel a deep interest in you, your husband, and your children. I thank my heavenly Father that He has given you grace to hold fast the faith under trying circumstances. But do not for a moment, my sister, distrust your heavenly Father.

Let your heart trust in God. Place your confidence in Him. His hand sustains you, and if you abide in Christ, you will grow stronger and stronger. Following on to know the Lord, you will know that His goings forth are prepared as the morning.

The knowledge of the truth is connected with the possession of that faith that works by love and purifies the soul. If you continue to trust in God, you will realize the most precious blessings in every time of need. The Lord sees, the Lord knows, how much you need His grace. You may depend upon Him. His mediation is assured in His promise, His everlasting pledge. "Them that honor me," He says, "I will honor." The Lord will reward your simple faith and trust in Him. You need not distrust the Word of God at any time. You have proved the promise of God. You have felt His hand upholding you. The Lord will hear your prayers.—Letter 82, 1898.

Invite the Softening,
Subduing Spirit of God to Settle Differences

Portion of a long letter written to Mrs. Mary Nelson on March 19, 1902. Ellen White tried to give the Nelsons counsel that would unite them as a family once again.

Your children need a father, you need a husband, and your husband needs a wife. You need the help of your husband, and you both need the help of the Saviour. Both of you should cultivate faith. Your children need a father who will wear Christ's yoke, a father who will submit his will to God's will, to be molded and fashioned by the divine hand.

My brother, my sister, for some time you have not been living together. You should not have pursued this course, and would not have done so, if both of you had been cultivating the patience, kindness, and forbearance that should ever exist between husband and wife. Neither of you should set up your own will and try to carry out your individual ideas and plans, whatever the consequences may be. Neither of you should be determined to do as you please. Let the softening, subduing influence of the Spirit of God work upon your hearts, and fit you for the work of training your children. Your work, under God, is to mold and fashion their characters. In order to lay hold on the strength and power that the Lord alone can give you, you must exercise faith. Appeal to your heavenly Father to keep you from yielding to the temptation to speak in an impatient, harsh, willful manner to each other—the husband to the wife, and the wife to the husband. Both of you have imperfect characters. Because you have not been under God's control, your conduct toward each other has been unwise.

I beseech you to bring yourselves under God's control. When tempted to speak provokingly, refrain from saying anything. You will be tempted on this point, because you have never overcome this objectionable trait of character. But every wrong habit must be overcome. Make a complete surrender to God. Fall on the Rock, Christ Jesus, and be broken. As husband and wife, discipline yourselves. Go to Christ for help. He will willingly supply you with His divine sympathy, His free grace. He who for thirty years was a faithful son, working at the carpenter's trade in order to do His share in bearing the burdens of the family firm, will give His followers strength faithfully to do their part in sharing the burdens of homelife.

My sister, Christ has committed to you the sacred work of teaching His commandments to your children. In order to be fitted for this work, you must yourself live in obedience to all His precepts. Cultivate a watchful observance of every word and action. Guard most diligently your words. Overcome all hastiness of temper; for impatience, if manifested, will help the adversary to make the homelife disagreeable and unpleasant for your children.

We are all the property of the Lord Jesus. He gave His life as a ransom to redeem us. By His gift every family—father, mother, and children—may be saved. My sister, will you neglect your home duties by not putting to tax your God-given power of will in an effort to help your children? In the name of the Lord, I charge you to make every effort, with your husband's help, to save your children.

Upon each of you, as parents, rests the equal responsibility of guarding every word and action, that neither your words nor your deportment shall disparage you in the estimation of your children. Bring into the household all the pleasantness and comfort and joy that you possibly can.

My dear Brother and Sister Nelson, repent before God for your past course. Come to an understanding and reunite as husband and wife. Put away the disagreeable, unhappy experience of your past life. Take courage in the Lord. Close the windows of the soul earthward and open them heavenward. If your voices are uplifted in prayer to heaven for light, the Lord Jesus, who is light and life, peace and joy, will hear your cry. He, the Sun of righteousness, will shine into the chambers of your mind, lighting up the soul-temple. If you welcome the sunshine of His presence into your home, you will not utter words of a nature to cause feelings of unhappiness.

Oh, Mary, I beg of you to stop and consider how much you are grieving the Holy Spirit of God! Seek the Lord with your whole heart, that the Sun of righteousness may shine into your soul, and work in you an entire transformation, sanctifying your every word and action.

How I wish I could cry with a loud voice to every mother in the land, "Sanctify your spirit through the grace that Christ freely gives to those who ask Him for grace. Practice tenderness. Manifest a sanctified love for your children. Interest yourself in their happiness. Teach them to exercise good sense. Acquaint them with God and His purpose for them. Make the religion of Jesus Christ attractive. Never offend the Lord God by dissension and unhappy differences. Seek for meekness and lowliness of heart. Cultivate affection."

Brother and Sister Nelson, while in the past you have disagreed, you are now under solemn obligation to God to make the most of your God-given abilities and powers. You should improve every opportunity you have for reaching a higher standard. It is God's purpose, signified to you through Sister White, His servant, that you should look to Jesus, and, by beholding Him, be changed into His likeness. The Lord desires that you shall no longer be children in your Christian experience, but, through the impartation of His grace, that you shall be complete in Him. If you take advantage of the present opportunity for reaching a higher experience, you can become strong and complete in Christ Jesus.

Brother Nelson, will you soften and subdue your nature? You may become like Jesus and be His missionary, His helping hand. He never prompts you to be exacting, dictatorial, and severe toward the members of your family and toward others with whom you associate. You can live this life only once. Will you not bring the pleasantness and the goodness of a perfect character into this life? The Lord wants you to be good and to do good. We can individually make life what we please. If we choose, we can honor God by using aright the talent of speech.

My brother, take up the care of your children. It will do no good to blame them; for they have received your disposition as an inheritance. In governing them, be firm, but not arbitrary. In talking with them, speak in a manner that will not create a feeling of stubborn resistance.

Brother and Sister Nelson, the example that you have set before your children has not been what it would have been had you been converted. If you were changed by the grace of Christ, you would show that you had overcome selfishness and the desire to have your own way, to consult your natural inclinations, and to do as you please. Now is the time to show that you do not live to please self. Bring into the character the fragrance of Christ's character. Put away the spirit of scolding, fretting, and repining. Cultivate purity of speech. Pray and sing to the glory of God. Let the peace of God rule in your hearts.—Letter 47a, 1902.

Courtship and Marriage Serious Step

Ellen White's grandniece, Addie Walling, was like a daughter to her. A distant cousin of Addie's apparently was interested in courting her. Mrs. White outlined her reasons for her lack of enthusiasm for such a courtship.

Since writing the foregoing I received a letter from you that has relieved me somewhat, but I am still some troubled. I think Reuben [Tapley]—I hope that there is no attachment between you. I should feel very sad if you had given him any decided encouragement. I like Reuben. I consider him an honest-hearted young man, but not one I would want to give you in marriage to for several reasons. One is, he is a consumptive, of a consumptive family, and I know too well what it is to have to battle with this terrible disease. We buried Nathaniel and Annie White with consumption. We buried Lumen Masten, foreman of the office, with consumption. We buried Robert Harmon, my next-oldest brother, with consumption. We buried Sarah Belden with consumption.

I would not favor, as you regard health and happiness, your connecting with one who is predisposed to consumption. His mother has escaped consumption because of a scrofulous swelling in her side. She has no health, but is liable to die any time. His mother's father, Samuel McCann, died of the long, lingering consumption, and my sister Harriet, his wife, took it of him, and her suffering was extreme. She died. Sarah, the eldest daughter, died of consumption. Melville, the next-eldest son, died of consumption. Lucy Ellen next died of consumption. Mary, the next, died of consumption, and only two of the children now live. It is the worst kind of consumption, and we feel deeply the need of care in this matter of connecting our interest with those whose blood is tainted with this dread destroyer.

As soon as I looked upon Reuben I knew he was marked. He will not live long. His slim neck, his large head, tell the painful story that his life is short. Now, Addie, there is still a more painful side to this question. While they are having a feeble hold on life, only one of this large family was religiously inclined; that was Sarah. Lucy Ellen made no preparation for heaven till on her deathbed; then with her expiring breath she called upon God. Melissa is religious. She has had all the light upon the Sabbath, yet has not kept it. This is Reuben's mother. Melville neglected religion just as Reuben does. [But he] did not oppose [it] when he was dying. His last breath was agonizing prayer. So, also, May neglected to give her heart to God till her very last dying days. Now this is worse to me than the dreaded disease of consumption. But I could not consent to have there be an attachment between you and Reuben. It is just and right that you should open your mind freely to me on this subject of courtship and marriage, for this concerns your happiness more than any other event of your life, and you need counsel and advice here more than on any other point. I hope to hear from you often.—Letter 95, 1886.

FAMILIES

Families on Earth to Be Symbols of Family in Heaven.—If the hearts were kept tender in our families, if there were a noble, generous deference to each other's tastes and opinions, if the wife were seeking opportunities to express her love by actions in her courtesies to her husband, and the husband manifesting the same consideration and kindly regard for the wife, the children would partake of the same spirit. The influence would pervade the household, and what a tide of misery would be saved in families! Men would not go from home to find happiness; and women would not pine for love, and lose courage and self-respect, and become lifelong invalids. Only one life lease is granted us, and with care, painstaking, and self-control it can be made endurable, pleasant, and even happy.—TDG 335 (1872).

Kindness Makes Home Pleasant Indeed.—By speaking kindly to their children, and praising them when they try to do right, parents may encourage their efforts, make them very happy, and throw around the family circle a charm which will chase away every dark shadow, and bring cheerful sunlight in. Mutual kindness and forbearance will make home a paradise, and attract holy angels into the family circle; but they will flee from a house where there are unpleasant words, fretfulness, and strife. Unkindness, complaining, and anger shut Jesus from the dwelling.—ST, Apr. 17, 1884.

HOSPITALITY IN THE HOME

A Plea for More Home Hospitality.—Even among those who profess to be Christians, true hospitality is little exercised. Among our own people the opportunity of showing hospitality is not regarded as it should be, as a privilege and blessing. There is altogether too little sociability, too little of a disposition to make room for two or three more at the family board without embarrassment or parade. Some plead that "it is too much trouble." It would not be if you would say: "We have made no special preparation, but you are welcome to what we have." By the unexpected guest a welcome is appreciated far more than is the most elaborate preparation.—6T 343 (1900).

Ready for the Unexpected Guest.—Some householders stint the family table in order to provide expensive entertainment for visitors. This is unwise. In the entertainment of guests there should be greater simplicity. Let the needs of the family have first attention.

Unwise economy and artificial customs often prevent the exercise of hospitality where it is needed and would be a blessing. The regular supply of food for our tables should be such that the unexpected guest can be made welcome without burdening the housewife to make extra preparation.—MH 322 (1905).[†]

For further reading see: The Adventist Home; Child Guidance; Testimonies on Sexual Behavior, Adultery, and Divorce.

---

[*]See Appendix E.

[†]In Ellen White's home there was no extra cooking for visitors. Abundant, simple food was served to family and guests alike. The menu was varied from meal to meal, prepared and served tastefully.

Mothers

18

In rightly training and molding the minds of her children, mothers are entrusted with the greatest mission ever given to mortals.
—Sons and Daughters of God, *p. 252*

To Shape Minds and Mold Characters.—Especially does responsibility rest upon the mother. She, by whose lifeblood the child is nourished and its physical frame built up, imparts to it also mental and spiritual influences that tend to the shaping of mind and character. It was Jochebed, the Hebrew mother, who, strong in faith, was "not afraid of the king's commandment" (Hebrews 11:23), of whom was born Moses, the deliverer of Israel. It was Hannah, the woman of prayer and self-sacrifice and heavenly inspiration, who gave birth to Samuel, the heaven-instructed child, the incorruptible judge, the founder of Israel's sacred schools. It was Elizabeth, the kinswoman and kindred spirit of Mary of Nazareth, who was the mother of the Saviour's herald.—MH 372 (1905).

Mother's Preparation Not to Be Neglected.—The child's first teacher is the mother. During the period of greatest susceptibility and most rapid development his education is to a great degree in her hands. To her first is given opportunity to mold the character for good or for evil. She should understand the value of her opportunity and, above every other teacher, should be qualified to use it to the best account. Yet there is no other to whose training so little thought is given. The one whose influence in education is most potent and far-reaching is the one for whose assistance there is the least systematic effort.—Ed 275 (1903).

Teach Your Children to Pray.—My brethren and sisters, I urge you to bring up your children in simplicity. Don't scold them when they do wrong, but take them to the Lord, and tell Him all about it. When you kneel before God with your children, Christ is by your side, and angels of God are all around you. Teach them to ask God to forgive them for being cross and impatient. Bring up your children in the nurture and admonition of the Lord. Let us be men and women of prayer. Let us take hold of the divine nature, and escape the corruption that is in the world through lust. Then we shall have the eternal life insurance policy, a life that measures with the life of God. Then when the ransomed are redeemed from the earth, the City of God will be opened to you, and you can present yourselves before the Lord, saying, Here am I and the children whom Thou hast given me. Then the harp will be placed in your hand, and your voice will be raised in songs of praise to God, and to the Lamb, by whose great sacrifice you are made partakers of His nature, and given an immortal inheritance in the kingdom of God.—RH, Jan. 14, 1909.

Mothers to Encourage Their Children.—Whenever the mother can speak a word of commendation for the good conduct of her children, she should do so. She should encourage them by words of approval and looks of love. These will be as sunshine to the heart of a child and will lead to the cultivation of self-respect and pride of character.—3T 532 (1875).

Teach Children Importance of Habits Formed When Young.— Children have claims which their parents should acknowledge and respect. They have a right to such an education and training as will make them useful, respected, and beloved members of society here, and give them a moral fitness for the society of the pure and holy hereafter. The young should be taught that both their present and their future well-being depend to a great degree on the habits they form in childhood and youth. They should be early accustomed to submission, self-denial, and a regard for others' happiness. They should be taught to subdue the hasty temper, to withhold the passionate word, to manifest unvarying kindness, courtesy, and self-control. Fathers and mothers should make it their life study that their children may become as nearly perfect in character as human effort, combined with divine aid, can make them. This work, with all its importance and responsibility, they have accepted, in that they have brought children into the world.—RH, Mar. 21, 1882.

A MOTHER'S SOURCE OF STRENGTH

Mothers to Look to God for Strength.—If woman looks to God for strength and comfort, and in His fear seeks to perform her daily duties, she will win the respect and confidence of her husband, and see her children coming to maturity honorable men and women, having moral stamina to do right. But mothers who neglect present opportunities, and let their duties and burdens fall upon others, will find that their responsibility remains the same, and they will reap in bitterness what they have sown in carelessness and neglect. There is no chance work in this life; the harvest will be determined by the character of the seed sown.—ST, Sept. 9, 1886.

Jesus a Mother's Best Friend.—If mothers would go to Christ more frequently, if they would trust Him more fully, their burdens would be lighter, and they would find rest. Jesus knows the burden of every mother. He is her best friend in every emergency. His everlasting arms support her. That Saviour whose mother struggled with poverty and privation sympathizes with every mother in her work, and hears her earnest prayers. That Saviour who went on a long journey for the purpose of relieving the anxious heart of a Canaanitish woman will do as much for the afflicted mother of today. He who gave back to the widow of Nain her only son as he was being carried to burial is today touched by the bereaved mother's woe. He who wept at the grave of Lazarus, who pardoned Mary Magdalene, who on the cross remembered His mother's needs, who after the resurrection appeared to the weeping women, and made them His messengers, is today woman's best friend, ready to aid her in her need if she will trust in Him.—ST, Aug. 20, 1902.

SOME WISE COUNSEL TO CHILDREN

Addie and May Walling, children of Ellen White's niece, lived in the White home, and Ellen White was like a mother to them. She cared for and counseled them as though they were her own. The girls were about 12 and 15 at the time this letter was written.

Dear Children, Addie and May: I have a few moments this morning and will write you a few words of counsel. In my absence I would have you kind and courteous to all who are employed in my house. Neither of you [must] feel that you have experience and wisdom to do things correctly without counsel and advice from those older than yourselves. I have observed in you both a want of respect to those older than you. This defect in your character will, if indulged, become confirmed upon you and grow stronger with every indulgence. Therefore subdue it, control it, overcome it entirely. . . .

I see, Addie, more especially in you a growing disposition to jealousy. Jealousy, the Scriptures tell us, "is cruel as the grave." Song of Solomon 8:6. You may inquire, "What is jealousy?" It is this: thinking that those around you do not think enough of you and appreciate your value. You imagine they talk about you and say things of you not correctly. You feel that others are favored and you are not. Many such feelings are the outgrowth of jealousy.

Now, Addie, you want to be a Christian, a child of God. And if you succeed, you will have battles to fight with your own natural imperfections. You must watch for these defects and war against them with all your powers. Jesus loves you, He died for you, my children, Addie and May, and He wants you to have His spirit and His grace that you may indeed be His lambs, His dear children. You want the grace of Jesus to subdue every unlovely trait of character that you may be approved of Jesus and the holy angels.

Addie, I observe you listen and watch to hear what others say, thinking they may say something in reference to you. Do not do this anymore. This you should overcome at once. Your mother did in this way when she was a girl, and she fancied that she was slighted and blamed and disliked, and this jealousy grew upon her until after she was married. She made the life of your father anything but pleasant. For your good, I enjoin upon you to nip this in the bud.

Again, I see in you a disposition to dictate to May and fret at her. This is growing upon you. Treat May kindly, make your requests patiently, not in an ordering manner, but just as one sister should treat another. You will be disliked by everyone unless you look well to these things.

You have both many things in your natural disposition that should be overcome. You must see these things, and then you will see how you despise them in others, and avoid them yourselves. You may grow up lovely in character, kind, gentle, meek, lowly of heart, or you may grow up peevish, fretful, unkind, self-sufficient, esteeming yourselves above that which you should. Read in the Bible what are the fruits borne by the Christian tree and then read the fruit borne by the evil tree. One is good, the other corrupt. Now I have no time to write further, but I know your defects of character. The Lord I love has shown me, and you, in His Holy Word that you may be His children, but you need His grace daily to overcome your errors of character.

All these things I have mentioned, or even one of them, if not overcome, will exclude you from heaven; for nothing can enter there but that which is pure and holy. I want that our labors for you, my children, should not be in vain. I want you to be happy in the beautiful world Jesus has prepared for those who love Him and seek to be like Him in character.

Do not neglect this matter. Be in earnest; battle with all your might against everything unlovely in character. You will be happier yourselves for this; you will make others happy around you, and you can, in your words and correct deportment, show that you are copying the Pattern, forming your character according to the character of Christ.

May, my dear child, I do not wish you to overwork, but I want you to be prompt and bear your share of responsibility. Those who do work only when compelled to do so will be worthless. You can do work with cheerfulness and not wait to be told. Be faithful in little things, and then it will be easy for you to be faithful in larger things. Remember, there are duties for you to perform [that are] just as important to perfect your experience as the duties those older have to do to perfect their experience. Do your work, not as though it were a burden, but a pleasure, as though done for Jesus. Your Saviour was an obedient child, working with His father at the simple trade of a carpenter. You must eat and drink in order to live, and then, as a natural result, the dishes must be washed, and floors swept, if you live in houses.

Now act your part with fidelity, doing your work for Jesus. I may write you again. I want you both to strive to excel in having the ornament of a meek and quiet spirit which in the sight of God is of great price. . . .

Well, goodbye, my dear children. Be kind, be respectful to others older than yourselves.—Letter 3, 1881.

CHILDREN'S RESPONSIBILITY TO CARE FOR AN ELDERLY MOTHER

Mary Chase was the sister of James White. During his lifetime he and Ellen had cared for his sister. After James died, Ellen White felt she could no longer bear this responsibility. She wrote to Mary's daughter, Adeline Savage, challenging her to fulfill her duty in caring for her mother.

Dear Niece, Adeline Savage: I think you should know how your mother [Mary Chase] is at the present time. She is quite feeble. She has needed care constantly. I cannot possibly have any care of her whatever.

We leave Battle Creek for Otsego today. Next week we shall be, I expect, at Chicago. The eighth we start on our long journey for California. I feel very sad to leave your mother in her present state of feebleness. I provide for her the very best I can. I purchased a house, which has cost me a thousand dollars, and furnished it simply with necessary articles for her use. We have let a family into the house— a mother, son, and daughter. They have the use of the house [in exchange] for your mother's board. I pay the taxes. Last year your mother paid the taxes, but she met with an accident in building a fire in the stove. The floor took fire and there was seventy-five dollars expense to me for repairs.

The son of the widow lady who has my house has been sick for five weeks. During this time your mother has been sick, attended by a physician and sometimes a nurse, for she could not receive attention from anyone in the house. It was in the bargain that your mother's fire should be made in the morning so that she could have a warm room to get up in, but further than this they could not do.

If she needed a nurse, she must provide it. She has only three hundred dollars, which will melt away very soon. She must have clothing. She must have wood. I have done all I can do, and more than I should do. I look to you, her children and her grandchildren, to act your part. I feel bad indeed at the present appearance of things, that strangers' hands have to do for your mother the duties which justly belong to you to perform. When the neighbors and friends inquire, "Has she no children to have a care for her?" how embarrassing to say, "She has two sons and a daughter and grandchildren and brothers." The question is asked, "Why do not her children take care of their aged mother in her feebleness?" I am not able to answer that question, but perhaps you can answer it.

I have my work, which is speaking and writing. I am in constant labor and ought not to have one thought or one care upon my soul for your mother. I have invested twenty-five dollars for clothing because your mother needed it. I have ordered wood for the winter because last winter I learned she lay abed hours in the daytime to save burning wood. The little money she has on hand, she is reluctant to use, thinking she might be sick for some time like her mother, and she dreads becoming a pauper. I cannot blame her for this, for judging from the past, she may feel she cannot depend at all on her children.

Your mother has been very economical. I shall not leave her to suffer if you do nothing; but if you feel conscience clear in this matter, if you wish your record to stand in the judgment in the future as it has in the past in regard to your poor old mother, I cannot help it. But God marks this unfeeling neglect.

God holds her children accountable for this neglected duty. I am sorry, so sorry, that the matter stands thus.

Christ will judge every man according to his works. He identifies His interest with His suffering, neglected children. He says to one class, "I was an hungered, and ye gave me no meat: I was thirsty, and ye gave me no drink: I was a stranger, and ye took me not in: naked, and ye clothed me not: sick, and in prison, and ye visited me not. . . . Then shall he answer them, saying, Verily I say unto you, Inasmuch as ye did it not to one of the least of these, ye did it not to me." The terrible word "Depart" is spoken.

To those on His right hand He says, "I was an hungered, and ye gave me meat: I was thirsty, and ye gave me drink: I was a stranger, and ye took me in: naked, and ye clothed me: I was sick, and ye visited me: I was in prison, and ye came unto me." The question is asked, "Lord, when saw we thee an hungered, and fed thee? or thirsty, and gave thee drink? When saw we thee a stranger, and took thee in? or naked, and clothed thee? Or when saw we thee sick, or in prison, and came unto thee?" He said, "Inasmuch as ye have done it unto one of the least of these my brethren, ye have done it unto me." Thus that which is done to His needy brethren Christ accounts as done unto Himself.—Letter 30, 1884.

Responsibilities of Parenthood

19

*E*llen White made many beautiful statements regarding the value of the family, children, and the home. She fully recognized their importance. At the same time she also recognized that young people contemplating marriage should take into consideration all that is involved in having children and rearing them to become all that God and the parents would like them to be.

Counsel Regarding Becoming Parents.—Those who assume the responsibilities of parenthood should first consider whether they will be able to surround their children with proper influences. The home is both a family church and a family school. The atmosphere of the home should be so spiritual that all the members of the family, parents and children, will be blessed and strengthened by their association with one another. . . .

Many who enter the marriage relation fail of realizing all the sacred responsibilities that motherhood brings. Many are sadly lacking in disciplinary power. In many homes there is but little discipline, and the children are allowed to do as they please. Such children drift hither and thither; there is nobody in the home capable of guiding them aright, nobody who with wise tact can teach them how to help father and mother, nobody who can properly lay the foundation that should underlie their future education. Children who are surrounded by these unfortunate conditions are indeed to be pitied. If not afforded an opportunity for proper training outside the home, they are debarred from many privileges that, by right, every child should enjoy. This is the light that has been presented to me.

Those who are unable to train their children aright should never have assumed the responsibilities of parents. But because of their mistaken judgment, shall we make no effort to help their little ones to form right characters? God desires us to deal with these problems sensibly.—3SM 214, 215 (1904).

Be Careful in Assuming Responsibility of Parenthood.—They [parents] should understand the principles that underlie the care and training of children. They should be capable of rearing them in physical, mental, and moral health. Parents should study the laws of nature. They should become acquainted with the organism of the human body. They need to understand the functions of the various organs, and their relation and dependence. They should study the relation of the mental to the physical powers, and the conditions required for the healthy action of each. To assume the responsibilities of parenthood without such preparation is a sin.—MH 380 (1905).

Women to Use God-given Abilities in His Work.—Letters have come to me from several, asking my advice upon the question, Should ministers' wives adopt infant children? Would I advise them to do this kind of work? To some who were regarding this matter favorably, I answered, No; God would have you help your husband in his work. The Lord has not given you children of your own; His wisdom is not to be questioned. He knows what is best. Consecrate your powers to God as a Christian worker. You can help your husband in many ways.

You can support him in his work by working for him, by keeping your intellect improved. By using the ability God has given you, you can be a homekeeper. And more than this, you can help to give the message.

There are women who should labor in the gospel ministry. In many respects they would do more good than the ministers who neglect to visit the flock of God. Husband and wife may unite in this work, and when it is possible, they should. The way is open for consecrated women. But the enemy would be pleased to have the women whom God could use to help hundreds, binding up their time and strength on one helpless little mortal, that requires constant care and attention.—5MR 325, 326 (1898).

TRAITS OF CHARACTER ARE PASSED ALONG IN CHILDREN

The following counsel was given to Elder and Mrs. E. P. Daniels in 1888 regarding the training of their children. Elder Daniels was a prominent minister and his children were an item for discussion. Ellen White felt it her duty to again remind Elder and Mrs. Daniels that they were not bringing up their children in the fear of God. E. P. Daniels is not to be confused with A. G. Daniells.

For years testimonies have followed you upon the subject of economy and the wise expenditure of means, but neither you nor your wife has made decided changes in your practices. You love display; you love indulgence of appetite; you love to gratify your taste. The same traits of character shown in yourself are reproduced in your children, and you will reap that which you have sown. There never can be sufficient means granted you for your labors to sustain you in your indulgence in extravagant, spendthrift habits. Why do you not learn from those brethren who comfortably support themselves and their families on less money than you receive for your labors? The reason that you are in embarrassed circumstances is not because your wages are not enough to support you as a Christian, but [because] you do not manage your means in such a way as to keep you from embarrassment. If you had twenty dollars a week, you would still complain of financial pressure.

In Healdsburg the Lord wrought through you, not because you were perfect, but in spite of your imperfections. Self was mingled with your work. When you realized that the Spirit and power of God were working with the people, if you had humbled yourself, if you had walked carefully and tenderly before God, feeling your unworthiness and His goodness, the influence you left in Healdsburg would have been far better than it now is. You charge all your financial embarrassment to circumstances.

You can talk well in regard to parents training their children.

Your wife, whom I love and respect in the Lord, would make an excellent lecturer upon this subject. But your practice contradicts the excellent principles that you have presented. She does not practice her own teachings. When your customs are seen and your home life practices revealed, the people become confused and disgusted. You do not train your children for usefulness, to practice self-denial, and to keep the way of the Lord. Why are you so irresolute in purpose, so feeble in action, so vacillating in principle, so weak in faith?

These things are a mystery to those who have an opportunity to become acquainted with you in the pulpit and at home. Elder Daniels, they see you one day strong and self-assured; next day they see in you a complete change. You affirm strongly things exactly opposite to what you affirmed as strongly the day before. . . .

When I was shown the great need of reform in the education and training of your children, I was filled with pain that I cannot express, because I saw that you did not act your part in bringing about the best good of your children. You need the work of the Spirit of God in your own heart, for right principles are not governing your life. If you were right with God, you would not be doing as you have been doing in reference to your children; you would not present such an example as you have in their management. You should depend far less upon self and far more upon Jesus. If you were closely connected with God, you would rule your children wisely.

Zua [Daniel's daughter] is impulsive; she lacks experience in the right direction; she needs to be guided and restrained instead of being indulged and flattered. If you were discerning, if your souls were imbued with the sanctifying power of the truth, you would need no advice in regard to her attending Snell's Seminary. If you were asked concerning the daughter of another, you would know just what course parents should pursue in relation to the education of their child. You have placed barriers in the way of Zua's salvation, for you have yourselves chosen as her associates the vain, the proud, the unbelieving. . . .

Sister Daniels, you have not met your solemn responsibilities as a mother . . . [when you have] aided your daughter to deceive her father in regard to her dress and expenditures. Both of you have been deceived and carried away with false ideas in regard to the training of your children. You must be thoroughly transformed by the grace of Christ, so that you can teach your children, by precept and example, the good and right way. Zua is full of affectation and deception. She is superficial in nearly all her attainments. Her school life has given her an outside polish, but her heart is unrenewed, for she has no love for God, no love for the society of Christians. She is in the ranks of the enemy, and should she die today she would not enter the kingdom of heaven.

Paul [the son] is in no better condition, and your youngest girl is far from having a lovely character. Your own training is in every way defective. May the Lord have mercy on you all, that you may not lose your soul and the souls of your children. . . .

Paul is a boy who has good qualities as well as objectionable traits of character that have been cultivated and indulged rather than restrained. You have not taught him the sinfulness of a sullen, stubborn disposition and firmly restrained this growing evil. Even in the expression of his countenance your indulgence is leaving its mold. The impressions made in youth are most abiding, and early life is the best time to cultivate correct habits.

Paul has been encouraged to be exacting and particular in his diet, but you should set the food before him and never allow him to turn from it in disdain, calling for something that you have not provided. He may cherish his exacting habits in regard to his diet until he shall be disagreeable to himself and all connected with him. If he were obliged to labor according to his strength, hunger would give him a relish for his food and remove his murmuring. Decided measures should be taken in this matter. I love this son of yours; he can be molded in the right way, for, if properly trained, he will respond after a time. . . .

Give your boy something to do. Teach him to be industrious. He has naturally no love for work; he loves indolence and seeks to shirk responsibility. If you want your children to bless you, teach them to be useful and self-denying. Restrict their reading. They should not be allowed to pore over the pages of novels or storybooks filled with the tales of lust and knavery, for it will not leave a heavenly influence on their minds. They are young and inexperienced and will be just what you make them. All such habits of reading will cut up by the roots the principles of virtue which enter into the formation of a good, firm character. Novel reading is like taking poison and will sooner or later reveal its bitter results.

The mark for good or evil made upon the characters of your children is not written in the sand, but is traced as on enduring rock. Their associations will have to be guarded, for what is learned from the words and habits of their companions will mold the whole after-life. The company your children keep, the principles they now adopt, [and] the habits they now form are settling the destiny of their future with an almost infallible certainty.

Heretofore, what I have said to you has left no lasting impression, but will you not now become a different man? If you do not, I greatly fear that you will depart from the faith. . . .

May the Lord give you such clear views of Jesus that your soul will be enraptured. I commit these plain words to you both, to tell you that one-half your usefulness is counteracted by defects that you can and must overcome. Make thorough work for eternity, as in the sight of God.

Elder Daniels, I am your friend because I tell you the truth. You are engaged in a solemn work, and as an ambassador of Christ, I desire that you should make no failure, but give full proof of your ministry. Pray much, my brother; talk less. Pray that you may be endowed with wisdom and courage necessary to accomplish the work, whatever it may be. Say before God, "I will do my duty with an eye single to Thy glory."—Letter 10, 1888.

Teach Children to Form Good Habits

Written to Mary Nelson on March 19, 1902, giving counsel on the education and development of her children.

Dear Sister Mary Nelson: As a Christian, you have duties to do that are left undone. You are not giving your children the education that they need. Your disposition is such that you are not molding and fashioning their characters after the divine similitude. You are in as much need of having your temper sweetened as is your husband.

Your harshness of voice and your disagreeable disposition should be entirely overcome. Although a mother, you have not been learning lessons of self-control. You should cultivate pleasing traits of character. You may and should cultivate sweetness of disposition. Do not delay; for your habits are becoming fixed.

You rule, but not in love. What an objectionable education your children are receiving! It is not right for you to bring up the younger members of the Lord's family as you are bringing up your children.

You should teach your children to form good habits. Will you spoil them for future usefulness by neglecting to train them as you should in habits of cleanliness and order? Will you not patiently teach and assist them always to keep their rooms and their clothing in order?

Fretting and scolding will not help to reform your children. In governing them, you should exercise firmness; but with this, kindness should be mingled. Diligently teach them how to be Christians. Never raise your voice in passion; never strike a blow in anger; for this, in the place of correcting their faults, will confirm them in a wrong course. Remember that they have inherited their parents' dispositions. You have now to meet in your children your own defects of character. Remember that if you speak harshly, you are giving them an example that they will learn to imitate. Sooner or later they will act toward you in the same harsh manner in which you have acted toward them, because in the home life you have set before them a wrong example.

Is it not time for you to take up your neglected duties, and try to please your husband and to train your children aright? My sister, the best thing you can do is to confess your mistakes to your husband and to your children. Tell the children that the harsh, rough spirit which you have cultivated is un-Christlike. Then say, "Children, by the strength and grace that Christ gives us, we will now make a decided change." Ask them to help you. Promise that you will help them.

Christ is ready to teach the father and the mother to be true educators. Those who learn in His school will never strike a child in passion. They will never speak in a harsh, unsympathetic tone; for words spoken in this manner grate upon the ear, wear upon the nerves, cause mental suffering, and create a state of mind that makes it impossible to curb the temper of the child to whom such words are spoken. This is often the reason children speak disrespectfully to parents.

Remember that children have rights which must be respected. Your self-will is very strong. You have given this trait of character to your children. You may be busy from morning till night, and yet fail of doing the work that God has appointed you to do. You need to act the part of a mother in guiding and training your little flock. . . .

My dear sister, you are in need of divine help. You must wear Christ's yoke yourself before you can properly teach your children that they are to give their hearts to Jesus. That you may be fitted to do this work, seek for God's special blessing. Let the Holy Spirit abide in your heart, making it a wellspring of love and joy. Pray most earnestly for a meek and quiet spirit. In the spirit of meekness, seek daily for God's blessing. If you daily receive blessings from above, you will be refreshed and will impart to your children that which you have received. And as your disposition and character change, you will have a beneficial influence over the disposition and character of your children.—Letter 47a, 1902.

PARENTS CAN BE TOO INDULGENT

In 1871 Ellen White wrote to her friends, Brother and Sister Bailey, about their indulgence toward their children.

Dear Friends, Brother and Sister Bailey: I have been feeling it to be my duty to write you since I have been writing for others the things that have been shown me in regard to them. I have had some things to write to you but have not felt free to write until now. When at your house if a favorable opportunity had presented, I should have spoken to you and relieved my mind. Since my returning home, I do not feel free unless I write to you.

I have had much writing to do in regard to the errors of parents in properly instructing their children and the result upon their children. Your course was opened before me. You have both been too indulgent to your children. Your dangers and errors are not seen and realized so fully as to lead you to take a position you should in your family and command your household after you.

God in His great mercy has brought the truth to your knowledge. You love the truth. You see its claims upon you. It has wrought a reformation in the life and has led you to have a deep interest in the spiritual welfare of your children. All this is in accordance with the Spirit of God. But while you feel thus anxious you fail seriously to do the work the Lord has left you as parents to do. Your children have not been restrained. They have been indulged to their injury. They have not been brought into subjection as God requires.

There has been a serious lack with you in the training of your children. Your daughter especially has been petted. Your sons have not been educated aright. Your daughter has been petted and indulged until her practical usefulness is very small. Her attention has been mostly directed to herself until her mind has become supremely selfish and centered upon herself. If she has had indisposition, she is averse to labor. She has been favored and excused from any exertion. You have talked before her that she was not well. Her imagination has been excited in this direction. The mother has borne the heavy burdens she should have shared with the daughter and with her sons. The mother would have been spared much suffering in consequence of acute attacks by disease, could she have had the help she might have had from her children, especially her daughter. Such labor would have been the greatest benefit to the daughter healthwise and saved her from sickness and been a blessing to her mother. . . .

Another evil which threatens to destroy the usefulness of your daughter is a love of the world, and pride of appearance. She has cherished an affectation which is death to spirituality.

Sister Bailey, you have committed a serious error in bringing up your children. Just as the twig is bent, the tree inclines. Your petting and excusing their errors and disrespect of your authority have stood directly in the way of their salvation. Children who are not trained to be courteous and to yield to the claims of their parents will not have a sense of their duty to God and His claims upon them for obedience and submission. . . .

Your children, who share your bounty and hospitality, should be made to understand that in return they must show obedience and respect for your authority. Your children will yet be without the grace of God; they will cause you heartaches and the keenest pangs of anguish without one feeling of remorse. They will consider the slightest restraint an invasion of their rights and will despise reproof.

Your children lost the benefits of the early training they should have had, but now you should change your discipline entirely and redeem your neglect. Your children lack those noble, desirable qualities of mind which right discipline and self-culture would have given them. Your children are not courteous, neither are they respectful. You listen to words from their lips that you should not permit under your roof. The young who are not restrained at an early age become their own masters and their own mistresses. They take the reins in their own hands. They are self-important, self-conceited, and impetuous, and do not have much taste or ambition for self-respect or to discipline their mind by close application to anything. They will not be restrained. They despise school discipline, for they have not been disciplined at home. . . .

God is not pleased with Sister Bailey's course in the management of her children. [She is] remiss in duty, weighed in the balance and found wanting. This is a serious defect in a mother—to be so tender of her children that she would allow sin upon them, allow them to be passionate, unthankful, disobedient, heady, high-minded—and yet excuse this and cover it from others' eyes and even from her own eyes. In this she is partaker of their wrongs and has been sustaining them in sin, and the blood of their souls will be in the skirts of her garments and their father's. They can now redeem the past by a reformation on their part, but they can never blot out the results of their great neglect as far as their children are concerned. God holds parents responsible for the conduct of their children in a great degree, for they have [responsibility for] the formation of their characters. . . .

Your daughter needs to be energized by active labor. She is far better able to work and bear her share of life's burdens than for her mother to bear them for her. Work, every day, that will bring into action her muscles and the organs of the body will be the best medicine your daughter can have. Delicate idleness is keeping her bilious and discontented and unhappy. . . . May God bless these lines to you, my brother and sister.—Letter 1, 1871.

A Knowledge of Practical Duties of Life

20

*C*hildren are God's precious heritage, to be disciplined, educated, and trained to lift burdens in their early years. These should be light at first; but children should be carefully educated to do their part, that they may understand how to do their work with willing aptitude.

—Review and Herald, *May 17, 1898*

USEFUL EMPLOYMENT ESSENTIAL

Example of Jesus as the Perfect Worker.—In His earth-life, Christ was an example to all the human family, and He was obedient and helpful in the home. He learned the carpenter's trade and worked with His own hands in the little shop at Nazareth. . . . The Bible says of Jesus, "And the child grew, and waxed strong in spirit, filled with wisdom: and the grace of God was upon him." As He worked in childhood and youth, mind and body were developed. He did not use His physical powers recklessly, but gave them such exercise as would keep them in health, that He might do the best work in every line. He was not willing to be defective, even in the handling of tools. He was perfect as a workman, as He was perfect in character.—FE 417, 418 (1896).

Young Women to Have Knowledge of Household Duties.—Many

ladies, accounted well-educated, having graduated with honors at some institution of learning, are shamefully ignorant of the practical duties of life. They are destitute of the qualifications necessary for the proper regulation of the family, and hence essential to its happiness. They may talk of woman's elevated sphere, and of her rights, yet they themselves fall far below the true sphere of woman.

It is the right of every daughter of Eve to have a thorough knowledge of household duties, to receive training in every department of domestic labor. Every young lady should be so educated that if called to fill the position of wife and mother, she may preside as a queen in her own domain. She should be fully competent to guide and instruct her children and to direct her servants, or, if need be, to minister with her own hands to the wants of her household.

It is her right to understand the mechanism of the human body and the principles of hygiene, the matters of diet and dress, labor and recreation, and countless others that intimately concern the well-being of her household. It is her right to obtain such a knowledge of the best methods of treating disease that she can care for her children in sickness, instead of leaving her precious treasures in the hands of stranger nurses and physicians.

The idea that ignorance of useful employment is an essential characteristic of the true gentleman or lady is contrary to the design of God in the creation of man. Idleness is a sin, and ignorance of common duties is the result of folly, which afterlife will give ample occasion to bitterly regret.—ST, June 29, 1882.

Children to Share Domestic Duties.—The faithful mother will not, cannot, be a devotee of fashion, neither will she be a domestic slave, to humor the whims of her children and excuse them from labor. She will teach them to share with her domestic duties, that they may have a knowledge of practical life. If the children share the labor with their mother, they will learn to regard useful employment as essential to happiness, ennobling rather than degrading. But if the mother educates her daughters to be indolent while she bears the heavy burdens of domestic life, she is teaching them to look down upon her as their servant, to wait on them and do the things they should do. The mother should ever retain her dignity.—HR, June 1, 1877.

A Knowledge of Practical Duties of Life

THE VALUE OF PRACTICAL EDUCATION

Why Work Before Play?—My mother taught me to work. I used to ask my mother, "Why must I always do so much work before I play?" "It is to educate and train your mind for useful labor, and another thing, to keep you out of mischief; and when you get older, you will thank me for it." When one of my little girls [a granddaughter] said to me, "Why must I knit? Grandmothers knit," I replied, "Will you tell me how grandmothers learned to knit?" "Why," [she said,] they began when they were little girls."—CG 124 (1887).

Teach Girls to Be Independent.—Many who consider it necessary for a son to be trained with reference to his own future maintenance seem to consider it entirely optional . . . whether or not their daughter is educated to be independent and self-supporting. She usually learns little at school which can be put to practical use in earning her daily bread,* and receiving no instruction at home in the mysteries of the kitchen and domestic life, she grows up utterly useless, a burden upon her parents. . . .

A woman who has been taught to take care of herself is also fitted to take care of others. She will never be a drug [a drag or burden] in the family or in society. When fortune frowns, there will be a place for her somewhere, a place where she can earn an honest living and assist those who are dependent upon her. Woman should be trained to some business whereby she can gain a livelihood if necessary. Passing over other honorable employments, every girl should learn to take charge of the domestic affairs of home, should be a cook, a housekeeper, a seamstress. She should understand all those things which it is necessary that the mistress of a house should know, whether her family is rich or poor. Then, if reverses come, she is prepared for any emergency; she is, in a manner, independent of circumstances.—HR, Dec. 1, 1877.

The child, the mere undisciplined immature schoolgirl, the Miss, dependent upon the discretion of parents and guardians, has no reason to listen to anything like courtship or marriage. She should decline all special attentions which would have the least likelihood to lead to any such results, and devote herself intently to making herself as perfect a woman as possible, that her life may be useful, and learn a trade that she will have employment and be independent.—TSB 21 (1880).

ALL, EVEN WOMEN, SHOULD LEARN A TRADE

All to Educate Themselves to Industrious Habits.—The custom of supporting men and women in idleness by private gifts or church money encourages them in wrong habits. This course should be conscientiously avoided. Every man, woman, and child should be educated to practical, useful work. All should learn some trade. It may be tentmaking, it may be some other business, but all should be trained to use their powers to some purpose. And God is ready to increase the capabilities of all who will educate themselves to industrious habits. We are to be "not slothful in business; fervent in spirit; serving the Lord." God will bless all who will guard their influence in this respect.—RH, Mar. 13, 1900.

Every Israelite Required to Teach Children a Trade.—In Israel, industrial training was regarded as a duty. Every father was required to teach his sons some useful trade. The greatest men in Israel were trained to industrial pursuits. A knowledge of the duties pertaining to housewifery was considered essential for every woman. And skill in these duties was regarded as an honor to women of the highest station.—MH 185, 186 (1905).

WOMEN OF SHARP INTELLECT NEEDED TO MANAGE BUSINESS

Following is a portion of a letter written in February 1884 to the matron of the St. Helena Health Retreat. Mrs. White pleads with this woman to make a decided impact on the work of God, to train young women to be useful, and to use her own talents to her best ability.

You should not follow your own inclinations. You should be very careful to set a right example in all things. Do not be inactive. Arouse your dormant energies. Make yourself a necessity to your husband by being attentive and helpful. Be a blessing to him in everything. Take up the duties essential to be done. Study how to perform with alacrity the plain, uninteresting, homely, but most needful duties which relate to domestic life. Your inactivity has been indulged and cultivated when it should be guarded against strictly and with a determined effort.

My sister, your mind will bear taxing. If you take up the burdens that you should, you can be a blessing to the [St. Helena] Health

A Knowledge of Practical Duties of Life

Retreat. But the indulgence of your sluggish temperament is a detriment to you, physically, mentally, and spiritually. You need the quickening, converting power of God. You need to stand firmly and truly for God and the right. You need to be vitalized by the grace of Christ. Will you wake up, and put to the task your almost-paralyzed energies, seeking to do all the good in your power? You must exercise the living machinery, or else you will not be able to throw off the waste matter, and you will fall short of gaining health. . . .

Time is precious, time is golden; it should not be devoted to little, unimportant things, which serve only to gratify the taste. You can be more useful, my sister, when you cease to allow unimportant things to take your golden moments, when useful and necessary things engage your attention and your time. There are many things to be done in this world of ours, and I hope you will not neglect the thoughtful, caretaking part of your work. You might have saved the institution with which you are connected hundreds of dollars, had you put your soul into the work. Had you spoken a word here, and done some planning there, you could have been a real blessing. Had you awakened your dormant energies by exercise in the open air, and done what it was in your power to do with cheerfulness and alacrity, you could have accomplished much more than you have, and been a real blessing.

I hope that you will devote your mind and your wisdom to the work. See that everything is run on an economical plan. This must be done, or debts will accumulate. Women of sharp, quick intellect are needed to discern where there is waste in little things and to rectify it. You have stood at the head of the Health Retreat as matron, and it was your duty to do this.

Much could be saved that is now wasted for the want of a [department] head to see and plan and tell what should be done, one who will take right hold, and by precept and example do this work. Girls will not be conscientious, diligent, and economical unless a right example is given them by the one standing at the head. If the girls are not willing to be taught, if they will not do as you wish them, let them be discharged. I know that much can be saved at our boarding house, and much at the sanitarium, if thoughtfulness and painstaking effort is brought into the work. . . .

By exerting a proper influence in these lines, you may educate girls for domestic service. This will be a great blessing to them.

All our talents should be used; they should not be allowed to rust through inaction. All our influence should be used to the very best account. After Christ fed the multitude, He said, "Gather up the fragments that remain, that nothing be lost." This lesson may apply to spiritual things as well as temporal. Those who do not appreciate and make the best use of their spiritual blessings, gathering up every precious ray of light, will soon become indifferent and inappreciative! Blessings are not given to those who do not value them. All our physical energies, as one of God's talents, should be used to the glory of God. Our influence is to be recognized and employed as belonging to God. God calls upon all to do their best.—Letter 5, 1884.

---

*This was written in 1877, when few girls acquired any higher education.

When Sorrow Comes

~

21

Lucretia Cranson was the daughter of old friends of the Whites. She married D. M. Canright in 1867. She died on March 29, 1879.

Dear Afflicted Sister: I would much prefer to be with you and converse with you, but this is impossible. I might say to you I sympathize with you in your feebleness, but when I think of you it seems ever sure to me and vivid before me that you are sustained by arms that never tire, and comforted with a love that is unchangeable, enduring as the throne of God.

I do not look upon you as repining in your feebleness, but as one upon whom the countenance of the Lord shineth, giving light and peace, whose soul is in fellowship with the Father and with His Son Jesus Christ, growing daily in the knowledge of the divine will, partaking of the divine nature, increasing in reverence, childlike holy trust, and confiding love. Never did the appreciation of Christ's blood, which pardons, seem to you so precious, so priceless as in your feebleness, when your hold is loosening upon the world.

You have been growing in inward experience, and others may profit by your counsel and your advice. Religion to you, my precious child, has become more and more beauteous. You now find so much comfort sitting at the feet of Christ and learning of Him. The fear of death is past. If there is any terror in the look of the last dread enemy, it is driven away by looking unto Jesus, for He has brightened the tomb by His sacred presence. There is that in your heart which will not rest unless enfolded in the arms of infinite love.

Dear child, your pilgrimage is nearly ended. We will not set up our wishes and our wills, but we will let you rest in hope till the Lifegiver shall call you forth from your prison house to a bright immortality. Jesus is just the Saviour for you now, the One whose bright presence will make, in any place, your heaven. Your life, my precious child, is hid with Christ in God, and when He who is your life shall appear, then will you also appear with Him, clothed with immortality and eternal life. Do you behold His glory in your failing strength, full of grace, mercy, and peace? And do you turn to Him like the needle to the magnet?

Your days may not all be clear and joyful, but let not this afflict you. In meekness, faith, and endurance, wait, hope, and trust. Your life is hidden with Christ in God. Your life, even now, may be a lesson to all, showing that one can be happy in the failing of strength under affliction. When the deep waters go over the soul, God's presence makes holy the chamber of His dying saints. Their patient endurance and joyful constancy, their support by an unseen power, is a powerful testimony in favor of the Christian's religion and the Christian's Saviour. These light afflictions will be a transforming power, refining, purifying, ennobling, and fitting for the courts above.

Oh, the Christian's last days may be fragrant because the beams of the Sun of righteousness shine through the life, diffusing a perpetual fragrance. Oh, what reason have we for joy that our Redeemer poured out His precious blood on the cross as an atonement for sin, and by His obedience to death brought in everlasting righteousness. You know that today He is at the Father's right hand, a Prince of life, a Saviour. There is no other name wherein you can trust your eternal interests, but in Christ you may rely fully, implicitly. Christ has been loved by you, although your faith has sometimes been feeble and your prospects confused. But Jesus is your Saviour. He does not save you because you are perfect, but because you need Him and in your imperfection have trusted in Him. Jesus loves you, my precious child.

When Sorrow Comes

You may sing,

> "Under the shadow of Thy throne
> Still may we dwell secure;
> Sufficient is Thine arm alone,
> And our defense is sure."

—Letter 46, 1879.

DEATH OF A HUSBAND

Written to Mrs. Fannie Ashurst Capehart, "Westmoreland," Washington Heights, Washington, D.C.

My Dear Sister: I have just read your letter. I will not delay writing, for perhaps a few lines may relieve your mind.

My husband died in Battle Creek in 1881. For a year I could not endure the thought that I was alone. My husband and I had stood side by side in our ministerial work, and for a year after his death I could not endure the thought that I was left alone, alone, to carry the responsibilities that in the past he and I had carried together. During the year, I did not recover, but came near dying. But I will not dwell upon this.

While my husband was lying in his coffin, our good brethren came to me and urged that we pray that he be raised to life. I told them, No, no. While living, he had done the work that should have been shared by two or three men, and now he was at rest. Why call him back to life to endure again that through which he has passed? "Blessed are the dead which die in the Lord from henceforth; Yea, saith the Spirit, that they may rest from their labours; and their works do follow them."

The year that followed my husband's death was filled with suffering for me. I did not think I could live, I became so weak. The idea came to members of my family that there would be a spark of hope for me if I could be induced to attend the camp meeting in Healdsburg. This meeting was to be held in a grove about half a mile from my home in Healdsburg. They hoped that on the campground God would reveal to me distinctly that I was to live. There was at the time no color in my face, but a deadly paleness. They took me to the campground one Sunday in an easy carriage. That day the large tent was full. It seemed as if nearly all Healdsburg was present.

A lounge was placed on the broad platform that served as a pulpit, and on it I was made as comfortable as possible. During the meeting, I said to my son, W. C. White, "Will you help me up, and assist me to stand on my feet while I say a few words?" He said that he would, and I got up. For five minutes I stood there, trying to speak, and thinking that it was the last speech I should ever make—my farewell message.

All at once I felt a power come upon me, like a shock of electricity. It passed through my body and up to my head. The people said that they plainly saw the blood mounting to my lips, my ears, my cheeks, my forehead. Before that large number of people I was healed, and the praise of God was in my heart and came from my lips in clear tones. A miracle was wrought before that large congregation.

I then took my place among the speakers, and before the congregation bore a testimony such as they had never before heard. It was as if one had been raised from the dead. That whole year had been one of preparation for this change. And this sign the people in Healdsburg were to have as a witness for the truth. . . .

My sister, no longer show any distrust of our Lord Jesus Christ. Go forward in faith, believing you will meet your husband in the kingdom of God. Do your very best to prepare the living to become members of the royal family and children of the heavenly King. This is our work now; this is your work. Do it faithfully, and believe that you will meet your husband in the City of God. Do what you can to help others to be cheerful. Uplift souls. Lead them to accept Christ. Never torture your soul as you have been doing, but be humble, true, faithful, and you have the word of God that you will meet when the warfare is ended. Be of good cheer.—Letter 82, 1906.

Written to Sister Chapman, an old friend in the faith, at the time of her life companion's death.

Dear Sister Chapman: I think of you every day and sympathize with you. What can I say to you in this, the greatest sorrow that has come to you in your life? Words fail me at this time. I can only commend you to God and to a compassionate Saviour. In Him is rest and peace. From Him you may receive your consolation. Jesus loves and pities as we have no power to do. Jesus Christ Himself does sustain you; His everlasting arms are beneath, His words can heal. We cannot possibly penetrate into the secret councils of God. The disappointments and distress and perplexities, the bereavements we meet, are not to drive us from God but bring us nearer to Him.

How we pant and are weary and agonized in carrying ourselves and our burden! When we come to Jesus, feeling unable to bear these loads one instant longer, and lay them upon the Burden-bearer, rest and peace will come. We do go stumbling along under our heavy loads, making ourselves miserable every day because we do not take to our hearts the gracious promises of God. He will accept us, all unworthy, through Jesus Christ. Never let us lose sight of the promise that Jesus loves us. His grace is waiting our demand upon it.

My dear afflicted sister, I know by experience what you are passing through. I have been going over the road with you that I have so recently traveled. Come near, my dear sister, to Christ the Mighty Healer. Jesus' love to us does not come in some wonderful way. This wonderful manner of His love was evidenced at His crucifixion, and the light of His love is reflected in bright beams from the cross of Calvary. Now it remains for us to accept that love, to appropriate the promises of God to ourselves.

Just repose in Jesus. Rest in Him as a tired child rests in the arms of its mother. The Lord pities you. He loves you. The Lord's arms are beneath you. You have not reined yourself up to feel and to hear; wounded and bruised, just repose trust in God. A compassionate hand is stretched out to bind up your wounds. He will be more precious to your soul than the choicest friend, and all that can be desired is not comparable to Him. Only believe Him; only trust Him. Your friend in affliction—one who knows.—Letter 1e, 1882.

Mrs. Parmelia Lane was the wife of Elder Sands Lane, who was a native of Michigan and a successful preacher. Later he became president of several conferences in the United States. He was conducting a tent meeting in Riseley when Mrs. White arrived in England. She and the Lane family were good friends through the years.

Dear Sister Lane: I have been afflicted as you now are, and I know how to sympathize with you. I can understand your feeling that you have sustained a great loss.

I want to tell you that we received a letter from your husband, written shortly before his death. At the time this letter was received, I was wrestling with the solution of many difficult problems and felt that I could not answer immediately. Later, I began to write in reply, but before my letter was finished, I learned that he was dead.

I prize this letter very highly, for in it Brother Lane gives an account of his personal experience, and gives me confidence to believe that he was a true child of God. Some of our brethren had been a little fearful that our brother did not see all things clearly, but his letter to us seems to indicate that he was conscientiously striving to follow in the right course.

My dear sister, I would be glad to receive a letter from you. I hope that you may be situated where you may be happy.

I am so glad to know that Jesus our Saviour is soon to come, and that then we may all meet around the great white throne. I mean to be there, and, if we are both true and faithful to the end, I believe that we shall meet your husband. We may have to pass through trying scenes, but we are safe as we hide our lives in Christ in God. Many will give heed to seducing spirits and doctrines of devils, and the only hope for every soul is to look constantly unto Jesus, the Author and the Finisher of our faith.

We must now do our part, as servants of Jesus Christ, in bringing to the world a knowledge of the truth. A short work is to be done in the world, and we must watch and work diligently. We must be instant in season and out of season. To the church of Christ belong our talents, both original and acquired. We are servants of the Lord Jesus Christ.

We are made sad as we see men and women lording it over those who should be the Lord's free agencies. Christ is the supreme ruler of His church. Let no man come between our soul and Him. Let us labor entirely for the Lord, allowing nothing to interpose between the soul and its highest interest—overcoming by the blood of the Lamb and the word of our testimony. . . .

When Sorrow Comes

Be of good courage in the Lord, my sister. Keep looking unto the Author and Finisher of our faith.—Letter 362, 1906.

WIDOWHOOD

Sister Lons was a recent acquaintance of Ellen White. Learning of Mr. Lons' death, Mrs. White wrote her new friend a letter of love and sympathy.

Dear Sister Lons: I am happy to have made your acquaintance, and have my heart linked with your heart, and also with the widow, Sister Brown. We have all three of us been left in widowhood, and we have been much blessed of God, in that He hath not failed us in our times of trial. He has been to us a present help in every time of need. There has been in our individual experience the proving of God—resignation under affliction, patience when tried most severely, and humble childlike reliance upon God.

We have learned in the midst of dark providences that it was not wise to have a will or way of our own, and to cast not reflection and surmises on the divine faithfulness. I feel that we are those who can understand and sympathize with each other. We are bound together by the grace of Jesus Christ and in the bonds of Christian sympathies made sacred by afflictions.

We will, if we meet no more upon earth, have tender, unforgotten memories of our short association with the family at Long Point. I am glad to have met you. I believe that in the providence of God that it is ordered that you be a member of the Brown family. In your association with them the Lord has made you an instrument of righteousness, a blessing especially to Sister Brown. I have very kindly, tender feelings for you, and especially for Sister Brown, understanding the sorrows of her life.

Afflictions are oft mercies in disguise. We know not what we might have been without them. When God in His mysterious providence overthrows all our cherished plans, and we may receive sorrow in the place of joy, we will bow in submission and say, "Thy will, Oh God, be done." We must and we will ever cherish a calm, religious trust in One who loves us, who gave His life for us. "The Lord will command his lovingkindness in the daytime, and in the night his song shall be with me, and my prayer unto the God of my life. I will say unto God my rock, Why hast thou forgotten me? why go I mourning because of the oppression of the enemy? . . . Why art thou cast down, O my soul? and why art thou disquieted within me? hope thou in God: for I shall yet praise him, who is the health of my countenance, and my God."

The Lord looks upon our afflictions. He graciously and discriminately metes them out and apportions them. As a refiner of silver He watches us every moment until the purification is complete. The furnace is to purify and refine, not to destroy and consume. He will cause those who put their trust in Him to sing of mercies in the midst of judgments.

He is ever watching to impart, when most needed, new and fresh blessings, strength in the hour of weakness, succor in the hour of danger, friends in the hour of loneliness, sympathy, human and divine, in the hour of sorrow. We are homeward bound. He that loveth us so much as to die for us hath builded for us a city. The New Jerusalem is our place of rest. There will be no sadness in the City of God. No wail of sadness. No dirge of crushed hopes and buried affection shall ever more be heard. God bless you, my dear much-respected sister.—Letter 37, 1893.

DEATH OF A CHILD

In a letter to Elder and Mrs. S. N. Haskell, Ellen White speaks of the death of her great-grandchild.

I have written many pages today. This morning I received a letter from Mabel Workman [her granddaughter]. About two weeks ago she gave birth to a ten-pound boy, but the little one died two days after his birth. Mabel has passed through a severe experience, but we are thankful that her life has been spared. Both father and mother have felt the trial severely, but they have accepted it as Christians should. Mabel's husband has proved himself to be a true Christian in this time of affliction, and the Lord has sustained them both. They feel that had they not had Mrs. Kress with them at the time, Mabel also might have lost her life. I feel thankful that Sister Kress could be with them; for she has great tact and skill. Had the mother's life been taken, all would have felt the affliction keenly.

225
When Sorrow Comes

We have been very anxious regarding Mabel for two weeks, for until today no word had come to us since the telegram telling of the death of the baby. I thank the Lord that Mabel's life has been spared, and I pray that she may live to be a blessing in the cause of God.—Letter 120, 1909.

Mrs. A. H. Robinson was an old friend in Michigan. Ellen White wrote to her immediately upon receiving news of the death of her child, sharing her own experience in the deaths of two of her sons.

My Dear Sister Robinson: I have just received my American mail. My secretary has read me my letters, many of which are of a very interesting character. I will answer your letter first.

As you relate your experience in the death of your child, and how you bowed in prayer, submitting your will to the will of your heavenly Father, leaving the matter with Him, my mother heart is touched. I have passed through an experience similar to the experience through which you have just passed.

When my eldest son was sixteen years old, he was stricken down in sickness. His case was considered critical, and he called us to his bedside, and said, "Father, Mother, it will be hard for you to part with your eldest son. If the Lord sees fit to spare my life, for your sake I will be pleased. If it is for my good and His name's glory for my life to close now, I will say, It is well with my soul. Father, go by yourself, and Mother, go by yourself; and pray. Then you will receive an answer according to the will of my Saviour, whom you love and I love." He was afraid that if we should bow together, our sympathies would strengthen, and we would ask for that which it would not be best for the Lord to grant.

We did as he requested, and our prayers were similar in every point to the prayers you offered. We received no evidence that our son would recover. He died, putting his full trust in Jesus our Saviour. His death was a great blow to us, but it was a victory even in death, for his life was hid with Christ in God.

Before the death of my eldest boy, my babe was sick unto death. We prayed, and thought that the Lord would spare us our darling. But we closed his eyes in death, and laid him away to rest in Jesus, until

DOG-8

the Lifegiver shall come to awaken His precious loved ones to a glorious immortality. . . .

But the Lord has been my Counselor, and the Lord will give you grace to bear your bereavement.

You inquire in regard to your little one being saved. Christ's words are your answer: "Suffer little children to come unto me, and forbid them not: for of such is the kingdom of God."

Remember the prophecy "Thus saith the Lord; A voice was heard in Ramah, lamentation, and bitter weeping; Rachel weeping for her children refused to be comforted. . . . Thus saith the Lord; Refrain thy voice from weeping, and thine eyes from tears: for thy work shall be rewarded, saith the Lord; and they shall come again from the land of the enemy. And there is hope in thine end, saith the Lord, that thy children shall come again to thine own border."

This promise is yours. You may be comforted and trust in the Lord. The Lord has often instructed me that many little ones are to be laid away before the time of trouble. We shall see our children again. We shall meet them and know them in the heavenly courts. Put your trust in the Lord, and be not afraid.—Letter 196, 1899.

DEATH OF A FRIEND

The following paragraphs are taken from a letter written to Edson and Emma White regarding an accident that took place near Avondale College.

On Monday morning I thought my family appeared unnatural. Some strange shadow seemed to hang over them. In the morning Sara and I drove to the station for Willie, but he did not come. Elder Gates, who had spoken to the people in Wallsend Sunday evening, drove up with us from the station, and Sara took him to the school, bringing back with her Elder Daniells and Brother Hare. Sara told me that these brethren would like to speak with me. I had a few words with Elder Daniells about the work in Maitland, and then Brother Hare drew his chair up close to mine and said he had something to tell me. Then he told me that the evening before an accident had occurred near the school.

Sister Peck, Miss Gates, and Sister Boyd's daughter were driving from Sunnyside to the school with a horse which we have always considered safe and manageable, though awkward. If we did not watch her while driving, she would turn to one side. The road to the school is not a permanent one, but is laid out for present use until a better [one] can be made. Under the management of Elder Haskell, the schoolboys made a log bridge over the creek. As the trap neared this bridge, those in it saw that a tree had fallen across the road, and Sister Peck, who had the lines, thought she would get out and lead the horse round it. But instead of standing still, the horse began to back, and tried to turn round toward home again.

No one anticipated any danger. But they were nearer to the edge of the creek than they supposed, and in a few seconds, the carriage and those who were in it, except Miss Peck, were in the river, which at that place is about fifteen feet deep. Sister Peck was thrown out on the bank, and the carriage in its descent passed over her. But she was not much hurt. She helped Ella Boyd out of the water, but Miss Gates was beyond their reach. Ella Boyd ran to the school and called out the men, and in about three minutes they had the body of Miss Gates out of the water. They carried her to the school, and did everything possible to restore her, but without success. She was dead. It is believed by all that she did not die from drowning, for she made no struggle to save herself. We think that the shock killed her. She was buried on Monday afternoon. . . .

Sister Gates was in delicate health. She had suffered much from lung difficulty. Only the day before her death, she spoke to Sister Hughes in reference to her case. She said that her lung difficulty had returned to her, and that she knew a long illness was before her. To her the future was a terrible dread, for her brother and his wife are both struggling with ill health, and she could not endure the thought of being a burden to them. Her father and mother, brothers and sisters, are all dead except this brother. We feel that it is well that she did not have to suffer from a lingering disease, and we have laid her away for a little while, till she shall be called forth to a glorious immortality.—Letter 203, 1899.

Woman
to Woman

22

It is the work of the heavenly angels to come close to the tried, the tempted, the suffering ones. They labor long and untiringly to save the souls for whom Christ has died.
—Review and Herald, *July 4, 1899*

Women Reaching Out to Other Women.—Women can learn what needs to be done to reach other women. There are women who are especially adapted for the work of giving Bible readings, and they are very successful in presenting the Word of God in its simplicity to others. They become a great blessing in reaching mothers and their daughters. This is a sacred work, and those engaged in it should receive encouragement.—MM 140 (1910).

Women as Messengers of Mercy.—We greatly need consecrated women who, as messengers of mercy, shall visit the mothers and the children in their homes, and help them in the everyday household duties, if need be, before beginning to talk to them regarding the truth for this time. You will find that by this method you will have souls as the result of your ministry.—RH, July 12, 1906.

Younger Women as Workers.—Women instructors should labor with the young women, not to see how much work can be gained from them, but to win their love and confidence. When this is won, there will be no difficulty about the work, for the workers will be filled with a desire to please.

The Lord calls upon those engaged in the sacred work of publishing the truth to give evidence that they have been purified by His grace. As the disciples of Christ reveal His character, they show forth His miraculous power, bearing a convincing testimony to the truth of His Word.—PM 259 (1901).

Women Can Enter Where Ministers Cannot.—Those women who labor to teach souls to seek for the new birth in Christ Jesus are doing a precious work. They consecrate themselves to God, and they are just as verily laborers for God as are their husbands. They can enter families to which ministers could find no access. They can listen to the sorrows of the depressed and oppressed. They can shed rays of light into discouraged souls. They can pray with them. They can open the Scriptures, and enlighten them from a "Thus saith the Lord."—5MR 327 (1898).

Women to Be Educated to Help Other Women.—If we can arrange to have regular, organized companies instructed intelligently in regard to the part they should act as servants of the Master, our churches will have a life and vitality that they have long needed. I have so longed for women who could be educated to help our sisters rise from their discouragement and feel that they could do a work for the Lord. This is bringing rays of sunshine into their own lives, which are reflected into the hearts of others. God will bless you and all who unite with you in this grand work.—WM 144 (1899).

SEEK OUT THOSE WHO ARE LONELY

Natural to Seek Companionship.—Everyone will find companions or make them. And just in proportion to the strength of the friendship will be the amount of influence which friends will exert over one another for good or for evil. All will have associates, and will influence and be influenced in their turn.

The link is a mysterious one which binds human hearts together, so that the feelings, tastes, and principles of two individuals are closely blended. One catches the spirit, and copies the ways and acts, of the other. As wax retains the figure of the seal, so the mind retains the impression produced by [communication] and association. The influence may be unconscious, yet it is no less powerful.—4T 587 (1881).

The Need for Association.—Many might be kept from sinful influences if they were surrounded with good associations and had words of kindness and love spoken to them.—4T 364 (1879).

Strength for Your Day.—Angels, who will do for you what you cannot do for yourselves, are waiting for your cooperation. They are waiting for you to respond to the drawing of Christ. Draw nigh to God and to one another. By desire, by silent prayer, by resistance of satanic agencies, put your will on the side of God's will. While you have one desire to resist the devil, and sincerely pray, Deliver me from temptation, you will have strength for your day.—RH, July 4, 1899.

OUR WILL AND OUR WAY SHOULD BE SUBMITTED TO GOD

A letter written on April 5, 1873, to Sister Billet, of San Francisco, California. Ellen White gives encouragement to her friend to stand fast on the platform of eternal truth. Sister Billet had not yet taken her stand as a Sabbathkeeper.

Dear Sister Billet: I would be much pleased to have a conversation with you today, but as this is impossible, the next best thing for me to do is to let the silent pen give expression to my thoughts and feelings. Very many hundred miles separate us, but you are not forgotten by us. We have deep interest that your soul should prosper even as your health.

My dear sister, does the truth grow more clear to your understanding? As you plant your feet upon the platform of eternal truth, do you feel that God is more precious and that you are in His sheltering care? We have precious, harmonious, sanctifying truth. We do not always consider that the sanctification we so earnestly desire and for which we pray so earnestly is brought about through the truth and, by the providence of God, in a manner we least expect. When we look for joy, behold there is sorrow. When we expect peace, we frequently have distrust and doubt because we find ourselves plunged into trials we cannot avoid. In these trials we are having the answers to our prayers. In order for us to be purified, the fire of affliction must kindle upon us, and our will must be brought into conformity to the will of

God. In order to be conformed to the image of our Saviour we pass through a most painful process of refining. The very ones that we regard the most dear upon the earth may cause us the greatest sorrow and trial. They may view us in the wrong light. They may think us in error, and that we are deceiving and degrading ourselves because we follow the dictates of enlightened conscience in seeking for the truth as for hid treasures.

The character and course of the Christian is in marked contrast to that of worldlings. The Christian cannot find pleasure in the amusements and in the varied scenes of gaiety of the world. Higher and holier attractions engage the affections. Christians will show that they are the friends of God by their obedience. . . .

Our prayers for conformity to the image of Christ may not be answered exactly as we desire. We may be tested and proved, for God sees it [is] best to put us under a course of discipline which is essential for us before we are fit subjects for the blessing we crave. We should not become discouraged and give way to doubt, and think that our prayers are not noticed. We should rely more securely upon Christ and leave our case with God to answer our prayers in His own way. God has not promised to bestow His blessings through the channels we have marked out. God is too wise to err and too regardful of our good to allow us to choose for ourselves.

The plans of God are always the best, although we may not always discern them. Perfection of Christian character can be obtained only through labor, conflict, and self-denial. We do not always count upon this, and do not consider the painful and often protracted process of purifying necessary for us in order that we may be conformed to the image of Christ. God frequently answers our prayers in a way we least expect. He brings us into positions which are the most trying to reveal what is in our hearts. To further the development of Christian graces He will place us in circumstances which will demand increased exertion on our part to keep our faith in lively exercise.

Let us bear in mind, dear sister, how inestimably precious are the gifts of God—the graces of His Spirit—and we shall not shrink from the trying, testing process, be it ever so painful or humiliating to us. How easy would be the way to heaven if there were no self-denial or cross! How worldlings would rush in the way, and hypocrites would travel in it without number! Thank God for the cross, the self-denial. The ignominy and shame our Saviour endured for us is none too humiliating for those saved by the purchase of His blood. Heaven will indeed be cheap enough.

Dear sister, it is for us to be patient, to choose the suffering part of religion. Your own precious child may not discern the mystery of godliness and may think you stubborn and foolish, that you will be odd and singular from the world. But faint not. If [you are] faithful to duty, God may touch the heart of your child and she may see the matchless charms of a Saviour's love. To the unbeliever whose happiness is in the things of the world, its pleasures and its vanities, the conscientious observers of the Lord's Sabbath seem wild and erratic. They may inquire why the great men, the ministers, the doctors, and the learned do not see these things if they are indeed the truth. Because of the cross! Popularity and worldly inducements are considerations too great for them to yield up. They have their minds darkened by the god of this world. . . .

We may have Christ with us while engaged in our daily avocations. Wherever we are, in whatever we are engaged, we may be indeed elevated because we are united to Christ. We may take up our humble life duties ennobled by and sanctified through the assurance of the love of God. Working from principle in the humblest calling invests it with dignity. The consciousness that we are indeed the servants of Christ will give a higher tone of character to our everyday duties—ever cheerful, patient, forbearing, and gentle. Says Christ, "I have yet many things to say unto you, but ye cannot bear them now." John 16:12. . . .

If you, my dear sister, are seen to be firm in principle, fearless in duty, zealous in seeking to exemplify Christ in your daily work, yet humble, lowly, gentle and tender, patient and forgiving, ready to suffer and to forgive injuries, you will be a living epistle known and read of all men. Your friends who are conforming their character to the world are not abiding in Christ, however high may be their profession. They do not discern the value and preciousness of the love of Christ. They cannot have a just sense of the great sacrifice made by the Captain of our salvation to redeem them from hopeless misery. The infinite sacrifice made on their account they cannot discern, therefore they are not willing to make any sacrifice themselves. . . .

Christ has bought us with a dear price, but yet He will recompense our service to Him. We may feel sad and weep over our poor service to Him who has given us such unmeasured evidences of His interest in and love for us. But the recompense will not be in exact proportion to the amount of work done, but in accordance with the motive and the love which prompted the doing of the work. The recompense will be of grace. His own abundant mercy will be displayed not because we have done anything worthy, but on account of His ummeasured love. Christ will say to the faithful, sincere worker, "Well done, good and faithful servant; . . . enter thou into the joy of thy Lord." Matthew 25:23. And even now angels of God take cognizance of our works of love and righteousness and we shall not be forgotten even in this life. In keeping His commandments there is great reward. "Great peace have they which love thy law: and nothing shall offend them." Psalm 119:165. Christ lays no more upon His servants than He gives them strength to perform. He will not cast them off in their adversity. When heart and flesh fail He will be the strength of their heart and their portion forever.

Sinners talk of the amusements of the world and the pleasures of sin, but when death is staring them in the face, they say nothing in praise of the beautiful life of sin they have led. The terrible, dark future is before them and if they could only know that their names were written in heaven, what a weight would be lifted from their sin-burdened souls! In every condition, under every circumstance, the Christian can say, "The path of holiness is a good way." However trying may be their position, they can say, "The Lord is good; 'his mercy endureth forever.'" Be of good courage, my sister. Trust wholly in God. He will sustain and comfort you in all your trials endured for His name's sake. . . . Good is the Lord and greatly to be praised.—Letter 9, 1873.

GOD WILL HEAR US

The following letter was written to Ellen White's dear friend, Lucinda Hall, whom she considered a member of her family.

Dear Lucinda: How very sad I was to have a letter from Asenath in regard to your sickness. Oh, may the Lord sustain you and relieve you of this affliction! . . .

Oh, Lucinda, I can't write much. A strange oppression is upon me. We will have a special season of prayer for you. God will hear us pray. He will raise you up to still act a part in His work. You have been faithful and true, but you have not had an easy lot. May God sustain you in your sickness and put His everlasting arms beneath you is my prayer.

I have missed you so very much since we parted. I feared when we left you that you would be sick. I could not explain your symptoms, only that a slow fever was upon you. Just trust yourself in the hands of God without anxiety, without fear. God is the rewarder of them who diligently seek Him. The fervent, effectual prayer of the righteous availeth much. Our prayers will not be in vain. "Ask, and ye shall receive." God alone can bring up Lucinda. She has given herself to God. She is His property. He will not forget the sacrifice she has made for the Lord. He will work for her and none can hinder. Only have faith. How I long to see you and make earnest intercessions for you. We are doing this where we are, far from you, but Jesus knows it all. He can hear from here and bless you there just as well. . . .

This morning, Sabbath, we called in Brother Haskell and Elbert Lane and engaged in prayer for our dear Lucinda. We felt that God did not turn away our prayer, but that His ears hearkened to our petition and that He would raise up the dear child to soundness. We shall continue to hold fast the arm of God. I have faith in no other power, no other skill. It is put within me. No arm but the Lord's can bring help to Lucinda. If she is raised up it will be by the prayer of faith. Jesus is our great deliverer. If we ask Him He will hear us. We shall plead with God. I hope dear Lucinda will take hold on the promises herself and not let go. I hope she will have unwavering faith.—Letter 69, 1874.

Prayer
for Service

*Y*ou need not go to the ends of the earth for wisdom, for God is near. It is not the capabilities you now possess or ever will have that will give you success. It is that which the Lord can do for you. We need to have far less confidence in what man can do and far more confidence in what God can do for every believing soul. He longs to have you reach after Him by faith. He longs to have you expect great things from Him. He longs to give you understanding in temporal as well as in spiritual matters. He can sharpen the intellect. He can give tact and skill. Put your talents into the work, ask God for wisdom, and it will be given you.

—Christ's Object Lessons, *p. 146*

At Simon's House

Appendix A

And one of the Pharisees desired him that he would eat with him. And he went into the Pharisee's house, and sat down to meat." Christ had no home that He called His own. Those who invited Him to their houses regarded Him as being too poor to possess a home. But every house was His property.

Simon thought that in making this feast he was doing Christ an honor. But, even though what he furnished had been his own, in partaking of his hospitality Christ would have given more than was bestowed on Him. As He sat at the Pharisee's table, He ate the provision furnished by His Father. Scribes and Pharisees were tenants in His home. His benevolence provided them with food and clothing. If He had not become man's surety, they would have enjoyed no blessings. And not only do temporal blessings come from Him, but to all who will receive it, He gives the bread of life.

Christ ate with publicans and sinners, as well as with Pharisees. When He was invited to their homes, He accepted the invitation. In this He offended the scribes and Pharisees, who thought that a Jew should not thus forget the wall of partition that tradition had erected. But with God there is no sect or nationality. When thus accused, Christ answered, "I came not to call the righteous, but sinners to repentance." He placed Himself in the very avenue where He could gain access to perishing souls, and plant in human hearts the seeds of truth, seeds that would spring up and bear fruit to the glory of God.

Christ never provided a luxury for Himself, but He allowed expressions of respect and love to flow to Him. This was His due. He had nothing in the world which He claimed as His own, yet He made the world and all that is therein. For our sake He became poor, that we through His poverty might be made rich. He bore the weakness of humanity. Could human eyes have been opened, they would have seen that He was stronger than the strong man armed; but He never forgot that in the estimation of the world He was a poor man.

There was no sham humility about Him. He was humility itself. "Being found in fashion as a man, he humbled himself." When anyone did Him a favor, with all courtesy and heavenly politeness He blessed the giver. He never refused the simplest flower plucked by the hand of a child and offered to Him in love. He accepted the offerings of children, and blessed the givers, inscribing their names in the book of life.

"And, behold, a woman in the city, which was a sinner, when she knew that Jesus sat at meat in the Pharisee's house, brought an alabaster box of ointment, and stood at his feet behind him weeping, and began to wash his feet with tears, and did wipe them with the hairs of her head, and kissed his feet, and anointed them with the ointment. Now when the Pharisee which had bidden him saw it, he spake within himself, saying, This man, if he were a prophet, would have known who and what manner of woman this is that toucheth him: for she is a sinner."

By curing Simon of leprosy, Christ had saved him from a living death. But now Simon questioned whether Christ was a prophet. Because Christ allowed this woman to approach Him, because He did not indignantly spurn her as one whose sins were too great to be forgiven, because He did not show that He realized that she had fallen, Simon was tempted to think that He was not a prophet. His heart was filled with mistrust and unbelief. Jesus knows nothing of this woman, who is so free in her demonstrations, he thought, or He would not allow her to touch Him.

But Simon could not read his Guest's heart. It was his ignorance of the only true God, and Jesus Christ, whom He had sent, that led him to think as he did. He had not yet been fully converted from his Pharisaism. He did not realize that on such occasions God's Son must act in God's way—with compassion, tenderness, and mercy. Simon's way was to take no notice of Mary's penitent service, her humble action. Her act of kissing Christ's feet and anointing them with ointment was exasperating to Simon. He thought that if Christ were a prophet, He would recognize sinners and rebuke them.

Reading Simon's thoughts, Christ answered them before he had spoken, thus showing that He was a prophet of prophets. "Simon," He said, "I have somewhat to say unto thee. . . . There was a certain creditor which had two debtors: the one owed five hundred pence, and the other fifty. And when they had nothing to pay, he frankly forgave them both. Tell me therefore, which of them will love him most? Simon answered and said, I suppose that he, to whom he forgave most. And he said unto him, Thou hast rightly judged."

As did Nathan with David, Christ concealed His home thrust under the veil of a parable. He threw upon His host the burden of pronouncing sentence upon himself. This way of presenting the matter made Simon feel very uncomfortable. He himself had led into sin the woman he now despised. She had been deeply wronged by him. By the two debtors of the parable Simon and the woman are represented. Simon's sin is shown to be tenfold greater than that of the woman, as much greater as the debt of five hundred pence is greater than a debt of fifty pence.

Simon now began to see himself in a new light. He saw how Mary was regarded by One who was indeed a prophet in every sense of the word. He saw that with keen prophetic eye Christ read her heart of love and devotion. Simon was ashamed. He felt that he was in the presence of a being superior to himself.

Simon had doubted that Christ was a prophet, but in His very knowledge of this woman, Christ gave evidence of His prophetic character. His mighty works bore witness of Him. His miracles, His wonderful instruction, His long patience, His humility, all were evidences of His divinity. Simon need not have doubted.

"I entered into thine house," Christ continued, "thou gavest me no water for my feet: but [with tears of repentance, prompted by love] she hath washed my feet . . . and wiped them with the hairs of her head. Thou gavest me no kiss: but this woman [whom you despise, since the time she entered in], hath not ceased to kiss my feet." The washing of the feet and the kiss of welcome were attentions that were not invariably shown to guests. It was customary to bestow them on those to whom it was desired to show special regard. These ministrations Christ should have received from His host, but He did not.

Christ recounted the opportunities Simon had had to show his love for his Lord, and his appreciation of what had been done for him. Plainly, yet with delicate politeness, Christ assured His disciples that His heart is grieved when His children neglect to express their gratitude to Him by words and deeds of love. Some may think that this scripture is no longer of force, but it is. Writing of those women who were to be honored, Paul said, "If she have lodged strangers, if she have washed the saints' feet, if she have relieved the afflicted, if she have diligently followed every good work" [1 Timothy 5:10].

Many need sympathy and appreciation. But those who would wash the saints' feet must have sanctified discernment, that they may be able to recognize a saint. The garment of God's messenger may be travel-stained and worn, but he may be an angel in disguise. Unrecognized, angels talk with men, speaking words that are to their souls as the water of life. Mary was looked upon as a great sinner, but Christ knew the circumstances that had made her thus. He saw that she had great capabilities for good. He saw the better place of her character, and knew that through His grace she would become a partaker of the divine nature, and would purify her soul by obeying truth.

Christ might have extinguished every spark of hope in Mary's soul, but He did not. The Heart-searcher read the motives that led to her actions, and He also saw the spirit that prompted Simon's words. "Seest thou this woman?" He said to him. "She is a sinner; I say unto thee, Her sins, which are many, are forgiven; for she loved much: but to whom little is forgiven, the same loveth little. And he said unto her, Thy sins are forgiven."

Those present, thinking of Lazarus, who had been raised from the dead by Christ, and who was at this time a guest in his uncle's house, began to question, saying, "Who is this that forgiveth sins also?" But Christ continued, "Thy faith hath saved thee; go in peace."

Jesus knows the circumstances of every soul. You may say, I am sinful, very sinful. You may be; but the worse you are, the more you need Jesus. He turns no weeping, contrite soul away. He does not tell to any all that He might reveal, but He bids every trembling soul take courage. He will not reject any who come to Him penitent and believing. Freely will He pardon all who come for forgiveness and restoration.

But to know Jesus requires a change of heart. No unconverted person, in his natural state of depravity, loves Christ. A love of Jesus is the first result of conversion. The proof of this love is given: "If ye love me, keep my commandments." "If ye keep my commandments, ye shall abide in my love; even as I have kept my Father's commandments, and abide in his love."

Christ might commission the angels of heaven to pour out the vials of wrath on our world, full of hypocrisy and sin, destroying those who are filled with hatred to God. He might blot this dark spot from His universe. But He does not do this. He is today standing at the altar of incense, presenting before God the prayers of those who desire His help. "Who is he that condemneth? It is Christ that died, yea rather, that is risen again, who is even at the right hand of God, who also maketh intercession for us."

Jesus is to be loved and trusted. All who will be obedient He leads upward step by step, as fast as they can advance, that, while standing by the side of the Sin-bearer, in the light that proceeds from the throne of God, they may breathe the air of the heavenly courts. Beside his great Intercessor, the repentant sinner stands above the strife and accusation of tongues. "Who is he that will harm you, if ye be followers of that which is good? But and if ye suffer for righteousness' sake, happy are ye: and be not afraid of their terror, neither be troubled."

No human being, even though united with evil angels, can impeach the souls who have fled to Christ for refuge. He has united the believing soul to His own divine-human nature. In His mediatorial office, His divinity and humanity are combined, and upon this union hangs the hope of the world.—ST, May 9, 1900.

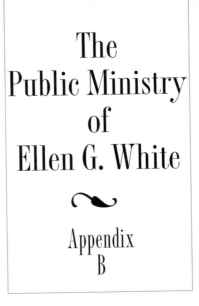

The
Public Ministry
of
Ellen G. White

Appendix
B

In her public ministry Ellen White effectively made appeals which called for a response. Presented here are accounts of a number of instances that reveal her method of appeal under varying circumstances.

At Battle Creek in the Early Days.—Attended meeting at the church at Battle Creek. Spoke to the people about one hour with freedom, in regard to the fall of Adam bringing misery and death, Christ bringing life and immortality to light through His humiliation and death. Felt to urge upon the people the necessity of entire consecration to God—the sanctification of the entire being, soul, body, and spirit. Spoke upon the death of Moses and the view he had of the promised land of Canaan. There was a depth of feeling in the congregation. . . . In meeting that evening we called those forward who had a desire to be Christians. Thirteen came forward. All bore testimony for the Lord. It was a good work (diary, Jan. 12, 1868).—1SM 144.

Earnest Work in Michigan.—Meetings were held all through the day. My husband spoke in forenoon; Brother Andrews in the afternoon. I followed with remarks quite at length, entreating those who had been interested through the meetings to commence from that day to serve God. We called forward those who wished to start in the service of the Lord. Quite a number came forward. I spoke several times, beseeching souls to break the bands of Satan and start then. One mother went to her son and wept and entreated him. He seemed hard, stubborn, and unyielding. I then arose and addressed Brother D, begged him to not stand in the way of his children. He started, then arose, spoke, said he would commence from that day. This was heard with glad hearts by all. Brother D is a precious man.

Sister E's husband then arose, testified that he would be a Christian. He is an influential man—a lawyer. His daughter was upon the anxious seat.* Brother D then added his entreaties to ours. Sister D's also to their children. We entreated and at last prevailed. All came forward. The fathers and all the sons and other fathers followed their example. It was a day of gladness. Sister E said it was the happiest day of her life (diary, Feb. 19, 1868).—1SM 144, 145.

A Good Response.—I spoke in the afternoon from 2 Peter. I had freedom in talking. After I had spoken one hour I invited those who wished to be Christians to come forward. Between thirty and forty came forward quietly without excitement and occupied the front seats. I spoke with them in regard to making an entire surrender to God. We had a praying season for those who came forward. We had a very precious season of prayer. Those who wished baptism were requested to signify it by rising. Quite a number arose (diary, June 9, 1873). —1SM 145.

After Some Hesitancy a Response.—I spoke in the afternoon [at Stanley, Virginia] from John 17:3. The Lord gave me much of His Holy Spirit. The house was full. I called those forward who wished to seek the Lord more earnestly and for those who wished to give themselves to the Lord a whole sacrifice. For a time not one made a move, but after a while many came forward and bore testimonies of confession. We had a precious season of prayer and all felt broken down, weeping and confessing their sins. Oh, that each may understand! (diary, Nov. 9, 1890).—1SM 145, 146.

Especially Blessed as She Began Work in Switzerland.—Sabbath and Sunday were precious seasons for those assembled. The Lord especially blessed in speaking Sunday afternoon. All listened with the deepest interest, and at the close of the discourse an invitation was given for all who desired to be Christians, and all who felt that they had not a living connection with God, to come forward, and we would unite our prayers with theirs for the pardon of sin, and for grace to resist temptation. This was a new experience for many of our brethren in Europe, but they did not hesitate. It seemed that the entire congregation were on their feet, and the best they could do was to be seated, and all seek the Lord together. Here was an entire congregation manifesting their determination to put sin away, and to engage most earnestly in the work of seeking God. . . .

After prayer, one hundred fifteen testimonies were borne. Many of these showed a real, genuine experience in the things of God.—RH, Nov. 3, 1885.

At Christiana (Oslo), Norway.—We spent two weeks in Christiana, and labored earnestly for the church. The Spirit of the Lord moved me to bear a very plain testimony. At our last meeting especially, I presented before them the necessity of a thorough change in the character if they would be children of God. When they come to worship before the Lord, it should be with subdued and reverent hearts. The house built for His worship is a sacred place, not a place for unholy feelings, malice, faultfinding, and bitterness of spirit. I urged upon them the necessity of deep repentance, confession, and forsaking of the sins which had shut away the sweet spirit of Christ from the church. We then called for those to come forward who would take a decided position on the Lord's side. Many responded. Some good confessions were made, and earnest testimonies were borne. We hope that this move is but the beginning of a decided advance on the part of many members of this church.—RH, Oct. 19, 1886.

Backsliders Reclaimed in Basel.—Sabbath, February 19, I spoke to the people at 9:00 a.m. The Lord gave me of His Holy Spirit as I presented before them the temptation of Christ in the wilderness. In the afternoon, at three o'clock, we assembled for social meeting. I was much blessed as I spoke to them again, upon the necessity of our coming up to greater sympathy and more decided contemplation of the great sufferings of Christ. We think of these altogether too little.

I requested those who desired prayers to come forward. The

seats were quickly filled, and my heart was stirred as I saw the whole congregation on their feet. I said, Sit down just where you are, and we will all seek the Lord together. Before the season of prayer, many testimonies were given in quick succession and with deep feeling, showing that hearts were touched by the Spirit of the Lord. Confessions were made with tears. We were glad to see this work going forward; for we knew it was just such a work as was needed to bring the people into that position of humbling their hearts and confessing their sins before God, that He would accept their repentance and their efforts to seek Him. "If we confess our sins, he is faithful and just to forgive us our sins, and to cleanse us from all unrighteousness."—RH, Apr. 19, 1887.

An Outstanding Experience in Australia.—On Sabbath, May 25, we had a precious meeting in the hall where our people meet at North Fitzroy. For several days before the meeting, I knew that I was expected to speak in the church on Sabbath; but unfortunately I had a severe cold and was quite hoarse. I felt inclined to excuse myself from this appointment; but as it was my only opportunity, I said, "I will place myself before the people, and I believe the Lord will answer my earnest prayers, and remove the hoarseness so that I can present my message to the people." I presented to my heavenly Father the promise, "Ask, and it shall be given you; seek, and ye shall find; knock, and it shall be opened unto you. For every one that asketh receiveth; and he that seeketh findeth; and to him that knocketh it shall be opened. . . . If ye then, being evil, know how to give good gifts unto your children, how much more shall your heavenly Father give the Holy Spirit to them that ask him?" Again, Christ says, "Whatsoever ye shall ask in my name, that will I do, that the Father may be glorified in the Son."

The Word of God is sure. I had asked, and I believed that I would be enabled to speak to the people. I selected a portion of Scripture; but when I rose to speak, it was taken from my mind, and I felt impressed to speak from the first chapter of 2 Peter. The Lord gave me special freedom in presenting the value of the grace of God. How much is His grace to be appreciated! The apostle says: "Grace and peace be multiplied unto you through the knowledge of God, and of

Jesus our Lord, according as his divine power hath given unto us all things that pertain unto life and godliness, through the knowledge of him that hath called us to glory and virtue: whereby are given unto us exceeding great and precious promises: that by these ye might be partakers of the divine nature, having escaped the corruption that is in the world through lust." . . .

At the close of my discourse, I felt impressed by the Spirit of God to extend an invitation for all those to come forward who desired to give themselves fully to the Lord. . . . About thirty came forward. Among these were the wives of the brethren A[†] who for the first time made manifest their desire to come near to God. My heart was filled with unspeakable gratitude because of the movement made by these two women.

I could then see why I was so earnestly moved to make this invitation. At first I had hesitated, wondering if it were best to do so when my son and I were the only ones whom I could see who would give us any help on that occasion. But as though someone had spoken to me, the thought passed through my mind, "Cannot you trust in the Lord?" I said, "I will, Lord."

Although my son was much surprised that I should make such a call on this occasion, he was equal to the emergency. I never heard him speak with greater power or deeper feeling than at that time. He called upon Brethren Faulkhead and Salisbury to come forward, and we knelt in prayer. My son took the lead, and the Lord surely indited his petition; for he seemed to pray as though in the presence of God. Brethren Faulkhead and Salisbury also presented fervent petitions, and then the Lord gave me a voice to pray. I remembered the sisters A, who, for the first time, were taking a public stand for the truth. The Holy Spirit was in the meeting, and many were stirred by Its deep movings.

At the close of the meeting many pressed their way to the platform, and taking me by the hand, requested me with tears in their eyes to pray for them. I answered heartily, "I will." The sisters A were introduced to me, and I found that their hearts were very tender. . . .

The mother of one of the sisters who has now taken her position on the truth has been a most bitter opposer, and has threatened that if her daughter did become a Sabbathkeeper, she would not allow her to enter her home, for the mother would look upon her as a disgrace to the family.

Mrs. A had often made the statement that she would never join the Seventh-day Adventists. She had been brought up in the Presbyterian Church, and had been educated to think that it was very improper for women to speak in meeting, and that for a woman to preach was altogether beyond the bounds of propriety. She enjoyed hearing Elders Daniells and Corliss, and thought them very clever speakers, but she would not listen to a woman's preaching. Her husband had prayed that God would so arrange matters that she might be converted under the ministry of Sister White.

When I made the appeal, and urged those to come forward who felt their need of drawing nearer to God, to the surprise of all, these sisters came forward. The sister who had lost her little one said that she was determined that she would not move forward, but the Spirit of the Lord so forcibly impressed her mind that she dared not refuse. . . .

I feel so grateful to my heavenly Father for His loving-kindness in bringing these two precious souls to unite with their husbands in obeying the truth.—RH, July 30, 1895.

The Lord Would Be Pleased to See a Similar Work Done in Every Church.—Sabbath, November 10, I visited San Francisco, and spoke to a churchful of people who had ears to hear and hearts to understand. They seemed to be hungry for the Word of the Lord, and I believe they heard to a purpose. As I spoke the word of life in plain, simple language, I knew that Christ was with us, softening and subduing hearts. The Holy Spirit was evidently at work. Oh, how my heart yearned for the precious souls whom I was inviting to look and live!

After I had finished speaking, Elder Corliss invited all who wished to give themselves to Jesus to come forward. There was a quick and happy response, and I was told that nearly two hundred persons came forward. Men and women, youth and children, pressed into the front seats. The Lord would be pleased to have a work similar to this done in every church.

Many could not come forward, because the house was so crowded, yet the animated countenances and tearful eyes testified to the determination, "I will be on the Lord's side. From this time I will seek earnestly to reach a higher standard."—RH, Feb. 12, 1901.

Response at General Conference Session of 1909.—My brethren and sisters, seek the Lord while He may be found. There is a time coming when those who have wasted their time and opportunities will wish they had sought Him. . . . He wants you to keep in the line of reason, and in the line of labor. He wants you to go forth to our churches to labor earnestly for Him. He wants you to institute meetings for those outside of the churches, that they may learn the truths of this last message of warning. There are places where you will be gladly received, where souls will thank you for coming to their help. May the Lord help you to take hold of this work as you have never yet taken hold of it. Will you do this? Will you here rise to your feet and testify that you will make God your trust and your helper? [Congregation rises.]

[Praying] I thank Thee, Lord God of Israel. Accept this pledge of this Thy people. Put Thy Spirit upon them. Let Thy glory be seen in them. As they shall speak the word of truth, let us see the salvation of God. Amen.—GCB, May 18, 1909.

Anxious seat: at a revival meeting, a seat, usually near the pulpit, occupied by persons concerned about their spiritual condition.

Two brothers who were church members, but whose wives were not.

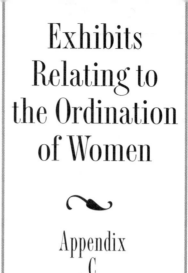

Exhibits Relating to the Ordination of Women

Appendix C

FROM THE LIFETIME AND EXPERIENCE OF ELLEN G. WHITE

A paper presented at the ministerial meeting at the 1990 General Conference session. Prepared by the White Estate staff.

1. A resolution to ordain women was discussed at the General Conference of 1881. No action was taken. The minutes include the following lines:

"Resolved, That females possessing the necessary qualifications to fill that position may, with perfect propriety, be set apart by ordination to the work of the Christian ministry.

"This was discussed by J. O. Corliss, A. C. Bourdeau, E. R. Jones, D. H. Lamson, W. H. Littlejohn, A. S. Hutchins, D. M. Canright, and J. N. Loughborough, and referred to the General Conference Committee."—RH, Dec. 20, 1881.

Ellen White did not attend the General Conference of 1881. Her husband died on August 6 of that year. Two weeks after his death she left Battle Creek, bound for California. She did not return to Michigan until August of 1883.

2. For many years Ellen White was voted ministerial credentials by the Michigan Conference (see e.g. RH, Sept. 10, 1872),

and then later by the General Conference. However, she was never ordained by human hands, nor did she ever perform a wedding, organize a church, or conduct a baptism.

3. In 1895 Ellen White recommended the ordination of women who would give themselves to a deaconess-type of work:

"Women who are willing to consecrate some of their time to the service of the Lord should be appointed to visit the sick, look after the young, and minister to the necessities of the poor. They should be set apart to this work by prayer and laying on of hands. In some cases they will need to counsel with the church officers or the minister; but if they are devoted women, maintaining a vital connection with God, they will be a power for good in the church. This is another means of strengthening and building up the church."—RH, July 9, 1895.

A number of women were ordained as deaconesses during Ellen White's Australian ministry. On August 10, 1895, the nominating committee at the Ashfield church in Sydney rendered its report, which was approved. The clerk's minutes for that date state: "Immediately following the election, the officers were called to the front where Pastors Corliss and McCullagh set apart the elder, deacons, [and] deaconesses by prayer and the laying on of hands."

Several years later, in the same church, W. C. White officiated at the ordination of the church officers. The minutes of the Ashfield church for January 7, 1900, state: "The previous Sabbath officers had been nominated and accepted for the current year, and today Elder White ordained and laid hands on the elders, deacon, and deaconesses.—AR, Jan. 16, 1986.

4. Women "Licensed to Preach" by the Seventh-day Adventist Church during Ellen White's lifetime included the following:

1878	Anna Fulton	Minnesota
	Ellen S. Lane	Michigan
	Julia Owen	Kentucky-Tennessee
1879	Libbie Collins	Minnesota
	Hattie Enoch	Kansas

	Libbie Fulton	Minnesota
	Lizzie Post	Minnesota
1880	Anna Johnson	Minnesota
1881	Ida W. Ballenger	Illinois
	Helen L. Morse	Illinois
1884	Ruie Hill	Kansas
1886	Ida W. Hibben	Illinois
1887	Mrs. S. E. Pierce	Vermont
1893	Flora Plummer	Iowa
1894	Margaret Caro	New Zealand
1895	Mrs. S. A. Lindsay	New York
1898	Sarepta Irish Henry	General Conference
	Lulu Wightman	New York
1899	Edith Bartlett	British Conference
1900	Hetty Haskell	General Coforence
	Mina Robinson	British Conference
1901	Carrie V. Hansen	Utah
	Emma Hawkins	Iowa
	Mrs. E. R. Williams	Michigan
1902	Mrs. S. N. Haskell	Greater New York
	Minnie Sype	Oklahoma
1904	Alma Bjdigg	Finland Mission
	Mrs. J. E. Bond	Arizona
	Bertha E. Jorgensen	South Dakota
1910	Pearl Field	Nebraska
	Mrs. Ura Spring	Nebraska

—*General Conference Archives and SDA yearbooks*

Some of the women listed above were employed by the church. Others, such as Margaret Caro, who was a dentist, were self-supporting.

5. Ellen White made three statements which are sometimes construed as evidence that she supported the concept of women as ordained gospel ministers.

In 1898 she declared that "there are women who should labor in the gospel ministry" (Ev 472). The context of this statement seems to indicate that she is speaking of ministers' wives. She wrote:

"Letters have come to me from several, asking my advice upon the question, Should ministers' wives adopt infant children? Would I advise them to do this kind of work. To some who were regarding this matter favorably, I answered, No; God would have you help your husband in his work. The Lord has not given you children of your own; His wisdom is not to be questioned. He knows what is best. Consecrate your powers to God as a Christian worker. You can help your husband in many ways. . . .

"There are women who should labor in the gospel ministry. In many respects they would do more good than the ministers who neglect to visit the flock of God. Husband and wife may unite in this work, and when it is possible, they should. The way is open for consecrated women. But the enemy would be pleased to have the women whom God could use to help hundreds binding up their time and strength on one helpless little mortal that requires constant care and attention."—5MR 325, 326.

In the year 1900 Ellen White published Testimonies, volume 6, which includes a section titled "The Canvasser a Gospel Worker." Here the author states:

"All who desire an opportunity for true ministry, and who will give themselves unreservedly to God, will find in the canvassing work opportunities to speak upon many things pertaining to the future, immortal life. The experience thus gained will be of the greatest value to those who are fitting themselves for the ministry. It is the accompaniment of the Holy Spirit of God that prepares workers, both men and women, to become pastors to the flock of God."—6T 322.

Finally, in September 1903 Ellen White wrote:

"The Lord calls upon those connected with our sanitariums, publishing houses, and schools to teach the youth to do evangelistic work. Our time and energy must not be so largely employed in establishing sanitariums, food stores, and restaurants that other lines of work will be neglected. Young men and young women who should be engaged in the ministry, in Bible work, and in the canvassing work should not be bound down to mechanical employment.

"The youth should be encouraged to attend our training schools for Christian workers, which should become more and more like the schools of the prophets. These institutions have been established by the Lord, and if they are conducted in harmony with His purpose, the youth sent to them will quickly be prepared to engage in various lines of missionary work. Some will be trained to enter the field as missionary nurses, some as canvassers, and some as gospel ministers."—8T 229, 230.

6. Ellen White made two statements about her own call to serve the Lord as His messenger. She declared:

"At the age of 78 I am still toiling. We are all in the hands of the Lord. I trust in Him; for I know that He will never leave nor forsake those who put their trust in Him. I have committed myself to His keeping.

"And I thank Christ Jesus our Lord, who hath enabled me, for that He counted me faithful, putting me into the ministry."—RH, July 26, 1906.

"In the city of Portland the Lord ordained me as His messenger, and here my first labors were given to the cause of present truth."—RH, May 18, 1911.

It will be recalled that Ellen White was given her first vision in December 1844, in Portland, Maine. Shortly thereafter she was prompted by the Lord to tell others what she had seen.

7. Ellen White did not concern herself with women's rights movements. When she was urged to join others in the crusade for women's suffrage, she declined the invitation. She wrote to her husband:

"I called upon Mrs. Graves. She had a burden upon her mind and ever since she knew I was at home she desired to see me. She said she felt that she must talk out her feelings to me. She is desirous that women's suffrage should be looked into by me. She says women ought to vote, and she related many things of a startling character which were legalized in France and St. Louis, and an effort was made to carry them out in Chicago this year, but [the effort] failed. Houses of ill fame are legalized. Women who travel alone through those cities, if they are the least suspicious of them, are taken up by the authorities and their cases are investigated. If they are diseased they are placed in the care of the doctors and cured. Then they are fit for the visits of men and are placed in the legalized home for men to satisfy their lusts upon. No examination is made of the men, and where this law is carried into effect the crime and immorality resemble the condition of the world which existed previous to the Flood.

"Mrs. Graves viewed the matter as I do in regard to the increase of crime and demoralization of society. She says women must vote if this law is [to be] withstood. We had a long talk in regard to temperance. I told her that my mind was unprepared for any such matter as women voting. She had been thinking and dwelling upon these things and her mind was ripe upon them, while my work was of another character. We were doing upon the point of temperance what no other class of people in the world were. We were as much in favor of a pledge against tobacco as liquor."—10MR 69.

8. It is likely that Ellen White did not suggest at any time that the Seventh-day Adventist Church should commence the practice of ordaining women to the gospel ministry. Her secretary, C. C. Crisler, says that she was very cautious on this point. Here is the correspondence relating to this question:

"March 12, 1916

"Mr. Clarence Crisler, Sanitarium [California]

"Dear Brother: Will you please inform me in regard to the setting apart of women who can give some time to missionary work, by laying on hands in prayer, found in *Review and Herald*, back in the early part of the nineties, probably back in about 1892 or 1893, from the pen of Sister White.

"The reason I ask for this, I was in a recent meeting where Elder Andross set aside women by the laying on of hands, and when I asked him for the authority for so doing, he referred me to you, and as I have been a Bible worker for a number of years and have recently been granted a ministerial license, I want this information.

"Please answer at once, as I want to hear from you before I go to the Southwestern Union Conference, which convenes April 7. Please send me two or three copies of her statement, as the president of our conference wants one."—Mrs. L. E. Cox, 134 Agarita Avenue, San Antonio, Texas.

"March 22, 1916

"Mrs. L. E. Cox, San Antonio, Texas

"Dear Sister: I have your letter of the twelfth, making inquiry regarding the ordination of women who give some time to missionary work—particularly to some statement which you believe to be found in a *Review* early in the nineties, from the pen of Mrs. Ellen G. White.

"As this query will require some study on my part, and searching, and as I must go to Mountain View in the morning for a few days, I am under the necessity of asking that you excuse me from answering for a few days. Upon my return, early next week, I will endeavor to send you a reply, accompanying same, if possible, with the extracts called for. However, I might say that I have not understood these extracts as teaching positively the ordination of women as ministers of the gospel. I have supposed, rather, that they refer primarily to the ordination of God-fearing women as deaconesses in local churches. But of this I will speak more fully when I write again.

"I hope to write you about the twenty-eighth, and will address you as above. If you are leaving San Antonio for other parts, it would be well for you to leave a forwarding order, so mail addressed as above will reach you in due time at the union conference."—Clarence Crisler.

"June 16, 1916

"Mrs. L. E. Cox

"Dear Sister: In my answer under date of March 22, I was unable to forward you copy of the *Review* article called for, but ventured to say, 'I have not understood these extracts as teaching positively the ordination of women as ministers of the gospel. I have supposed, rather, that they refer primarily to the ordination of God-fearing women as deaconesses in local churches.'

"Since writing the above, I have found the article in question and have had same copied. Enclosed find a copy of this article. [RH, July 9, 1895]. I am also forwarding a copy to your local conference president, Elder E. L. Neff, and to the president of your union, Elder J. W. Christian, that they may know what I am sending to you.

"While I do not make it a part of my work to presume to interpret that which has been written, yet I may be pardoned for expressing as my conviction the thought that this article published in the *Review* does not refer to the ordination of women as ministers of the gospel, but rather touches upon the question of setting apart, for special duties in local churches, God-fearing women in such churches where circumstances call for such action.

"And may I add that Sister White, personally, was very careful about expressing herself in any wise as to the advisability of ordaining women as gospel ministers. She has often spoken of the perils that such general practice would expose the church to by a gainsaying world; but as yet I have never seen from her pen any statement that would seem to encourage the formal and official ordination of women to the gospel ministry, to public labor such as is ordinarily expected of an ordained minister.

"This is not suggesting, much less saying, that no women are fitted for such public labor, and that none should ever be ordained; it is simply saying that so far as my knowledge extends, Sister White never encouraged church officials to depart from the general customs of the church in those matters."—C. C. Crisler.

CONCLUSION

The question of women's ordination was not high on Ellen White's agenda during her lifetime. Her best energies were directed toward achieving a greater unity and a deeper spirituality in the church.

Use
of the Tithe

Appendix
D

Portion of a letter written by Ellen White on March 16, 1897, from her home, "Sunnyside," at Cooranbong, New South Wales, to A. G. Daniells, concerning the use of the tithe. The entire letter is published in Manuscript Releases, *vol. 13, pp. 281-286.*

I send you this morning a letter written for America, and sent there yesterday morning, which will show you how I regard the tithe money being used for other purposes. This is the Lord's special revenue fund, for a special purpose. I have never so fully understood this matter as I now understand it. Having had questions directed here to me to answer, I have had special instruction from the Lord that the tithe is for a special purpose, consecrated to God to sustain those who minister in the sacred work as the Lord's chosen, to do His work not only in sermonizing but in ministering. They should understand all that this comprehends. There is to be meat in the house of God, a treasury well supplied, and it is not to be diverted to other purposes. There is to be special labor given to awaken the people of God who believe the truth, to give a faithful tithe to the Lord, and ministers should be encouraged and sustained by that tithe.

257
Use of the Tithe

That there will always be a temptation to divert the tithe money to other channels, we know; but the Lord has guarded this, His own portion, to be sacredly used for the support of the gospel ministers. There may be such measures taken as shall reduce the working force that bears the message of truth, as is being done, and in America has been done, to meet the measurement of the tithe in the treasury; but this is not the Lord's plan, and if entered upon and continued will reduce God's blessing to the churches that work upon such a plan. There may be a great dearth of means if there is a departing from the Lord's plan.

The Lord regards the tithe as His own, to be used for a certain purpose, and it is an easy matter, in the place of practicing the self-denial that we should, to help in educating students, or in the temporal matters, as providing conveniences for the church, which is necessary, to dip into the Lord's consecrated portion which should be used only to sustain the ministers in new fields as well as in other places. And this should not be done in a niggardly way. All the inconveniences that the laborers must wrestle with in these new fields should be taken into consideration. The expense of living is greater in some localities than in others.

Special efforts should be made for those who are where fruit is scarce, for they could live so much cheaper if they were where they could get fruit. When they are sent to fields where they are deprived of nearly everything because of the expense, a careful consideration should be made of these matters, and the lack should be supplied as far as possible, but not by withdrawing from his salary for these extra things. Those who are more favorably situated should share their prosperity with those who are in need of the very things that they are so abundantly supplied with in their locality.

We shall become very narrow, conceited, and selfish if we are not guarded and do not watch against the foe we have to meet and contend with. I shall do something for Brother Robert Hare. I will supply some things which will relieve the situation of want of fruit. I will get a couple of hundred pounds of grapes, and make [them] into jelly, that they can use on their bread. Now see what others can do. Each can do a little, and send to Brother Hare. When you visit the place, you can take some things, and we will prepare some things and send them before that time. We will make this a thank offering to God because we are permitted to live in localities where we can obtain these things and enjoy them. I think the Lord would bless us in doing this.

Now in regard to educating students in our schools. It is a good idea; it will have to be done; but God forbid that in the place of practicing self-denial and self-sacrifice our individual selves, to do this work, we should subtract from the Lord's portion, specially reserved to sustain the ministers in active labor in the field, and . . . to [keep] at work those who are already ordained for the work. We can easily consider these matters, how much it requires to support our own families according to the members of that family. Then let those whose business it is act in accordance with this rule. Look not upon our own things but upon the things of others. Let us practice the golden rule, and do unto others as we would that they should do unto us were we in like circumstances.

The fibrous roots of selfishness will root themselves wherever they are given a chance. We want to cut out and exterminate every fiber of the root of selfishness.

If one is appointed to a field where he is deprived of many things, and is sent into that field by the decision of the conference, that same power is to bear its share of the burden of making this messenger of God in that field as nearly as possible as comfortable and as pleasantly situated as the members of this power are in their several localities. The Lord will bless all such love expressed toward His workers in hard places.

But there is not that careful, tender regard, that thoughtful discrimination, in such cases, as there ought to be. If all who have anything to do with these matters would let the bright beams of the Sun of Righteousness shine fully into their hearts, they would open the windows on heaven's side and then diffuse in every way possible the light to others, in a variety of ways.

All these things are to be done, as you propose, to help students to obtain an education; but I ask you, Shall we not all act in this matter unselfishly and create a fund, and keep it to draw upon on such occasions? When you see a young man or a young woman who is a promising subject, advance or loan the sum needed, with the idea that it is a loan, not a gift. It would be better to have it thus. Then when it is returned, it can be used to educate others. But this money is not to be taken from the tithe, but from a separate fund secured for that purpose. This would exert a healthy uprightness and charity and patriotism among our people. There must be thoughtful consideration and a skillful adjustment of the work in the cause of God in all its departments. But let there be no meager, stingy plans in using the consecrated portion for the sustaining of the ministry; for then the treasury would soon be empty.

The management of the case of Brother Hickox is after human methods, not after the methods which the Lord has ordained. I have had this matter so presented to me that I see the danger of diverting the tithe to any such purpose as you have suggested. The Lord is not pleased with your management of this case. May the Lord help you all to have the heavenly anointing, that no such thing may be repeated.

Brother Farnsworth is ready to voice the decisions of human minds without looking on all sides of the question to see if there might not possibly be mistakes made. It is a very serious matter how anyone handles one of the Lord's disciples, one who has been dedicated to His service, to do His work. What made you do this kind of work? The Lord is not in it. You were faithless because there was an empty treasury. Now, in the name of Jesus Christ of Nazareth, I charge you not to devote the means that should be used in sustaining the gospel to any other purpose, and that your faith fail not as you see a lack in the supply of tithes, gifts, and offerings.—13MR 281-285 (1897).

James and
Ellen White's
Relationship

Appendix
E

For the first time the White Estate is publishing in their entirety letters 64, 65, 66, and 67, 1876. The letters, like others written by James and Ellen White, were written without any thought that they would be published someday. But in these letters we gain uncommon insights into how committed Christians handled marital stress. Through these letters we believe that other couples can take heart and learn how to handle their own tensions and conflicts.

We have endeavored to put the letters in a setting that shows the genuine love and affection between James and Ellen White during their long marriage, both before and after James's strokes. To understand the background of the letters, we ask that you read this complete section, including the covering statement.

JAMES AND ELLEN WHITE
The Saviour's Eye Is on James White—We will present your case to God, dear James, every time we pray, and will press our petitions to the throne. At times I have had a blessed assurance that God heard me pray through His dear Son and that His blessing rested on you there at Dansville. I feel the sweet presence of God at times when I pray, and feel such an evidence that God has set His love upon you, and although you are afflicted, Jesus is with you, strengthening and supporting you by His all-powerful arm. He that stretched out His hand to save sinking Peter upon the troubled water will save His ser-

vant who has labored for souls and devoted his energies to His cause. Yes, James, the eye of the compassionate Saviour is upon you. He is touched with the feelings of your infirmities. He loves you. He pities you as we cannot. He will make you to triumph in His own dear name. Be of good courage, my poor suffering husband, wait patiently a little longer and you shall see of the salvation of God. We know in whom we have believed. We have not run as uncertainly. All will come out just right in the end.—10MR 28 (1865).

Ellen Misses James's "Manly Arm"—During His Illness.— Yesterday after I left the cars I rode twelve miles in the stage. The scenery was beautiful. The trees with their varied hues, the beautiful evergreens interspersed among them, the green grass, the high and lofty mountains, the high bluffs of rocks—all are interesting to the eye. These things I could enjoy, but I am alone. The strong, manly arm I have ever leaned upon is not now my support. Tears are my meat night and day. My spirit is constantly bowed down by grief. I cannot consent that your father [James White] shall go down into the grave. Oh, that God would pity and heal him! Edson, my dear boy, give yourself to God. Wherein you have erred, frankly acknowledge it by confession and humility. Draw nigh to God and do unite with me in pleading with God for his recovery. If we chasten our souls before God and truly repent of all our wrongs, will He not be entreated, for the sake of His dear Son, to heal your father?—10MR 28, 29 (1866).

Edson Urged to Treat His Father Tenderly.—Dear Edson, do not on any account move rashly in regard to the letter written by your father.* Keep quiet; wait and trust; be faithful; make every concession you can, even if you have done so before; and may God give you a soft and tender heart to your poor, overburdened, worn, harassed father.— 10MR 29 (1871).

James White Very Attentive.—My husband is very attentive to me, seeking in every way to make my journeyings and labor pleasant and relieve it of weariness. He is very cheerful and of good courage. We must now work and with carefulness preserve our strength, for there are thirteen more camp meetings to attend.— 10MR 33 (1875).

After several strokes, James White had some personality changes, sometimes becoming unreasonable and thinking that everybody was against him. He was harsh and severe toward Edson and wrote him a very unkind letter. He later apologized to Edson for his criticism.

Letters

❧

(Written May 10, 12, 16, and 17, 1876)

*I*n 1973 a collection of approximately 2,000 letters, written between 1860 and 1899, was acquired by the Ellen G. White Estate. Originally addressed to Lucinda Hall, one of Ellen White's closest friends, the letters were written by such well-known Adventists as James and Ellen White, Kellogg, Loughborough, Amadon, and Haskell. The story of how the collection came to the White Estate was told by Elder Arthur White in the Review and Herald of August 16, 1973.

Among the collection were 48 previously unknown Ellen White letters. Most are the newsy-type letters that one friend would write to another. But Ellen considered Lucinda more than just a casual friend. On July 14, 1875, she wrote:

"I wish I could see you, Lucinda. . . . How I have missed you on this journey. Not but that I have friends, but you are nearest and dearest, next to my own family, and I feel no differences than that you belonged to me and my blood flowed in your veins."—Letter 48, 1875 (10MR 33).

Because of her special closeness to Lucinda, Ellen White poured out her heart to her friend about some family matters in a series of four letters written between May 10 and 17, 1876. Considering the circumstances she was trying to cope with at the time, that was a very human thing for Ellen White to do. But only a day after writing the third letter, she had second thoughts about what she had done. In the last of the series, dated May 17, 1876, Ellen White began by saying:

"I am sorry I wrote you the letters I have. Whatever may have been my feelings, I need not have troubled you with them. Burn all my letters, and I will relate no matters that perplex me to you. . . . I will not be guilty of uttering a word again, whatever may be the circumstances. Silence in all things of a disagreeable or perplexing character has ever been a blessing to me. When I have departed from this, I have regretted it so much."—Letter 67, 1876.

But Lucinda did not destroy the letters as requested. Thus they came into the possession of the White Estate in 1973. The Estate, being uncertain as to how to deal with these four letters, laid them aside, and did not place them in the regular file. Since then, some have suggested that the White Estate should have burned the letters, in harmony with Ellen White's original request. But others have felt that the letters should be preserved, for two reasons: 1. The situation confronting the White Estate is different from that which faced Lucinda Hall. Lucinda was the one who was asked to burn the letters. Since she did not, the White Estate board must consider the request in the light of its own situation. Critics might accuse the Estate of destroying not merely these letters, but other correspondence and manuscripts; 2. The account of how Ellen White related to an extremely difficult time in her life could be of help to individuals facing similar circumstances today.

Because many are aware of the situation in the White family that Ellen White was wrestling with at the time, and with the hope that others facing similar circumstances today may find encouragement from them, the letters, with adequate background to help understand them, are herewith being made available.

THE SETTING OF THE LETTERS

Anyone who has dealt with stroke victims can identify with Ellen White when she wrote, "I have not lost my love for my husband, but I cannot explain things."—Letter 67, 1876. A week earlier she had written, "I can but dread the liability of James's changeable moods."—

Letter 64, 1876. The change in personality exhibited by James White in the years after 1865, during which he experienced several strokes, was very difficult for his wife and associates to understand.

Before his illness, James White was a dynamic and forceful leader. But after his strokes, he experienced serious personality changes. From time to time he seemed much like his former self, but often he was suspicious and demanding. Such was the situation Ellen White was facing at the time she wrote these four letters to Lucinda.

Never one to mince words, James White frequently expressed himself forcefully. In his autobiography he wrote about a man who had criticized him:

"To see a coarse, hard-hearted man, possessing in his very nature but little more tenderness than a crocodile, and nearly as destitute of moral religious training as a hyena, shedding hypocritical tears for effect, is enough to stir the mirthfulness of the gravest saint."—LI 115, 116 (1868).

The force of James White's personality was an invaluable asset during the formative years of the Seventh-day Adventist Church. With his wife's visions constantly challenging him, Elder White started publications, built institutions, promoted church organization, and spiritually fed the flock. In addition, for 10 years he served as president of the General Conference. (His life story is told by Virgil Robinson in a biography entitled *James White*, published by the Review and Herald Publishing Association in 1976.)

But when that strong personality, altered by a series of strokes, was turned on his family and associates—including his wife—Ellen found her strength and patience stretched nearly to their limits. A person who reads only these four letters will certainly obtain a distorted picture of the relationship between James and Ellen White. One must keep in mind statements such as the following, written by James about Ellen:

"Marriage marks an important era in the lives of men. 'Whoso findeth a wife findeth a good thing, and obtaineth favour of the Lord,' is the language of wisdom. Proverbs 18:22. . . . We were married August 30, 1846, and from that hour unto the present she has been my crown of rejoicing."—LS 125, 126 (1880).

Even in his illness, James realized at times that his actions were not in harmony with his good intentions. In 1879 he wrote his children:

"I wish now to call your attention to a subject of graver importance. Probably, dear children, I may have erred in some sharp things I have written relative to the mistakes of younger heads. It is my nature to retaliate when pressed beyond measure. I wish I was a better man."—James White to Willie and Mary, Feb. 27, 1879.

We do not know all that happened after the fourth letter was written, but in less than 10 days Ellen was by her husband's side at the Kansas camp meeting.

On May 16, the same day on which the third of the four letters was written to Lucinda, Ellen wrote, in part, to her husband:

"It grieves me that I have said or written anything to grieve you. Forgive me and I will be cautious not to start any subject to annoy and distress you."—Letter 27, 1876.

Unfortunately, James never completely recovered from his illness. He had some good days, but these were intermixed with periods of depression. A comment made by the president of the General Conference two years after James White's death indicates the charitable interpretation that his close associates placed on his illness-induced actions:

"Our dear Brother White thought we were his enemies because we did not see things as he did. I have never laid up anything against that man of God, that noble pioneer who labored so hard for this cause. I attributed it all to disease and infirmity."—G. I. Butler to J. N. Andrews, May 25, 1883.

This overview of the circumstances under which Ellen White wrote the four letters to Lucinda Hall (May 10-17, 1876) is brief, but we believe it provides a needed perspective for readers who examine the only letters that Ellen White requested to be burned.

Ellen G. White Estate, August 6, 1987.

Dear Sister Lucinda:

We received your letter last evening. We also received one from James. Lucinda, I have no idea now of exchanging a certainty for an uncertainty. I can write more, and am free. Should I come east, James's happiness might suddenly change to complaining and fretting. I am thoroughly disgusted with this state of things, and do not mean to place myself where there is the least liability of its occurring. The more I think of the matter, the more settled and determined I am, unless God gives me light, to remain where I am. I can never have an opportunity such as God has favored me with at the present. I must work as God should direct. I plead and entreat for light. If it is my duty to attend the camp meetings, I shall know it.

Mary is now secured. I may lose her if I should go east. Satan has hindered me for long years from doing my writing, and now I must not be drawn off. I can but dread the liability of James's changeable moods, his strong feelings, his censures, his viewing me in the light he does, and has felt free to tell me his ideas of my being led by a wrong spirit, my restricting his liberty, et cetera. All this is not easy to jump over and place myself voluntarily in a position where he will stand in my way and I in his.

No, Lucinda, no camp meetings shall I attend this season. God in His providence has given us each our work, and we will do it separately, independently. He is happy; I am happy; but the happiness might be all changed should we meet, I fear. Your judgment I prize, but I must be left free to do my work. I cannot endure the thought of marring the work and cause of God by such depression as I have experienced all unnecessarily. My work is at Oakland. I shall not move east one step unless the Lord says "Go." Then, without one murmur, I will cheerfully go, not before.

A great share of my life's usefulness has been lost. If James had made retraction, it would be different. He has said we must not seek to control each other. I do not own to doing it, but he has, and much more. I never felt as I do now in this matter. I cannot have confidence in James's judgment in reference to my duty. He seems to want to dictate to me as though I was a child—tells me not to go here, I must come east for fear of Sister Willis' influence, or fearing that I should go to Petaluma, et cetera. I hope God has not left me to receive my duty through my husband. He will teach me if I trust in Him.

I am cheerful and happy. My nerves are getting calm. My sleep is sweet. My health is good. I hope I have not written anything wrong, but these are just my feelings, and no one but you knows anything about it.

May the Lord help me to do and feel just right. If things had been different, I might feel [it was my] duty to go to camp meetings. As they are, I have no duty. God blesses me in doing my work. If I can get light in [a] dream or in any way, I will cheerfully follow the light. God lives and reigns. I shall answer to His claims, and seek to do His will.

In love.—Letter 64, 1876 (May 10, 1876).

Dear Sister Lucinda:

I wish you would write some news. Write often.

I have decided to remain here, and not attend any of the camp meetings. I dare not go east without an assurance that God would have me go. I am perfectly willing to go if the light shines that way. But the Lord knows what is best for me, for James, and the cause of God. My husband is now happy—blessed news. If he will only remain happy, I would be willing to ever remain from him. If my presence is detrimental to his happiness, God forbid I should be connected with him. I will do my work as God leads me. He may do his work as God leads him. We will not get in each other's way. My heart is fixed, trusting in God. I shall wait for God to open my way before me.

I do not think my husband really desires my society. He would be glad for me to be present at the camp meetings, but he has such views of me, which he freely has expressed from time to time, that I do not feel happy in his society, and I never can till he views matters entirely differently. He charges a good share of his unhappiness upon me, when he has made it himself by his own lack of self-control. These things exist, and I cannot be in harmony with him till he views things differently. He has said too much for me to feel freedom with him in prayer or to unite with him in labor, therefore as time passes and he removes nothing out of my way, my duty is plain never to place myself where he will be tempted to act out his feelings and talk them out as he has done. I cannot, and will not, be crippled as I have been.—Letter 65, 1876 (May 12, 1876).

Dear Lucinda:

A letter received from my husband last night shows me that he is prepared to dictate to me and take positions more trying than ever before. I have decided to attend no camp meetings this season. I shall remain and write. My husband can labor alone best. I am sure I can.

He writes [that] Walling wants me to bring the children over the plains to attend the Centennial. But they have crossed the plains for the last time, to pay out fifty dollars. If he wants them, he can come and get them. I could send them by Brother Jones, but it would be to have them no more under my charge. I have too much care to prepare these children even for a journey. James did not express his mind in the matter. He takes exceptions to the sketches of life in *Signs*. Shall stop just here. He only mentions one thing, the putting in of [Israel] Dammon's name. I think he would be satisfied if he had the entire control of me, soul and body, but this he cannot have. I sometimes think he is not really a sane man, but I don't know. May God teach and lead and guide. His last letter has fully decided me to remain this side of the mountains.

He has in his letters to me written harshly in regard to Edson, and then told me that he did not write to call me out. He did not want me to make any references to Edson. I wrote thus—I give you the words, for he has returned the letter: "Will you, please, if you are happy, to be thankful and not agitate disagreeable matters which you feel called upon to write me, to make no reference to them. Please take the same cautions yourself. When you wish to make these statements in reference to your own son, please lay down your pen and stop just there. I think God would be better pleased, and it would do no harm to your own soul. Leave me to be guided by the Lord in reference to Edson, for I still trust in His guiding hand and have confidence He will lead me. The same guiding hand is my trust."

He has felt called upon to press upon me the danger of being drawn in by Edson and deceived by him. He has felt called upon to write in regard to my danger of being deceived by Sister Willis, in regard to my being called to Petaluma, et cetera. I hope [that] when my husband left he did not take God with him and leave us to walk by the light of our own eyes and the wisdom of our own hearts.

In his last [letter] he repeats [that] he does not want me to make any references to what he writes till "you see things differently. And be assured of this, that none of these things sink me down a hair. I shall be happy to meet you and Mary at the Kansas camp meeting provided that, with the exception of a direct revelation from God, you put me on a level with yourself. I will gladly come to that position and labor with you, but while entrusted with the supervision of the whole work I think it wrong to be second to the private opinions of anyone. The moment I come to this I can be turned by the will of others' infallibility. When I cannot take this position I can gracefully cast off responsibilities. I shall have no more controversies with my dear wife. She may call it a 'mouse or a bat' and have her own way. If she doesn't like my position in reference to Edson or other matters, will she please [keep] her opinion to herself and let me enjoy mine? Your remarks called me out. And now that you cannot endure my speaking as plainly as you do, I have done.

"As to your coming to Kansas, I am not the least anxious. Judging from what I can gather from that last page, I think we can better labor apart than together until you can lay down your continual efforts to hold me in condemnation. When you have a message from the Lord for me, I hope I shall be where I shall tremble at His word. But aside from that, you must let me be an equal, or we had better work alone.

"Don't be anxious about my dwelling on disagreeables anymore. I have them in my heart. But while on the stage of action I shall use the good old head God gave me until He reveals that I am wrong. Your head won't fit my shoulders. Keep it where it belongs, and I will try to honor God in using my own. I shall be glad to hear from you, but don't waste your precious time and strength lecturing me on matters of mere opinions."

There is considerable more of the same kind.

Now, Lucinda, my course is clear. I shall not cross the plains this summer. I would be glad to bear my testimony in the meetings, but this cannot be without worse results than we could gain.

Will you not write me something in reference to these things? Why do you keep so silent? How is James's health? I had a dream that troubled me in reference to James.

What is your mind in reference to the children?

In haste.—Letter 66, 1876 (May 16, 1876).

[The following sentences were written in the margin of the first page of the letter:] "This arrangement of Walling's to have his family go to the Centennial, May does not like. She does not want to see Walling, and is opposed to going east. I shall not go east. I am decided. I get no light to go anywhere. EGW."

Dear Sister Lucinda:

I am sorry I wrote you the letters I have. Whatever may have been my feelings, I need not have troubled you with them. Burn all my letters, and I will relate no matters that perplex me to you. The [Sin]bearer is my refuge. He has invited me to come to Him for rest when weary and heavy laden. I will not be guilty of uttering a word again, whatever may be the circumstances. Silence in all things of a disagreeable or perplexing character has ever been a blessing to me. When I have departed from this, I have regretted it so much.

You knew when you left that there was no one I could speak with, however distressed I might be; but this is no excuse. I have written to James a letter of confession. You may read all letters that come from Oakland to him, and remail [them to him] where he is. I know not who to send letters in the care of at Kansas.

I received last night a letter from James expressing a very [different] tone of feelings. But I dare not cross the plains. It is better for us both to be separated. I have not lost my love for my husband, but I cannot explain things. I shall not attend any of the eastern camp meetings. I shall remain in California and write.

The last letters have fully decided me. I regard it the light that I have asked for. I would have come to the Kansas meeting but felt forbidden to start. It is all right. The Lord knows what is best for us all.

I have no confidence that it was your duty to go east when you did. Had you remained, I might have accomplished much more. But I understand all the circumstances, and have not a word of censure to lay on you or my husband or anyone.

I am writing frequently twenty pages a day. I have dropped *Sketches of Life.* [We] have got off two more forms [of] the testimony. One more form will complete it. Mary Clough is just the same; she works with interest and cheerfulness. She proves to be a precious help; I don't know how we could keep house without him. He makes bread, just excellent pies, buns; and cooks vegetables. All that they have paid him as yet is two dollars each week, till last two weeks, two and [a] half. Shall pay three in two weeks more. Mary [is] teaching him to cook. He is neat; takes care of the whole house.

Where is Frankie Patten? Is she coming or not? Why do you not say something about these things?

Love to all.—Letter 67, 1876 (May 17, 1876).

The following was written to "Dear Husband," May 16, 1876, from Oakland, California, the same day the third letter was written to Lucinda Hall.

It grieves me that I have said or written anything to grieve you. Forgive me and I will be cautious not to start any subject to annoy and distress you. We are living in a most solemn time and we cannot afford to have in our old age* differences to separate our feelings. I may not view all things as you do, but I do not think it would be my place or duty to try to make you see as I see and feel as I feel. Wherein I have done this, I am sorry.

I want a humble heart, a meek and quiet spirit. Wherein my feelings have been permitted to arise in any instance, it was wrong. Jesus has said, "Learn of Me; for I am meek and lowly in heart; and ye shall find rest unto your souls." Matthew 11:29.

I wish that self should be hid in Jesus. I wish self to be crucified. I do not claim infallibility, or even perfection of Christian character. I am not free from mistakes and errors in my life. Had I followed my Saviour more closely, I should not have to mourn so much my unlikeness to His dear image.

Time is short, very short. Life is uncertain. We know not when our probation may close. If we walk humbly before God, He will let us end our labors with joy. No more shall a line be traced by me or expression made in my letter to distress you. Again I say, forgive me every word or act that has grieved you.

I have earnestly prayed for light in reference to going east and I have now decided my work is here, to write and do those things that the Spirit of God shall dictate. I am seeking earnestly for the higher life. Mary and myself are at work as hard as we can. God in His providence has given me my work. I dare not leave it. We will pray that God may sustain you, but I see no light for me east.—20MR 23 (1876).

[A few days later Ellen apparently changed her mind and joined her husband for the 1876 summer camp meeting season. They met 14 camp meeting appointments, working in perfect harmony. Returning to Battle Creek, they met publishing deadlines for Spirit of Prophecy, *volume 2. They went back to California together, where they again took up the work there.]*

James White Recovering After Another Stroke.—Our camp meeting has ended. We are all at home again. Father endured the camp meeting as well as we could expect. He comes up very slowly—cannot eat enough to sustain strength. We have very precious seasons of prayer in his behalf and our faith is tested, but we do not become discouraged.

I am now satisfied that he had a stroke of paralysis. He is very quiet, not exacting, patient, tender and kind. The care falls principally upon me. He seems to feel that if I am with him he is at rest. But our faith claims the promises of God for his complete restoration. We believe it will be done. God has a great work for him and me. We shall have strength to perform it.

God has sustained me in bearing my double burden at the five camp meetings I have attended. I feel of the best of courage. I have labored exceedingly hard and God has helped me. I now mean to complete my book and then let writing go for the present.—10MR 36, 37 (1877).

James White Like Himself Again.—I had great freedom in speaking one hour. All were deeply attentive. But the best part of the matter was that Father went into the stand, sang and prayed like his own self. This is God's doing and His name shall have all the glory.—10MR 36 (1877).

A Few Weeks After James White's Death.—I miss Father more and more. Especially do I feel his loss while here in the mountains. I find it a very different thing being in the mountains with my husband and in the mountains without him. I am fully of the opinion that my life was so entwined or interwoven with my husband's that it is about impossible for me to be of any great account without him.—Letter 17, 1881.

Years After James White's Death.—My husband, the faithful servant of Jesus Christ, who had stood by my side for thirty-six years, was taken from me, and I was left to labor alone. He sleeps in Jesus. I have no tears to shed over his grave. But how I miss him! How I long for his words of counsel and wisdom! How I long to hear his prayers blending with my prayers for light and guidance, for wisdom to know how to plan and lay out the work!—2SM 259 (1899.)

My husband died in 1881. Since that time I have done more work than in all my life before in carrying responsibilities and in writing and publishing books. When my husband was dying, I promised him that with the help of my two sons I would carry on the work that he and I had done unitedly, if the Lord would be pleased to give me strength. I have not studied my ease. I have refused to fail or become discouraged. And I have not been told in words that I shall see my husband in the City of God. I hope that I should not need the evidence of words to give me this assurance. I have the evidence of the Word of God that my husband loved the truth and kept the faith. And I have the assurance that if I follow on trustingly, faithfully, doing God's will as a faithful messenger, my husband and I will be reunited in the kingdom of God. I have not one particle of doubt regarding my husband's preparedness to lay off the armor.

The year [after]† my husband's death was the most trying one I ever experienced. But since the life-giving power came to me as I stood in the large tent at the Healdsburg camp meeting, I have felt in a special sense that the Lord spared my life that I might bear a definite message, and that the angels of God are by my side. Were it not for the evidence that the Lord is my helper, I could not work as I do. While He spares my life, I shall faithfully discharge my duty. I am not doing my work, but the work of the Lord.

Now, my sister, we have a right to take the Lord at His word. I have never asked God to reveal to me whether I should be saved, or whether my husband will be saved. I believe that if I live in obedience to all the commandments of God, and do not become discouraged, but walk in the light as Christ is in the light, I shall at last meet my Saviour and see His face. For this I am striving. I will not trust in man or make flesh my arm. I have the promise that if I am faithful in bearing the messages God gives me, I shall receive the crown of life. My gaining this crown depends on my believing the message of truth, and holding by faith the promise of God that I shall have His grace to sustain me in discharging the duties He requires of me. If I discharge faithfully my duty, what others choose to do will not be charged to my account because I did not warn them.—Letter 82, 1906.

---

*Ellen White was 48 years of age and her husband was 54 when this letter was written.

†This word was previously transcribed as "before," but internal evidence suggests that it should have been "after."

Notes

Notes

Notes

Notes

~

Notes

Notes

~

Notes

Notes

Notes

Notes

Notes

Notes

Notes